Mothering from the Field

Mothering from the Field

The Impact of Motherhood
on Site-Based Research

EDITED BY BAHIYYAH MIALLAH MUHAMMAD
AND MÉLANIE-ANGELA NEUILLY

Rutgers University Press

New Brunswick, Camden, and Newark, New Jersey, and London

Library of Congress Cataloging-in-Publication Data

Names: Muhammad, Bahiyyah Miallah, 1980– editor. | Neuilly, Mélanie-Angela, 1977– editor.
Title: Mothering from the field : the impact of motherhood on site-based research / Bahiyyah
Miallah Muhammad, Mélanie-Angela Neuilly, editors.
Description: New Brunswick : Rutgers University Press, [2019] | Includes bibliographical
references and index.
Identifiers: LCCN 2018043050 | ISBN 9781978800564 (pbk.) | ISBN 9781978800571 (hbk.)
Subjects: LCSH: Women college teachers. | Women social scientists. | Women scientists. |
Research—Methodology. | Social sciences—Fieldwork. | Science—Fieldwork. | Working
mothers. | Work and family.
Classification: LCC LB2332.3.M68 2019 | DDC 378.1/2082—dc23
LC record available at https://lccn.loc.gov/2018043050

A British Cataloging-in-Publication record for this book is available from the British Library.

∞ The paper used in this publication meets the requirements of the American National Standard for Information Sciences—Permanence of Paper for Printed Library Materials, ANSI
Z39.48-1992.

www.rutgersuniversitypress.org

Manufactured in the United States of America

To our families, near and far

Jaelah, Jian, and Grace, may you grow up to change the world

Contents

Mothering from the Field

Introduction

• •

MÉLANIE-ANGELA NEUILLY AND
BAHIYYAH MIALLAH MUHAMMAD

Two Mothers Birthing an Idea . . .

It all started on Facebook. Isn't that how everything starts these days? Mélanie, a classic Facebook oversharer, had been posting breathtaking pictures of her family while she was "conducting field research" in Nice, France. These pictures did not involve Mélanie's research (medico-legal practices in France and in the United States), thankfully, but rather presented the image of an idyllic summer vacation on the Côte d'Azur: a visit to Monaco, her husband and baby playing on the beach, French food, posing by a medieval fountain in a medieval village, and so on. These dreamy posts, however, were accompanied by much less dreamy status updates. The first two updates from the trip to her field site are as follows:

> May or may not have broken a toe in the middle of the night . . . (May 31, 2014)

> Let the record show that between the hours of 2 and 5 this morning, my child was a spawn of evil and parenting straight out sucked. Now let's go back to looking at how cute she is and all . . . (May 31, 2014)

> A fairly quick browsing yields such gems as

> Sometimes you just have to go to bed with a little bit of vomit in your hair . . . (June 19, 2014)

1

Let's go see an autopsy, of a decomposed body, bright and early, happy birthday to me! (June 22, 2014)

You know what you really don't need when you have an infant with unpredictable sleep patterns? A crazy drunk loud neighbor arguing on the phone between 3 and 5 in the morning, especially not after a night of football cheering by some other neighbors... I hate this place. There, I said it. (June 27, 2014)

And for the final post,

Tomorrow is my last day at the medical examiner's office! It has been the most challenging six weeks of field research in my life! Now to write something meaningful... (July 10, 2014)

Bahiyyah, a very conservative Facebook sharer, was comforted to see Mélanie's posts about her field research experiences because she would also be spending her summer abroad conducting a research project in Africa with her husband and babies. Although she had previous field experiences with her children and family, none of them were as long as a summer. Most of Bahiyyah's preparations for her trip consisted of written journal entries and random conversations with colleagues who had field experiences with babies or knew of others who did. Much of the information derived from these conversations was either not applicable or downright scary. Bahiyyah's early journal notes read,

Today I was told to watch the movie 'Mary and Martha' which is about two mothers who lose their sons to malaria. Not sure this was helpful advice since malaria is an issue in many of my field site locations... (April 8, 2014)

I spoke with a colleague who conducted anthropological research in Africa with her son and they both survived. I'm feeling hopeful. (May 3, 2014)

During a presentation a professor spoke of her fieldwork with her daughter in tow. She identified a teenaged sitter in the host country and her baby survived. Although she laughed about it today, she knew her baby was not safe and she vowed to never do that again. (May 8, 2014)

For an entire semester, Bahiyyah was silently battling various doubts about how she would approach her first long-term research experience with her family. It wasn't as if she really had a choice. Being on the tenure track doesn't leave one with much time to collect data and publish on one's findings. It was Bahiyyah's goal to use this summer-long research experience to provide data for the bulk of the publications she would use for her upcoming tenure and promotion application. Mélanie's posts served as motivation and a turning point for Bahiyyah. Her last month of preparing for travel became strategic. The strategy would be to complete a successful research trip and coauthor a book-length manuscript from this experience as well as others. This would be in addition to building family memories and bonding in a foreign country in ways that would be cherished for years to come.

Bahiyyah was learning a lot from Mélanie, whether Mélanie knew it or not. Mélanie's six weeks of nursing and researching at a morgue spoke of life, not death. It was very inspiring. As a result, Bahiyyah's journal entries shifted to include practical tools for surviving fieldwork with babies:

Identify child friendly locations near research site . . . (June 1, 2014)

It's okay to have fun . . . (June 3, 2014)

Purchase a durable stroller for various terrains. Remember that it must fold easily and fit in tight places and spaces. It should have a hood to protect baby from the sun and should be big enough for two babies but not too bulky. (June 5, 2014)

The following November, Bahiyyah was in San Francisco with her husband and two daughters for a conference when she spotted Mélanie's distinctive "well-traveled" stroller, Mélanie's baby, and Mélanie in the conference hotel. She immediately lit up. It was more than the happiness of seeing an old graduate school friend—it was the relief of realizing that she was not alone. Others—more senior faculty—had brought their families along. They could also talk about their shared experience of conducting international field research with family in tow. And thus the conversation started.

These conversations are necessary indeed, as it is only when we confront the reality of our experiences in friendly exchanges with our peers that we can truly come to grasp the true pregnancy of our actions as mother-researchers. Only when we come out of the shadows of "imposter syndrome" and encounter others like us can we change the narratives about what it means to be a field researcher, a professional, and a mother. As we empower each other, we also find solace in the sisterhood we create, and most importantly, we pave the way for others to join us.

During the summer of 2014, Bahiyyah was in Africa and Mélanie was in France. Our stories held their similarities. In November 2014, Mélanie had just completed a short essay relating her experience for the American Society of Criminology's professional association newsletter (Neuilly, 2015). It explained how difficult the experience was and yet how deliberate the

Facebook façade had been in capturing memory-worthy moments to look back on fondly instead of acrimoniously. Mélanie's publication highlighted her seriousness in getting her experience out there for others to learn from, and this was enough for Bahiyyah to use as a conversation starter. The hallway conversation led to participating in a conference roundtable and then a collaboration with some more friends sharing the experience of conducting field research with young children for a panel at the University of Idaho's 2015 Women's Leadership Conference. And just like that, we had a call out for chapter proposals, and this book was born. The more we continued to discuss the book project and work on its content, the more it became a source of empowerment.

Delivering Content

In what felt like it was beginning to be a crowded area of scholarship (Hargittai, 2015; Mason, Wolfinger, & Goulden, 2013; Ward & Wolf-Wendel, 2012, just to name a few), we wanted to dig deeper into the issues women and mothers face in academia. Certainly, those are many and complex, but aside from Ramage Macdonald and Sullivan (2008), we did not see our experience as field researchers recognized or our questions answered (Mose Brown and Dreby's volume came out after we had already started writing this book). Therefore, this book aims to meet that need—our need—a need we felt was mostly unmet during the onset of our research travels with children. Here we build onto what is already known about women and mothers in academia and the sciences. We add to this base of knowledge the lived experiences of mothers doing field research. We acknowledge and embrace the difficulties, we share what works and how, and most importantly, we bring to the table an in-depth policy discussion that taps into the fact that beyond women and family-friendly policies, reform must include methodology and a variety of epistemological approaches to science. We have to fundamentally rethink the delineation between public and private spheres and between the supposedly opposed objective rigor required by science and the emotional work involved in nurturing children and oneself (the researcher).

Here, using feminist methodology as the framework, we challenge such dichotomies and offer evidence that alternatives exist and simply need to find a broader audience in order to become recognized and formally supported. Here we lend our voices in hopes that all mother-researchers will hear us when we say it is possible, we have done it, and hopefully, through our struggles, advances will be made to allow you to do it more easily!

Practically speaking, part 1 of this volume focuses on establishing the state of women and mothers in academia and the sciences (physical and social) in particular. Here we rely on renowned scholars of gender in higher education,

Kelly Ward and Lisa Wolf-Wendel, along with Lindsey Marco for an overview of the state of women and mothers in science, technology, engineering, and math (STEM) and site-based fields. Because a discussion of women who mother children while conducting field research is incomplete without acknowledging the primacy of field-centered anthropology, Stacey Camp's chapter provides a very exhaustive overview of the gendered nature of the history of field research in anthropology all the while weaving in her personal narrative. This first section introduces the reader to the necessity to understand site-based research as endlessly diverse and, at the same time, as having been profoundly limited by patriarchal notions of ideal fieldworkers and field destinations.

Part 2 of the volume focuses on the difficulties of conducting field research for mothers. While we are all proof that mothering from the field can be done, it would be irresponsible of us to pretend as though it were easy. In this second section, we draw the reader's attention to the hardships and heartaches that field research can all too often entail for women with children. Rather than using these narratives as cautionary tales, we embrace them as part of a full and complex life, allowing mothers to start stepping away from an often oversimplified and masculine-dominant narrative of success achieved through self-reliance and self-determination. Whether they went into the field as single mothers or experienced traumatic events while in their research context, Kelley Sams, Lydia Zacher Dixon, and Cecilia Vindrola-Padros embody the resilience and persistence that women everywhere know so intimately. They also bring the importance of experiences to bear on the validity of their research, showing how being mothers, far from limiting their outcomes, led to broadening their skillset and deepening their accomplishments. This really sets the tone for the entire book and speaks volume not only for the need to discuss this topic but also for the importance of addressing this particular common thread whenever debating policy solutions.

Part 3 presents how some mothers have made it work, mostly through their use of extensive networks and support systems. Here we introduce some of the key feminist concepts that make mothering from the field successful. We put the emphasis on networks of support, whatever shape they may take. By doing so, we build on the difficult experiences discussed in section two and define an alternative narrative. In this section, voices other than mothers' emerge and weave into the complexity of the argument. Contributors include Bahiyyah and her husband, Muntaquim Muhammad; Grace Karram Stephenson and her family, husband John Stephenson and mother Joanne Karram; and Brian Wolf, Mélanie's husband. To use a metaphor based on Bahiyyah's husband's experience as a documentarian, in each chapter of this section, the lens gets turned away from the researcher and back toward the supporting team, be he or she behind the camera, dad, caretaker, or grandma extraordinaire.

We continue poking holes in patriarchal narratives and shine a bright light on the underbelly of fieldwork. Because women and mothers have typically been the ones responsible for making men's fieldwork possible, this underbelly, all the support, the team effort, the networked quality of the endeavor, has, until now, remained invisible. We bring it to the surface, personalize it, and examine every component of its existence. As in part two, we are not interested in only showing the perfect results of our seemingly flawless studies or, put simply, "the good side" of things. We want to demystify fieldwork, make it real, and embody it in its glorious, flow-inspired moments as well as in its gritty, painful, mundane, necessary, and yet rich and fecund details. We also want to highlight that this messy research nonetheless rests on strong scientific backing, methodologically sound strategies, and acceptance or rejection of hypothesized explorations. Indeed, it is all science and must be considered as such. Whether the principle investigator is man or woman (with child or children) we show the end result of data collected, findings analyzed, peer-reviewed publications secured, tenure and promotion accepted, and senior status in the academy obtained.

In part 4, we transition from the characteristics of the researcher and her team to how these characteristics evolve through the life course. Based off a popular saying, heard many times by many mothers, "This too shall pass," focus here is on the transiency of experiences as field researchers and mothers. Mélanie, Anne Hardgrove, and Kimberly Garland-Campbell each illustrate a specific stage of the life of a mother-researcher. Mélanie's experience highlights the difficulties of field research with an infant while both Hardgrove and Garland-Campbell showcase mothering from the field through a longer-term parenting lens. And while both Mélanie and Hardgrove contrast the reality of their fieldwork experience before and after having children, Garland-Campbell's narrative is that of one who only started knowing child-free field research once her children were adults. This section is meant to serve as a reminder that mothering from the field is not something for which we can design one-size-fits-all policy solutions, nor is it something mother-researchers can ever really claim to have figured out. As Mélanie's husband Brian came to realize early on in the parenting process, "just when you think you got your child's needs figured out, she grows and you get a different child."

Drawing from all the preceding chapters, part 5 presents a set of in-depth discussions on how motherhood can be conceptualized as the cornerstone of a methodological revolution. At the heart of the argument, we use a basic feminist and critical approach to question the very notion of the ideal field researcher. We posit that mother-researchers invite a quintessentially different perspective. If these perspectives are not embraced, it can be prejudicial not only toward women who wish to be both mothers and field researchers but also to science as an enterprise as well as to the children we bring along with us. Contributors Sarah Kelman, Marylynn Steckley, Deirdre Guthrie, Aprille Ericsson, her sister Dawn Ericsson Provine, and their children and adult nephew, Arielle, Mikae, and Pierre, respectively, offer a reconceptualization of field researchers and their methodology based on redefinitions of the separations of the public and private spheres. This methodological revolution is not proposed without its tools. Therefore, specific policy suggestions are offered to solidify a possible transition from the currently very masculine-dominant approach to field research and science to a more feminist-driven and balanced one. In addition, we not only uncover how definitions of what is considered "the field" are truly at stake but also propose the need to consider the impact we, as mothers, have on the field, whatever it is, and the impact the field has on our children. Whether in the social or physical sciences, close to or far away from home, in the outdoors or in an urban environment, site-based research is endlessly varied, as are those who conduct it. This is indeed important as we discuss, within academia at large, the ways in which we ought to make institutions more family-friendly and more inclusive of diversity. Low diversity among today's researchers translates to low diversity in tomorrow's researchers.

Finally, part 6 is a "how-to" section, presenting practical solutions to a complex problem. Here we focus on tips for successfully navigating the duality of fieldwork and motherhood. We continue to provide a counternarrative to the self-reliance trope and also introduce concrete policy solutions that shift the responsibility of mothers' success in the field from the individual to the institution. Ryanne Pilgeram illustrates how mothers sometimes have to let go of some unrealistic ideas of what doing field research really means and find interests closer to home in order to manage responsibilities. Bahiyyah Muhammad provides a financial breakdown of the true and hidden costs of doing research with a family in tow.

The voices in this volume are diverse, representative of all ranks and types of positions in the academy and among research practitioners, inclusive of the journey from doctoral student to full professor, and from a wide variety of fields, including aerospace engineering, anthropology, criminal justice, geography, health sciences, higher education, history, obstetrics, plant genetics, and sociology. We conduct research all over the world, speak a broad range of different languages, and represent different racial and ethnic backgrounds. Some of us are single mothers, some of us are first-generation college students, some became mothers while young, and others waited longer. While there are still many who go unrepresented here, we are all eager to share our experiences of conducting field research while raising children and get the conversation started.

References

Hargittai, M. (2015). *Women scientists: Reflections, challenges, and breaking boundaries.* Oxford, UK: Oxford University Press.

Mason, M. A., Wolfinger, N. H., & Goulden, M. (2013). *Do babies matter? Gender and family in the ivory tower.* New Brunswick, NJ: Rutgers University Press.

Mose Brown, T., & Dreby, J. (2016). *Family and work in everyday ethnography.* Philadelphia, PA: Temple University Press.

Neuilly, M.-A. (2015). The reality of field research with a family: Turning a nightmare into memories. *The Criminologist, 40*(6). Retrieved from http://www.asc41.com/ Criminologist/2015/Nov-Dec_2015_TheCriminologist.pdf

Ramage Macdonald, J., & Sullivan, M. E. (2008, October 24). Mother in the field. *Chronicle of Higher Education.* Retrieved from https://www.chronicle.com/article/Mothers-in-the -Field/45801

Ward, K., Wolf-Wendel, L. (2012). *Academic motherhood: How faculty manage work and family.* New Brunswick, NJ: Rutgers University Press.

Part I

Women and Mothers
Doing Field Research

• •

What Do We Know?

MÉLANIE-ANGELA NEUILLY

Before we start, let's pause and take a moment to acknowledge that we are the few, the select, the mothers who have jumped through the hoops and tackled the obstacles and made it all the way. Most of us here have a graduate degree. Most of us have obtained not just jobs in our fields but one of the most desirable types: tenure-track jobs. Some of us are tenured, and a few of us have even managed to check all the boxes by being promoted to full professor. We recognize that this path we have chosen is not necessary to live a fulfilled life, and some might read on and think, *No thank you, this is not for me*, and there is nothing wrong with that. But for those who are dedicated to this path, remember that there is a reason there are so few of us around: it is harder for women and even harder for mothers.

Our goal with this book is to make it a bit easier for mothers to get involved in site-based research and thus increase parity in academia and site-based research fields in general. But before we can do that, we need to go in with our eyes wide open, knowledgeable of all the ways in which women in general and mothers in particular struggle not only in academia but also when it comes to doing field research.

This first section of the book is focused on just that: surveying the state of women in site-based fields, STEM first and anthropology second. We begin

with renowned experts on gender equity in academia and academic motherhood, Lisa Wolf-Wendel and the late Kelly Ward. In their chapter with Lindsey Marco, they provide a comprehensive overview of the "woman problem" in
STEM. They cover site-based, research-specific issues but also couch the entire
book within the larger context of gender equity in academia. They emphasize
the need to switch the perspective from a "woman problem," an individual-
centric perspective, to an institutional problem.

Stacey Camp, in turn, focuses on contextualizing the issues faced by women
in archaeology in particular, an exemplary site-based discipline. Providing a
historical framework for the gendered nature of fieldwork as defined in
archaeological archetypes and borrowing from feminist frameworks, Camp
addresses the negative impact of the stereotype of the lone white male hero
in the field. Much like Ward, Wolf-Wendel, and Marco, Camp also emphasizes the detrimental effect the underrepresentation of women and female narratives has on methodological rigidity and the knowledge-building endeavor
in archeology, let alone its demoralizing effect on prospective or current
female archaeologists. Peppering her chapter with first-person narratives illus-
trating her own struggles as a mother conducting archaeological research in
the field, Camp opens up the first-person-centric rest of the anthology.

Section-Specific Takeaways

- To solve the "woman problem" in STEM and related field-based disciplines, college is not where we need to focus our efforts. It is too late
  by then. We need to start in early elementary school and focus on math
  because women are the most absent from mathematics-reliant fields.
- To create an academic research environment that is more diverse and
  family-friendly, we need to recognize that diversity is a complex issue
  in academia: women, mothers, and minorities should not just all be
  thrown in the same basket. Understanding the varied needs of each
  underrepresented group is a necessary first step to finding solutions
  that actually work.
- For women and mothers to thrive in academia in general and site-based
  research disciplines in particular, we need to reject ideal worker norms
  and recognize that there is more than one way of being an academic
  and conducting research, even field research.
- Finally, we need to recognize that when the pipeline leaks, it is not the
  leaking fluid's fault—it is the pipeline that needs fixing. As such, solutions to academia's inclusivity in general, and the retention of women
  and mothers in particular, should be institutional, not individual. In this
  volume, we will offer individual-level practical solutions based on our
  experiences, but we will always put the focus on institutional reform.

1

Women Working
in the Field

●●●●●●●●●●●●●●●●●●●●●

Perspectives from
STEM and Beyond

KELLY WARD, LISA WOLF-WENDEL,
AND LINDSEY MARCO

This chapter examines recent literature that contributes to the ongoing understanding of women in STEM and related field-based disciplines. An important perspective offered in the chapter is related to where and how people conduct research and how women's roles as mothers shape their experiences. We posit that who conducts research and the setting for the research are important factors to consider as part of larger conversations about women in STEM.

Women are underrepresented at all stages of the STEM pipeline, including undergraduate and graduate degree programs. Women are also less likely than their male counterparts to pursue prestigious postdocs, less likely to be hired in tenure-track positions, underrepresented at the highest ranks of the professoriate, and underrepresented at the department chair and dean levels (Bilimoria & Xiangfen, 2011; Blickenstaff, 2005; Chen & Soldner, 2013). At each stage of the pipeline, women in the STEM fields "leak" (Blickenstaff, 2005). Of those women who do pursue academic careers, women are overrepresented in less prestigious institutions and in non-tenure-track and part-time positions and are found in lower paying jobs (Allen, 2011). Many believe that under-representation will remedy itself and that time alone will solve the problems. Some believe that as more women enter the STEM pipeline, representation at each level will solve itself. However, the passage of time alone is not sufficient to fix gender inequities, as the problems are complex and deeply rooted in structural inequities in society and education and within disciplines. Given the current makeup of the faculty, it would take between thirty-five and fifty years for women to achieve parity at the higher academic ranks (Curtis, 2011; Hargens & Long, 2002). There are a number of factors that make even this parity projection unlikely, including delayed faculty retirements and institutions replacing vacant tenure-track positions with part-time and/or adjunct faculty on annual contracts (Kezar & Sam, 2010).

The Representation of Women in STEM Fields

To understand the underrepresentation of women in STEM-related disciplines, it is helpful to look at concrete numbers. Between 2003 and 2009, around 28 percent of bachelor degree students were attracted to STEM fields, which was a larger percentage than those interested in non-STEM fields. Approximately 64 percent of students entered STEM fields; however, after one year of study, only 36 percent remained (Chen & Soldner, 2013). About half of those who left STEM majors switched their area of study to a non-STEM field, and the other half dropped out of college before earning a degree. Within the STEM fields of engineering and technologies and computer or information sciences, engineering and technologies had the largest attrition rate with 50 percent of students leaving after one year of study. Approximately 32 percent of females who started studying in the STEM field switched to a non-STEM major, and 14 percent left without a degree (Chen & Soldner, 2013).

According to the National Science Foundation (NSF), in 2013, women received approximately 32 percent of all doctoral degrees in STEM fields broadly defined. At the same time, women held 24 percent of full-time faculty positions at four-year universities and colleges and held 15 percent of full-time professorships in engineering (NSF, 2013). The representation of women has improved since a prior survey in 2003. However, numbers are slightly inflated due to the significant entry of foreign nationals at the graduate student level. International students received roughly 56 percent of doctorates in engineering in 2013 (NSF, 2013).

Gender and Differences within STEM

One of the things that differentiates fields within STEM has to do with how (and where) research is conducted. In general, STEM academics can be divided into three groups based on where they work: laboratory based, field based, and theoretically based. Laboratory-based scientists require significant institutional infrastructure (space, equipment, staff, students, postdocs) to maintain their work. Laboratory-based sciences often require that individuals be physically present in the lab. The work must be done at a specific place. There is also a community orientation to the work that is carried out in most labs—with other colleagues, undergraduates, graduate students, and postdocs often involved in the research process. There is a heavy focus on grant funding for laboratory-based scientists, as they need to pay not only for the infrastructure but also for all the personnel needed to carry out their work.

In contrast, field-based scientists, like those studying oceanography, geology, and anthropology, for example, are also unique in that they must go into the field to do their work. Being in the field for days, weeks, months, and even years at a time is clearly a requirement and is important to maintaining productivity. For women, especially those with children, field-based settings can be challenging and require attention to logistics, field assistants, and childcare (Brown & Dreby, 2013; McGuire, Primack, & Losos, 2012). There is also a time intensity to doing field-based research. For example, the ethnographer studying schools or hospitals may not physically leave their home for extended periods like an ocean-going oceanographer who leaves for three months at a time, but there is still intensive time spent in the field (Rothman, 2013). It is important to think broadly about the very notion of doing field-based research because it can vary significantly across disciplines. Funding is an important element to consider, as grants are necessary to fund place-based research. Collaboration can also be an important component to field-based work, but for women in fields like the geosciences, collaboration can manifest positively if it is inclusive or negatively if it is exclusive (Macfarlane & Luzzadder-Beach, 1998). As one example, in oceanography, it was not until the late 1960s that women were even allowed on sea-going research vessels (O'Connell & Holmes, 2005).

In contrast, those who do more theoretical work might also collaborate and require funding, but their work is done more independent of place and time. Theoretical scientists might be able to carry out their work with more flexibility and autonomy than their colleagues in lab- or field-based specialties. Again, the positive side of this for women in male-dominated fields (and most STEM work that is theoretically oriented tends to be male dominated) is that there is not the same reliance on others to get grants and get work done as in lab or collaborative settings, but the downside can be isolation and lack of support (Herzig, 2004). The research literature on STEM and gender typically does not account for these important distinctions within STEM on how and where "work" gets done and how that might affect women and men in the field.

Given the nuances associated with STEM and the nuances of doing STEM research, it is important to consider in any given context, study, or report what comprises STEM. In some studies, STEM is actually limited to physics, chemistry, math, and biology and omits geosciences (Macfarlane & Luzzadder-Beach, 1998), and technology-related fields are left out altogether. Furthermore, not all STEM research is related to laboratories, another misnomer often associated with doing STEM research. While the acronym of STEM is helpful in providing general information (as we do here), it is important to consider the complexity within and among fields typically included in STEM nomenclature.

When talking about underrepresentation of STEM, the literature often refers to "women and minorities" as if they are one and the same (Burke & Mattis, 2007; Fealing, Lai, & Meyers, 2015). In fact, whatever progress has been made in the STEM fields in terms of access have been made mostly by white women and not by women (or men) who represent historically underrepresented minority groups (Armstrong & Jovanovic, 2017). Although women and minorities share a common history concerning STEM (they both have a legacy of exclusion; Alegria & Branch, 2015), the causes of the current disparities and solutions for increasing their numbers in STEM are not necessarily the same. Rather than grouping all women and underrepresented groups together, it is more appropriate to study the complexities of race and gender and understand the similarities and differences among and between groups (Seymour & Hewitt, 1997). Relatedly, there has been an increase in STEM scientists, some of whom are women, who immigrate to the United States from other countries to pursue academic careers. These international scientists bring cultural diversity to the field that is often not accounted for in the research but also bring with them gendered norms and expectations that are unique to their own cultural upbringing (Englander, Yáñez, & Barney, 2013; González Ramos & Bosch, 2013). The practice of labeling all women and minorities as one group acts as an erasure of extensive diversity of backgrounds and concerns (Lewis, Menzies, Najera, & Page, 2009). It is important to remain cognizant of the difference that diversity makes when addressing issues associated with women in STEM. There is not one "woman," and *STEM* is an umbrella term that needs to be contextualized.

Pipelines and Progressions

The pipeline representation of women in higher education is prevalent throughout literature and practice related to women in STEM (overall and within particular disciplines; e.g., Ceci et al., 2014; Mattis, 2007; O'Connell & Holmes, 2003). The pipeline visual conveys a steady stream, and in the case of women in higher education, the pipeline has "leaks." A perusal of topics and titles related to the "woman problem" in STEM fields leave many to ask, "Where are the women?" The pipeline model illustrates how the representation of women is stronger at incoming levels but lessens as careers progress (i.e., there are more women as undergraduate students than as full professors). Women leak from the pipeline at many stages, and women leak more than men (Blickenstaff, 2005; Burke & Mattis, 2007). These leaks "create a sex-based filter that removes one sex from the stream and leaves the other to arrive at the end of the pipeline. No one in a position of power along the pipeline has consciously decided to filter women out of the STEM stream, but the cumulative effect of the many separate but related factors results in the sex imbalance in STEM that is observed today" (Blickenstaff, 2005, p. 369). Discourses associated with problems, leaks, and drops from the pipeline perpetuate a deficit mind-set instead of one focused on capacity and development (Patton, 2014). The continued use of the metaphor of the pipeline may itself contribute to problems associated with underrepresentation of particular groups in science.

Another challenge associated with the pipeline visual is that it conveys a fixed, linear, and one-way progression; yet some careers in STEM disciplines present a lot more opportunity. There is more than one way to succeed and more than one desired end. Students can leave the pipeline to pursue fulfilling careers in science even if they leave academia (Main, Prenovitz, & Ehrenberg, 2017). These scientists would be considered leaks, but if they work in STEM careers and reenter at a later date, would that still be a leak? It is possible that alternative ways to view the pipeline are needed. In fact, it may be advantageous to expand pathways and provide alternative paths to increase diversity in STEM (Dean & Fleckenstein, 2007; NAS, 2007). Career development for women may be more idiosyncratic than fixed (Ward & Wolf-Wendel, 2012).

At the faculty level, a simple view of the pipeline suggests that an influx of women into assistant professor positions will lead inevitably to a greater number of women in associate, senior, and administrative ranks. A detailed analysis shows that while women have made progress in some fields at the incoming levels of academic ranks, they do not steadily progress into associate and senior ranks (Kulis, Sicotte, & Collins, 2002; NSF, 2013). Women tend to be older than men when they receive their doctorates; therefore, they enter the academic workforce later. Women also enter into faculty positions at a slower rate than men relative to the number of doctorates earned (Hargens & Long, 2002). In some fields like the geosciences, for example, the number of women entering the workforce has declined, further contributing to a pipeline problem—if fewer women enter the pipeline, the "woman problem" cannot be remedied with time (Holmes & O'Connell, 2003; Thompson, Perez, &

Shevenell, 2011). Recent research about women's experiences in STEM pipelines suggests that overt discrimination in terms of hiring is not to blame for the underrepresentation of women in sciences. Instead it is more a matter of transitions across the life course (i.e., early math education, gender socialization, transition to college, choice of major, graduate school, entry into the profession) as the root of the problem (Ceci et al., 2014). In short, at critical transition points, women are vulnerable when it comes to navigating transitions, given societal expectations and larger organizational complexities.

Explaining Leaks in the Pipeline

We now turn to a discussion of some of the challenges that exist in STEM-related disciplines that are specific to women. In particular, we talk about sexist science cultures, work-family concerns, and career choices and how each of these influences progression in the academic career pipeline. We also offer theoretical considerations to help explain women's experiences as faculty in higher education.

Sexist Cultures

Gender discrimination remains a major issue for women in all of higher education with particular concerns related to STEM fields. Given the history of STEM fields as largely male domains, it is not surprising that women can find "chilly" climates in classrooms, fieldwork settings, and laboratories (Settles, Cortina, Malley, & Steward, 2006). It is critical not just to focus on getting women into STEM fields but also to examine the field itself as a means to examine what women encounter once in the pipeline (Macfarlane & Luzzadder-Beach, 1998; Settles et al., 2006). The culture of science that permeates many STEM fields has been described as competitive, exclusive, and sexist, leaving women to feel unwelcome, lacking mentors or role models, and like outsiders (De Welde & Laursen, 2011). The general climate within STEM fields is, in part, tied to paradigmatic beliefs about knowledge creation and the use of particular kinds of methods to generate knowledge. Scientific pursuits tend to be associated with the objective and can minimize the subjective. The chasm between the objective and subjective can be particularly troublesome for women because they have historically been associated with subjectivity, whereas men are associated with objectivity (Valian, 2000). Research using scientific methods also privileges objectivity (Harding, 1986).

Science as a profession tends toward total dedication to the pursuit of knowledge. This brings up two issues for women in STEM fields. One, STEM fields that are rooted in objectivism can exclude those with more subjectivist orientations and research approaches that value connection and reflexivity (Brown & Dreby, 2016). To be sure, not all women are subjective and men objective, but scientific structures can create such binaries (Harding, 1986). Two, the sole focus on science and research pursuits that can characterize research in STEM fields can be exclusive of women. This is particularly relevant for women with children and responsibilities beyond work. Science is "greedy" and calls for exclusive dedication and devotion that can conflict with women who have children. Williams (2001) refers to ideal worker norms as those that call for total dedication to the job with the exclusion of all else. Such a view is based on the assumption that people do not have outside pursuits or responsibilities and that science comes first. Furthermore, traditional notions of work separate work and family, which can lead to exclusive structures (Brown & Dreby, 2016). The "either you have a career or you have children" mind-set has clearly affected women to a greater extent than men given the physical and biological aspects of maternity (Ward & Wolf-Wendel, 2012). Sexist cultural milieus tied to knowledge creation and work norms can subtly or overtly contribute to the exclusion of women in all fields, in particular in academic STEM fields.

Work and Family

Women's place on the margins of academic life can, in part, be attributed to their seeking to combine work and family. To be sure, not all women faculty have children, and not all women academics with children are unable to succeed professionally (by standards put forth either personally or professionally), yet, as a group, work and family issues are part of what puts women academics in marginalized positions (Williams, 2001). A longitudinal study completed by Mason, Wolfinger, and Goulden (2013) examines how family formation influences academic careers. They found that caretaking for both men and women negatively impacts career outcomes (e.g., tenure, promotion). For women, in particular, having children means less likelihood to acquire faculty positions and earn tenure, a pattern that persists across disciplines (Moyer, 2012). Additional research also illustrates how motherhood penalizes academics who are also mothers (e.g., Kelly & Grant, 2012). In terms of understanding "leaks" in the pipeline, having children is a predictor of women leaving academic trajectories particularly early in their careers (Mason, Wolfinger, & Goulden, 2013). In addition to the negative career outcomes associated with having children that needs attention, there are also other aspects related to work and family that warrant consideration for women in STEM.

In our study of academic motherhood, we found that women with children in STEM fields can and do have satisfying careers, but they achieve these through their own sense of agency rather than through the support and assistance of institutional policies, mentors, or role models (Ward & Wolf-Wendel, 2012). Our data also suggests that where people do their research shapes career outcomes. For example, we found that academic mothers with research agendas that involve significant travel or extended research time in the field find that such commitments are challenging with families, especially young children. In some instances, these women opt for other research topics and methods that are more compatible with parenthood. We also found that long-term decisions about family shape career outcomes short and long term. Since the publication of our book in 2012, we have continued with our longitudinal project and see additional patterns of how work and family shape career experiences and outcomes even when children are no longer in the home (Ward & Wolf-Wendel, 2017).

Women in STEM tend to be partnered or married to other STEM academics. For example, in the natural sciences, approximately 83 percent of women academics are part of a dual career academic couple. Eighty percent of women in mathematics and 64 percent of women in engineering are in dual career couples (Schiebinger, Henderson, & Gilmartin, 2008). Dual careers can limit people in terms of their progression in the pipeline, applying for positions, and career advancement. Research is clear about dual careers in academic settings—women are more likely to forgo career advancement than men due to dual career couple concerns (Schiebinger et al., 2008).

Career Choices

For doctoral recipients in STEM fields, there are multiple opportunities that can influence where people work. Choosing to leave academic science is an option, and people in STEM fields have more career options beyond academia than people in other academic disciplines (Monosson, 2008). Given the structural barriers discussed throughout this chapter, women clearly can and do opt out of academic science and into other work settings.

The term *opting out* suggests that given competing options, women choose to leave the workforce. There are push and pull factors associated with the choice to leave work or to work in a setting outside of a tenure-track position. For some it is the pull to be at home with children, but for many it is the push to leave a workforce that is not very friendly to the notion of children and not very friendly for women (Herr & Wolfram, 2009; Stone, 2007). The structural barriers discussed throughout this paper can be part of the push to leave academic science. Mason, Wolfinger, and Goulden's (2013) work suggests that women with children opt out of tenure-line positions at greater rates than their male counterparts due to the perceived clash in culture between work and family in academia. Findings from a study of doctoral students in a broad array of disciplines suggest that as a career choice, academia is not always viewed as viable based on market conditions or attractive based on work-family concerns (Golde & Dore, 2001).

Another aspect related to women in STEM is the strong identity that women in STEM have with their field of study (Monosson, 2008). A scientist identity appears to carry people through other options in terms of careers. This, in part, explains the leaky pipeline between graduate school and throughout the early academic career (Ceci et al., 2014). Unlike in other disciplines, women in STEM fields tend to have options outside of academe that are attractive and often similar to the work they would do within the academic context (Monosson, 2008). For doctoral students and faculty dealing with informal and formal barriers, options in industry or in the public or private sector may be more attractive than academic settings (Main, Prenovitz, & Ehrenberg, 2017). The goal for many people is to do science—they are not always particular about *where* they do it.

What gets lost in explaining the status of women in higher education as a matter of individual choice is a critical examination of those choices from perspectives that include consideration of gender, power, and social structures (Ward & Wolf-Wendel, 2008; Ward & Wolf-Wendel, 2017). The goal is to avoid having campuses and disciplines exonerate themselves from responsibility for fixing the structures that perpetuate gender inequity by determining that leaks in the pipeline are only about individual choice (e.g., Susie left her tenure-track job because she wanted to be closer to family; Tonia left her PhD program to be home with her baby). Clearly, individual choice is part of any equation about career decisions, but organizational and disciplinary milieu are also important factors to consider (yet are often overlooked as part of the landscapes and circumstances related to women's faculty recruitment and retention; Herr & Wolfram, 2012; Stone, 2007). To blame the drop of water for leaking out of the pipe is clearly problematic; instead, it is critical to understand why the pipe is leaking.

Theoretical Perspectives

In addition to the barriers already mentioned, there are also theoretical views that help explain women's participation in academic careers. In particular, we discuss the disconnect between ideal worker norms prevalent in science and gendered norms, the concept of cumulative (dis)advantage, and the metaphor of glass ceilings and mazes.

Ideal worker norms and gendered norms. The academic tenure system favors ideal workers—those who can dedicate themselves to their academic pursuits above all else. The professorship is based on a monastic tradition, and the tenure system tends to reward those who sublimate private concerns to their jobs (Finkelstein, 1984). The "up or out" nature of the tenure process creates considerable pressure for novitiates. The culture of tenure has created an environment of competition that appears to reward dedication to the position—the professorship—above all else in life. This is the very description of the ideal worker. These norms are characteristic of the notions put forth by Moen in her work on career mystique (Moen & Roehling, 2005). She argues that it is a myth that hard work leads to career success and that career failure is a result of simply not working hard enough. Faculty members, like individuals in other professions, have created an expectation that does not allow individuals time out from their careers without being seen as nonproductive. Furthermore, if they take too many breaks, workers (i.e., faculty members) are viewed by their colleagues as not working hard enough. Moen explains that part of career mystique is the idea that "clocking in" and being present is often more important than actual productivity. This career mystique is particularly acute in the academic profession because of stereotypes and beliefs about faculty members held by those outside the profession (and even by some in the profession) that the career is easy and requires little commitment (Jaschik, 2013), and the need to counteract that belief by maintaining that it is a strenuous job requiring untiring commitment.

Ideal worker norms shape how people think about work and careers. Given the history of the academic workplace as a male enclave, it is important not only to consider norms that govern faculty life but also to keep in mind how gender plays into these norms at work and at home. In our society, both men and women face gendered expectations and norms. One such norm faced by women is that if they are to have children, then they must fulfill their role as primary caregiver and ideal mother. As the literature portrays, ideal mothers are dedicated solely to the care of their children, a proposition that would exclude women from full participation in the workforce (Somerville, 2000).

Cumulative (dis)advantage. One explanation for the underrepresentation of women in many disciplines, in the highest ranks, and at the most prestigious institutions can be attributed to the concept of cumulative (dis)advantage. The earliest conceptualization of cumulative disadvantage related to female faculty was in a study conducted by Clark and Corcoran (1986), who theorized that just as individuals accumulate and compound wealth, they can also accumulate and compound advantage and disadvantage in their careers. Success as a faculty member is really an accumulation of advantage over time, in which faculty members exploit small gains to obtain greater gains (Merton & Rossi, 1968). This is also known as the "Matthew effect," where the "rich get richer and the poor get poorer." For female faculty, as Valian (2000) also points out, this means that small inequities can build up over time to create fairly large disparities and inequities between men and women. Professional women, including faculty members, who end up at a slight disadvantage in interactions with colleagues, senior faculty, department chairs, and deans can accumulate a fairly significant disadvantage over time that can impact career progression (Valian, 2000).

Glass ceilings and mazes. The notion of the glass ceiling suggests that a "ceiling" of unstated norms and distorted expectations hinders women from reaching the top rungs of the career ladder (Cotter, Hemsen, Ovadia, & Vanneman, 2001). The greater the progressions along the academic ladder, the less women are represented. A large body of work deals with the various barriers faced by women in academia (e.g., Fox & Mohapatra, 2007; Rosser & Lane, 2002). There are several explanations for the glass ceiling, including sexism, workplace discrimination, cultural inequities, career choices, work-family conflict, lack of mentoring, and workplace priorities that are not valued (e.g., in higher education, engaging in service over research; Cotter et al., 2001). In STEM fields, the glass ceiling is manifest similarly in that opportunity for women is greatest at the lowest levels of the fields, with opportunities diminishing as careers progress. Women have opportunity and higher representation at "lower" levels as research assistants, lab technicians, and adjunct professors, but their representation lessens as the academic ladder progresses and where the barriers that limit ongoing advancement are present. It is important to note that these barriers may not always be formal (i.e., people or institutions purposefully blocking entry) but may instead be informal (i.e., women opting out because they perceive it to be incompatible with other life choices; Ceci et al., 2014). An extension of the glass ceiling metaphor is that of glass mazes, walls or obstacle courses, which all suggest that barriers are evident not just in moving up the career ladder but also throughout the process and, in particular, in graduate school (De Welde & Laursen, 2011). A commonality that exists across the various glass metaphors that represent women's lack of progress in STEM and academic careers is that of inequality and blocked career advancement (De Welde & Laursen, 2011).

Charting the Course: Tips for What's Next

The review of literature related to women in STEM-related disciplines makes clear that progress for women has been slow. There is opportunity to improve not only the representation of women but also their experiences at all stages of the educational and academic career. The intent of the chapter has been to provide background and context about academic women. We close the chapter with ideas to prompt and guide ongoing thinking and further action to address the problems associated with women in STEM and at the institutions where they work and study.

Given the amount of attention and money dedicated to the topic, if it were an easy fix, gender equity and parity would already be achieved. Instead, the problem is slow to budge. Making progress requires sustained attention to formal and informal structures at all stages of the pipeline and attention to the nuances associated with "women" (not all women are the same) and disciplinary norms (not all disciplines are the same). Addressing issues associated with women in STEM calls for sustained efforts to understand the problem differently and to recognize the role of power, gender, and difference in the problem and its remedy.

Starting early in the educational experience (as early as elementary school), efforts need to be maintained to keep girls engaged in science and, more important, math since it is competence and familiarity with math that is the gateway to ongoing progress in all areas of STEM (Ceci et al., 2014). Elementary- and high-school-aged students need access and awareness to the types of careers and experiences that are associated with the pursuit of different classes and majors. At the undergraduate level, ongoing efforts need to focus on the recruitment and retention of women in STEM disciplines. It is vital for campuses to have role models, both men and women, who can show students different aspects of scientific careers. Classes, especially gateway classes that tend to "make or break" participation in particular disciplines, need to shift from a focus on teaching to one that is geared to student learning and development (Brainard & Carlin, 1997). Another important element of the undergraduate experience is the role that faculty members and advisors play in providing research experiences for students and preparation for graduate school (Golde & Dore, 2001).

The graduate school stage is crucial for ongoing progression in STEM career and academic progressions. The literature makes clear that the experiences of men and women can differ and, accordingly, interventions need to address unique needs. Students need mentorship as part of their graduate experience, and mentoring relationships need to be monitored to assess their ongoing effectiveness in helping student progress. One promising practice is to have programs focused on helping with retention that can assist with making sure student needs are being met. It is also important for mentors to recognize how gender can affect experience. Collaboration is vital to success for graduate students and early career faculty. While many of these collaborations can and do evolve naturally, there may also need to be intentionality to assure that people are not excluded. Such connections are particularly important for women working in disciplines or research programs that require field-based work. It is critical that women have access to the research skills learned through advising and collaborative experiences.

In addition to collaboration, early career faculty and graduate students need to see and be introduced to not only different careers but also the way people can carry out their careers. There is no one way to be a scientist or a faculty member. Advisors and mentors play such an important role in early career socialization that it is easy to see only one way to be a professor or scientist or researcher, and ideal worker models often prevail (Ward & Wolf-Wendel,

2012). In reality, there are multiple paths to success and ways to keep women with children in the academic pipeline. Ideal worker norms pose one model for success, but it is not the only one. Many people in STEM are successful using a more expansive and flexible approach to their work lives. One-size-fits-all models in STEM careers tend to model what has historically been true for men. Such tropes may no longer be useful to men or women seeking to fulfill careers and life outside of work.

Cultures need to change. One of the problems with using metaphors like pipelines and glass ceilings is that it puts the onus on the person navigating those spaces as the key actor. It is easy to look at individuals who "leak" out of the pipeline as exercising individual choice. It is not uncommon to hear colleagues talk about a female faculty member who left her job to be closer to family or that someone opted for a clinical position to avoid grant pressures or that a female colleague does not want to go up for full professor because it is too political. To be sure, choices and gumption are important to academic career progression, but more important is self-reflection about work settings that foster inclusion, equity, and excellence.

Transforming outcomes associated with women in STEM disciplines calls for solutions that are as complex as the problem. Paying attention to gender, power, policies, and practices at all stages of the educational and academic career is critical. Further maintaining a keen eye on the unique needs, challenges, and opportunities present for women (especially those who are mothers) will not only help remedy problems associated with representation; it will also make for better experiences while at different career stages and ultimately make for better research, teaching, and service in higher education.

References

Alegria, S., & Branch, E. H. (2015). Causes and consequences of inequality in the STEM: Diversity and its discontents. *International Journal of Gender, Science, and Technology*, 7(3), 321–342.

Allen, E. (2011). Women's status in higher education: Equity matters. *ASHE Higher Education Report*, 37(1), 1–163.

Armstrong, M. A., & Jovanovic, J. (2017). The intersectional matrix: Rethinking institutional change for URM women in STEM. *Journal of Diversity in Higher Education*, 10(3), 216–231.

Bilimoria, D., & Xiangfen, L. (2011). *Gender equity in science and engineering: Advancing change in higher education*. Florence, KY: Routledge, Taylor & Francis.

Blickenstaff, J. (2005). Women and science careers: Leaky pipeline or gender filter? *Gender and Education*, 17(4), 369–386.

Brainard, S., & Carlin, L. (1997). A longitudinal study of undergraduate women in engineering and science. *Frontiers in Education Conference, 27th Annual Conference. Teaching and Learning in an Era of Change* (pp. 134–143).

Brown, T. M., & Dreby, J. (Eds.). (2013). *Family and work in everyday ethnography*. Philadelphia, PA: Temple University Press.

Burke, R. J., & Mattis, M. C. (Eds.). (2007). *Women and minorities in science, technology, engineering, and mathematics: Upping the numbers*. Cheltenham, UK: Edward Elgar.

Ceci, S. J, Ginther, D. K., Kahn, S., & Williams, W. M. (2014). Women in academic science: Explaining the gap. *Psychological Science in the Public Interest, 15*(3), 75–141.

Chen, X., & Soldner, M. (2013). STEM attrition: College students' paths into and out of STEM fields. *National Center for Education Statistics*. Retrieved from http://nces.ed .gov/pubs2014/2014001rev.pdf

Clark, S. M., & Corcoran, M. (1986). Perspectives on the professional socialization of women faculty: A case of accumulative disadvantage. *Journal of Higher Education, 57*, 20–43.

Cotter, D. A., Hermsen, J. M., Ovadia, S., & Vanneman, R. (2001). The glass ceiling effect. *Social Forces, 80*(2), 655–681.

Curtis, J. (2011, April). *Persistent inequity: Gender and academic employment*. Paper presented at the meeting of New Voices in Pay Equity AAUW, Washington, D.C.

Dean, D., & Fleckenstein, A. (2007). Keys to success for women in science. In R. Burke & M. Mattis (Eds.), *Women and minorities in science, technology, engineering and mathematics* (pp. 28–46). Cheltenham, UK: Edward Elgar.

De Welde, K., & Laursen, S. (2011). The glass obstacle course: Informal and formal barriers for women Ph.D. students in STEM fields. *International Journal of Gender, Science and Technology, 3*(3), 571–595.

Englander, K., Yáñez, C., & Barney, X. (2013). Doing science within a culture of machismo and marianismo. *Journal of International Women's Studies, 13*(3), 65–85.

Fealing, K. H., Lai, Y., & Meyers, S. L. (2015). Pathways vs. pipelines to broadening participation in the STEM workforce. *Journal of Women and Minorities in Science and Engineering, 21*(4), 271–293.

Finkelstein, M. J. (1984). *The American academic profession: A synthesis of social science inquiry since World War II*. Columbus, OH: Ohio State University Press.

Fox, M. F., & Mohapatra, S. (2007). Social-organizational characteristics of work and publication productivity among academic scientists in doctoral-granting departments. *The Journal of Higher Education, 78*(5), 542–571.

Golde, C. M., & Dore, T. M. (2001). At cross purposes: What the experiences of today's doctoral students reveal about doctoral education. Retrieved from http://www.wcer.wisc .edu/phd-survey/golde.html

González Ramos, A. M., & Bosch, N. V. (2013). International mobility of women in science and technology careers: Shaping plans for personal and professional purposes. *Gender, Place & Culture, 20*(5), 613–629.

Harding, S. (1986). *The science question in feminism*. Ithaca: Cornell University Press.

Hargens, L. L., & Long, J. S. (2002). Demographic inertia and women's representation among faculty in higher education. *The Journal of Higher Education, 73*(4), 494–517.

Hargens, L. L., McCann, J. C., & Reskin, B. F. (1978). Productivity and reproductivity: Fertility and professional achievement among research scientists. *Social Forces, 57*(1), 154–163.

Herr, J. L., & Wolfram, C. D. (2012). Work environment and opt-out rates at motherhood across high-education career paths. *ILR Review, 65*(4), 928–950.

Herzig, A. H. (2004). 'Slaughtering this beautiful math': Graduate women choosing and leaving mathematics. *Gender and Education, 16*(3), 379–395.

Holmes, M. A., & O'Connell, S. (2003). Where are the women geoscience professors? *Papers in the Earth and Atmospheric Sciences*. Paper 86.

Jaschik, S. (2013). Least stressful job? Really. *Inside Higher Ed.* Retrieved from https://www.insidehighered.com/news/2013/01/07/claim-college-professor-least-stressful-job-infuriates-faculty

Kelly, K., & Grant, L. (2012). Penalties and premiums: The impact of gender, marriage, and parenthood on faculty salaries in science, engineering and mathematics (SEM) and non-SEM fields. *Social Studies of Science, 42*(6), 869–896.

Kezar, A. J., & Sam, C. (2010). *Understanding the new majority of non-tenure-track faculty in higher education: Demographics, experiences, and plans of action.* San Francisco, CA: Jossey-Bass.

Kulis, S., Sicotte, D., & Collins, S. (2002). More than a pipeline problem: Labor supply constraints and gender stratification across academic science disciplines. *Research in Higher Education, 43*(6), 657–691.

Lewis, J., Menzies, H., Najera, E., & Page, R. (2009). Rethinking trends in minority participation in the sciences. *Science Education, 93*(6), 961–977.

Macfarlane, A., & Luzzadder-Beach, S. (1998). Overview: Achieving equity between women and men in the geosciences. *Geological Society of America Bulletin, 110*(12), 1590–1614.

Main, J. B., Prenovitz, S., & Ehrenberg, R. G. (2017). In pursuit of a tenure-track faculty position: Career progression and satisfaction of humanities and social sciences doctorates. *Cornell Higher Education Research Institute.* Working paper.

Mason, M., Wolfinger, N. H., & Goulden, M. (2013). *Do babies matter? Gender and family in the ivory tower.* New Brunswick, NJ: Rutgers University Press.

Mattis, M. (2007). Upstream and downstream in the engineering pipeline: What's blocking US women from pursuing engineering careers? In R. Burke & M. Mattis (Eds.), *Women and minorities in science, technology, engineering and mathematics* (pp. 334–362). Cheltenham, UK: Edward Elgar.

McGuire, K. L., Primack, R. B., & Losos, E. C. (2012). Dramatic improvements and persistent challenges for women ecologists. *BioScience, 62*(2), 189–196.

Merton, R. K., & Rossi, A. S. (1968). Contributions to the theory of reference group behavior. In R. K. Merton (Ed.), *Social theory and social structure* (pp. 229–235). New York: Free Press.

Moen, P., & Roehling, P. (2005). *The career mystique: Cracks in the American dream.* Lanham, MD: Rowman and Littlefield.

Monosson, E. (Ed.). (2008). *Motherhood, the elephant in the laboratory: Women scientists speak out.* Ithaca, NY: Cornell University Press.

Moyer, M. W. (2012). The motherhood gap. *Scientific American, 306*(6), 16.

National Academy of Sciences (NAS), Committee on Maximizing the Potential of Women in Academic Science and Engineering and Committee on Science, Engineering, and Public Policy. (2007). *Beyond bias and barriers: Fulfilling the potential of women in academic science and engineering.* Washington, D.C.: National Academies Press.

National Science Foundation (NSF). (2013). Survey of earned doctorates. Retrieved from http://www.nsf.gov/statistics/srvydoctorates/

O'Connell, S., & Holmes, M. A. (2005). Women in oceanography: Women of the academy and the sea. *Oceanography, 18*(1), 12–17.

Patton, S. (2014, October 27). STEM stories: Diversity in academe. *Chronicle of Higher Education.*

Rosser, S. V., & Lane, E. O. N. (2002). Key barriers for academic institutions seeking to retain female scientists and engineers: Family-unfriendly policies. Low Numbers, stereotypes, and harassment. *Journal of Women and Minorities in Science and Engineering, 8*(2).

Rothman, B. K. (2013). Theorizing the field: Beyond blurred boundaries and into the thick of things. In T. M. Brown & J. Dreby (Eds.), *Family and work in everyday ethnography* (pp. 17–28). Philadelphia, PA: Temple University Press.

Schiebinger, L., Henderson, D. A., & Gilmartin, S. (2008). *Dual career couples: What universities need to know*. Michelle R. Clayman Institute for Gender Research, Stanford University.

Settles, I. H., Cortina, L. M., Malley, J., & Stewart, A. J. (2006). The climate for women in academic science: The good, the bad, and the changeable. *Psychology of Women Quarterly, 30*, 47–58.

Seymour, E., & Hewitt, N. (1997). *Talking about leaving: Why undergraduates leave the sciences*. Boulder, CO: Westview Press.

Somerville, J. (2000). *Feminism and the family: Politics and society in the UK and USA*. New York, NY: Palgrave Macmillan.

Stone, P. (2007). *Opting out? Why women really quit careers and head home*. Berkeley, CA: University of California Press.

Thompson, L., Perez, R. C., & Shevenell, A. E. (2011). Closed ranks in oceanography. *Nature Geoscience, 4*(4), 211–212.

Valian, V. (2000). *Why so slow? The advancement of women*. Cambridge, MA: The MIT Press.

Ward, K., & Wolf-Wendel, L. (2008). Choice and discourse in faculty careers: Feminist perspectives of work and family. In Glazer, J. (Ed.), *Unfinished business: New and continuing gender challenges in higher education*. Baltimore, MD: Jossey-Bass.

Ward, K., & Wolf-Wendel, L. E. (2012). *Academic motherhood: Managing work and family*. New Brunswick, NJ: Rutgers University Press.

Ward, K., & Wolf-Wendel, L. (2017). Mothering and professing: Critical choices and the academic career. *NASPA Journal about Women in Higher Education, 10*(3), 229–243.

Williams, J. (2001). *Unbending gender: Why family and work conflict and what to do about it*. Cambridge, UK: Oxford University Press.

2

Fieldwork and Parenting
in Archaeology

●●●●●●●●●●●●●●●●●●●●●●●

STACEY L. CAMP

> Anxiety is the other inheritance that
> trails women who write
> —Behar, 1995, 15

Introduction

In the wee hours of a morning in the spring of 2013, I found myself wide awake
with the overwhelming and completely irrational fear that this could be the last
time I see my children, a fear that follows me with every trip I take. My bags had
been carefully packed the night before as my children observed with concern
and curiosity, too young to understand that mama was going on a long journey.
The months leading up to the trip were filled with persistent, painful reminders
that it was coming, such as vaccination appointments and meetings to determine my itinerary, but now that the day had arrived the idea of leaving my toddler and preschooler was terrifying. An oppressive guilt I had been fighting for
weeks had now clouded my usually pragmatic mind, one that had just as easily
swiftly and unemotionally rationalized the scholarly and professional benefits
that would come with such a trip. But now my mind was fixated on the little
ones I was leaving and the things I was sacrificing for academic work; I had made
the choice to wean my nearly 2-year-old son over the course of the two weeks
leading up to the trip, a process punctuated by hormone-infused sobs on my
part, and relatively no complaints on his.

Though I knew there would be a few opportunities to communicate while away, I was spending at least a week in a place where I would not be able to talk with my family on a daily basis; phones were expensive, the time differences were difficult to manage with my work schedule and my husband's schedule, the internet was unpredictable, and the power was intermittent and unreliable. Heart heavy with this knowledge and an anxiety many working parents know well, I gently kissed both of my children goodbye and whispered "I love yous" as they lay in peaceful slumber. I slipped out of the warm bed and tip-toed into the living room, solemnly awaiting the 5:00am cab that would begin my days-long journey to Asia from the United States and trek far away from the ones I love.

As an archaeologist, my work life is characterized by mobility and travel. Such professional expectations are the genesis of a discipline historically rooted in international travel and isolation from the outside world, including the neglect of one's parental, spousal, and familial obligations. The formative days of archaeology were populated by charismatic, privileged white men whose upbringing afforded them the financial support to undertake such adventures. Their social milieu encouraged and rewarded the colonization and plundering of other cultures for the benefit of the Western world. From its onset, archaeology was defined as a masculine endeavor. Root's account of pioneering females in archaeology illustrates that the history of archaeological practice has been dominated by "the heroic great man 'cowboy' model of archaeological visionary and adventurer" (2006, p. 9); this has resulted in "synthetic histories of the field" being "written by these men, and they are for the most part about men often cast quite explicitly as heroes and adventurers" (Root, 2006, p. 9).

Such accounts have been revisited by historians of archaeology, with the important discovery that "the 'fathers of archaeology' did not routinely engage in excavations themselves but rather had artifacts and materials brought to them for study in the comfort of their homes and museums" (Tomášková, 2007, p. 272; Lucas, 2001). Physically excavating soil as a lone archaeologist or as an archaeologist working on a team did not become a hallmark of the discipline until the twentieth century (Tomášková, 2007, p. 272). This "romanticization of fieldwork" haunts contemporary archaeology. Fieldwork continues to be a principle characteristic of the profession, a practice that is ableist and glorifies "its physicality, its emphasis on exploration and adventure, and its attendant hardships and ordeals" (Moser, 2007, p. 249). You can hear echoes of such sentiments in my earlier narrative; it is part of who I am as a white, middle-class female archaeologist enculturated in a profession that places a high value on fieldwork.

Historic and contemporary media have also played into these disciplinary narratives regarding the gendered, racialized, sexualized, ableist, and classed identity of an archaeologist. With the exception of the hypersexualized film series *Tomb Raider* starring Angelina Jolie, Indiana Jones remains the poster child of archaeology. Indiana Jones is a far cry from a professional role model, especially for archaeologists who have families. "Indy" is emotionally detached, unable to maintain successful relationships with his family, students, and paramours. He is untethered to anything but his pursuit and plundering of the past. In the latest installment in the *Indiana Jones* franchise that made its theatrical debut in 2008, Indy discovers that he has a teenage son sired with one of his former romances, an intelligent globe-trotter who sacrificed her own professional aspirations due to her assumption that Indy could not handle the task of parenting while pursuing his archaeological vocation. Upon first appearance, these images may seem innocuous, but stereotypes have power: they define and articulate social possibilities for individuals interested in pursuing archaeology as a profession. Yet scholars still neglect to address the gendered nature of these representations, instead blaming archaeologists for narcissistically obsessing over such distortions (Marwick, 2010, p. 395). If archaeologists wish to form a more inclusive discipline, we must consider how this visual culture is received by others and how it limits the types of individuals who pursue archaeology as a profession. For instance, Battle-Baptiste, one of the few African American women practicing archaeology in academia, notes that "the popular imagery of the 'Indiana Jones factor' has never related to me as a woman of African descent, nor does it capture a lot of clout with my community" (2011, p. 70).

One of the ways feminists in other fields have sought to undermine powerful stereotypes defining their professional identities is by adopting a first-person narrative style in their writing. Following these writing traditions, I interrupt my academic narratives with my own parenting stories as an academic archaeologist. My accounts are by no means an attempt to represent any one woman's experience as a parent and archaeologist, and I acknowledge that my position as a tenured academic at a United States–based university is one of privilege nearly all other professions do not afford women in this world. This stance is in line with feminist thought, which acknowledges "that no position is innocent, whether it be feminist, minority, marginal, 'other' or mainstream" and "demands accountability for the process of knowledge production" (Engelstad, 2007, p. 230; Levine, 1994, p. 10). I began writing this piece because discourses regarding managing parenting and fieldwork obligations remain suspiciously absent from scholarly literature, which is likely due to the perception that first-person narratives are less "scientific" or "objective" forms of knowledge production. When I found myself unexpectedly pregnant in my first year of a tenure-track job while being ABD (all but dissertation), I scoured the web and library for anything remotely close to a narrative about how women fared in similar shoes; the limited literature on motherhood and academia was not comforting. First-person narratives are critical to share, as they open up dialogue on how archaeologists handle their childcare in a travel- and fieldwork-demanding career. In writing this, I wish to evoke further scholarly discussion on how current and future generations of archaeologists manage the demands of a family life with the expectations of an archaeological practice still deeply tethered to its colonial legacy of fieldwork.

Scholarship on the professional experiences of female archaeologists as well as on how these entrenched stereotypes have influenced archaeological interpretations began to flourish in the 1990s and continues into the present. A recent example of such work is anthropologist Kathryn Clancy's study of the sexual harassment female anthropologists have experienced at anthropological field sites (Bohannon, 2013). Clancy's research revealed that 63 percent of women had experienced "inappropriate or sexual remarks" while at a field site (Bohannon, 2013). This chapter thus begins by examining the historical conditions that privileged a specific set of archaeological practices—fieldwork and extensive travel—methodologies that have historically been wedded with masculinity in the West. These practices neglect other forms of equally critical archaeological labor—such as laboratory work—that have been traditionally relegated to female archaeologists.

The Gendering of Archaeological Method, Practice, and Interpretation

While other academic disciplines began to explore gender dynamics within their profession and in their interpretations of data as early as the 1970s, archaeology in the United States did not engage with gender in any substantive way until the early 1980s (Hays-Gilpin & Whitley, 1998, p. 5; Gilchrist, 1999, p. 4; Conkey & Spector, 1984; Wylie, 1991, p. 31). The first significant publication on gender and archaeology was Conkey's and Spector's now canonical 1984 "Archaeology and the Study of Gender," which identified androcentrism in the field of archaeology and archaeology's lack of scientific rigor in discussions of gender in the past. Archaeological accounts of the time portrayed men occupying active, aggressive, and economically productive roles in the past, while women were assigned domestic tasks. This article was followed by Joan Gero's seminal 1985 publication, "Socio-politics and the Woman-at-Home Ideology." In it, Gero observed that academic female archaeologists were encouraged to pursue "indoor work" such as laboratory research. In contrast, the majority of male doctoral candidates were advised to carry out fieldwork, or outdoor projects. Gero attributes this discrepancy to Western ideologies about women belonging in the home. Gero also found that the NSF preferred to fund fieldwork over laboratory research. When female archaeologists applied for field-based research funding from NSF, they were much less successful than their male colleagues (Gero, 1985, p. 347).

While fieldwork has been historically gendered male, preservation, conservation, and laboratory work has been gendered female. The latter activities are seen as "passive," consisting of "doing nothing, as opposed to fieldwork excavation, which involves risk, danger, and adventure" (Beaudry & White, 1994, p. 139; Woodall & Perricone, 1981). Such a binary—male is to female as fieldwork is to laboratory research—stems from Victorian culture, where women were assumed to be biologically well-suited for indoor work (such as childrearing, cleaning, food preparation, and household management), while men were born to work in the outdoors. This concept is known as the "separate spheres ideology," and while a number of archaeologists have demonstrated that it was much more complex in practice, it still has traction in the contemporary Western world.

Feminist archaeologists writing in the 1980s began with revisionism. They wrote historiographies detailing the presence of female archaeologists in the past and documented women archaeologists' previously invisible contributions to the field. First-wave archaeologists challenged archaeological narratives that cast women as "passive" actors, fulfilling their domestic duties within the confines of the home or their village, while men, in contrast, brought home the lion's share of food via hunting. Some of the earliest published feminist scholarship was criticized for inverting androcentric interpretations of the past rather than emphasizing the fluid and "localized" nature of gender identities (Conkey & Gero, 1991, p. 10). Second-wave feminist archaeology generated more nuanced, data-driven theories of gender relations in the past, rooting their analyses in what archaeologists call a multiscalar analysis. Multiscalar analyses involves triangulating disparate sets of data—such as oral histories, multimedia (e.g., photographs, film, etc.), literature (e.g., prescriptive manuals on everything from pregnancy to manners), archaeological data, and other documentary sources—to form a more informed picture of the past. Third-wave feminism broadened explorations of gender by highlighting the situational, fluid nature of gender and sexuality as well as by untethering gender from sexuality (Schmidt & Voss, 2000; Meskell & Joyce, 2003; Joyce, 2008). This body of work, which continues to grow, emphasizes that sexuality is not always a reflection of one's gender identity. This literature likewise questions the historical and sociocultural conditions that permit certain sexual and gender identities to flourish; for instance, Casella (2000a, 2000b) conducts the archaeology of all-female, convict-era prisons in Australia to explore how institutionalized settings can shape inmates' sexual behavior and associated material practices.

Feminist archaeologists have also noted how "theory" has been relegated to men, while gender studies has been posited as outside of theory, associated with the "lunatic fringe" of mostly female authors (Wright, 1998, p. 53). Conkey's 2007 study of four newly published archaeology theory edited volumes documents an alarming trend; though there are 102 individual authors in these readers, only 27 percent are women (Conkey, 2007, p. 293). Especially concerning is the ghettoization of scholarship on the archaeology of gender, with 85 percent of the chapters on gender archaeology authored by women in these volumes (Conkey, 2007, p. 293). Hutson's (2002) study of citational practices within the journals *American Antiquity*, *Journal of Field Archaeology*, *Ancient Mesoamerica*, and *Southeastern Archaeology* provides a ray of hope. In terms of publications in *American Antiquity*, Hutson discovered that gender equity in citational practices was achieved starting in 1982, which is when women began serving as editors of the journal (2002, p. 333).

These publications ushered in a new era of exploring problematic gender issues within the profession of archaeology and an examination of archaeological interpretations of gender relations in the past, though these United States–based contributions were slow to hit the press when contrasted with literature of the same subject matter in "Scandinavia and the United Kingdom" (Hays-Gilpin & Whitley, 1998, p. 5). The relative archaeological silence on gender issues stemmed from the lack of women working in the field—what Claassen describes as a "century of isolation" for women in the discipline (1995, p. 5). In the United States alone, Gero estimated that only 20 percent of archaeologists were female in 1991 (1991, p. 97, in Gilchrist, 1999, p. 23). The figure was a bit higher for England and Australia in the mid-1990s, where "approximately 35 per cent of archaeologists" was made up of women (Morris, 1994; Beck, 1994, cited in Gilchrist, 1999, p. 23).

How do we continue to shift the tide of archaeological practice so that the discipline is more equitable? It is within the walls of the academy that archaeology can be defined in broader terms. A quick glance of 2015's job advertisements suggest that being a principal director of a large field project and directing field schools are still prerequisites for obtaining a tenure-track job. With the overwhelming backlog of uncatalogued artifacts—a situation known as the "curation crisis"—that began accumulating in state, federal, and private museums and universities as early as the mid-1800s, academia must find a way to reconfigure its expectations for archaeological research. One way to do so is by decolonizing archaeology's focus on fieldwork—a practice that is colonial in origin—as the primary indicator of academic success. Many decades worth of unanalyzed artifacts sit dormant in laboratories due to archaeology's incessant emphasis on fieldwork (Lipe, 1974; Marquardt, Montet-White, & Scholtz, 1982). Voss's work (2012) on the Market Street Chinatown Collection is an example of how previously abandoned archaeological collections can breathe new life into our understandings of marginalized histories and generate publications. Revising and reevaluating our expectations regarding fieldwork might likewise bring new individuals into the field of archaeology and help the discipline move away from its androcentric past.

Writing Culture, Writing Archaeology

My daughter was born in August 2009 in the small town of Moscow, Idaho. The morning after she was born a nurse came into my hospital room with a local newspaper; it detailed a grant I had been awarded—the first big federal grant of my career. I politely thanked her for the paper and immediately discarded it next to my bed, out of sight. This grant would fund and mark the first of my archaeological fieldwork projects as a tenure-track faculty member. I obsessed over the picture of me in the paper—done up, thin, healthy. I didn't even know that person anymore even though the photo was taken less than a year before my pregnancy. It looked nothing like me in that hospital bed—bloated from pre-eclampsia and months of bed-rest, in extreme pain from a complicated delivery; sick and exhausted from painkillers; hair matted from a days-long labor; bleeding profusely as I painfully tried to get my daughter to latch and successfully nurse amidst her colicky screams that would characterize our relationship many months following her birth. As the photo and the newspaper incident attested, I could not escape my academic identity in the eyes of others. Less than 16 hours after giving birth to my firstborn, I was forced to confront the unending struggle of reconciling my motherly and scholarly identity.

Flash forward to summer 2010: my first attempt to manage the expectations of archaeological fieldwork and motherhood with my now 1-year-old daughter. Since she was born, I had been frantically working on publications, grant proposals, new course preps, and managing my second year on the tenure-track. Money was a challenge for me and my husband, meaning that we could not afford full-time childcare during this period of time. I cobbled together full-time childcare for four weeks of fieldwork, relying on my out-of-state mother who is a primary caretaker for her mother, my out-of-state full-time employed mother-in-law, my husband's vacation time, and a nanny to cover my time in the field away from my daughter. I ran the field project over the weekends and three days of the work week so that my husband could handle care on his days off. I came home on the days we were "off" of work and immediately jumped into my role as full-time mommy. It gave me a reprieve from the stress of managing people and allowed me to connect with her, if only for a few days.

One morning on my day "off" from the project and back home with my daughter, I discovered I was pregnant. I was overcome with joy after experiencing years of infertility and a miscarriage a few months earlier. A day later, I headed back into the field. A few days later, I rolled out of bed and made my way to the bathroom to discover I was bleeding. As someone who is RH negative, I realized that this meant I needed to be at a hospital for an injection to protect myself and future pregnancies within 24 hours of bleeding. The only problem was that the hospital was 3 hours away, back at home. I worked in the field that day, warned my field crew that I might have to take it easy, and at the end of the work day I headed back home to get my injection and blood panels done that night. The latter confirmed what I already knew; my hormone levels were low, too low to sustain a viable pregnancy.

Because field projects are short in duration, housing and work permits are secured months, sometimes years, in advance, and staff and student workers are employed during the brief period of time, the project must go on even in the midst of crisis. As a director, I had no choice. I miscarried in the field for a week, constantly changing pads of tissue and heavy blood. In the field, I was filled with emotions that are still difficult to articulate and diffuse in content; the loss, the worry of not being able to have another child; the awkward silences from students who were unsure how to talk to me after the word had spread I was suffering from a miscarriage; the exhaustion of working and keeping it together while miscarrying during what had already been a rough summer of sacrificing parental duties over my fieldwork obligations. I felt resigned for the rest of the summer and wondered how I would ever manage something that big and exhausting again as a mother.

In the late 1980s, cultural anthropology—a subfield of anthropology and sister to archaeology—underwent a literary revolution and postmodernist shift that appeared to be paving the way for new forms of ethnographic description and writing, such as the narrative above. This transition involved anthropologists considering their own biases and subjectivity in relationship to their informants (known as "reflexivity") or individuals they studied and including informants' voices in their ethnographies (also known as "multivocality").

Some scholars argued that this literary revolution had been long in the making, however, and that it started with the advent of feminist thought. Though feminist theory had been present since the late 1940s, it was neglected by those wishing to forge a new discipline out of what feminists argued was already a well-trodden scholarly path: "However, despite these similarities, when anthropologists look for a theory on which to ground the new ethnography, they turn to postmodernism, dismissing feminist theory as having little to teach that anthropology does not already know" (Mascia-Lees, Sharpe, & Cohen, 1989, p. 12–13). As feminists pointed out, this was certainly not the first moment in anthropological history when anthropologists had toyed with different narrative techniques. When anthropology was first establishing itself as a field separate from the writings of "colonial officials, missionaries, traders, explorers, members of learned societies," anthropologists adopted a more objective, sterile tone (Visweswaran, 1994, p. 5). Some of the first female ethnographers also "portrayed women's lives through the use of third-person objective accounts" (Visweswaran, 1994, p. 21). Rather than being acknowledged for introducing unique narrative forms, early female anthropologists' voices were repackaged and renamed, "reclassified in more academically favorable terms" (Behar, 1995, p. 4) or neglected altogether as confessional and not objective accounts of culture.

When new theories are generated in cultural anthropology, they tend to have a ripple effect on archaeology. Archaeology's equivalent of cultural anthropology's "postmodernist turn" took place during the late 1980s, and it looked different in practice. While cultural anthropologists turned toward self-reflexivity and writing as an ethnographic act, postprocessualist archaeologists deconstructed the method of archaeology (e.g., Hodder, 1986; Shanks & Tilley, 1987), examined public and community archaeology as a tool of political engagement (Leone et al., 1987; Little & Shackel, 1991; La Roche & Blakey, 1997; McDavid, 1997), and investigated the sociopolitics of archaeological practice (Trigger, 1989; Gathercole & Lowenthal, 1990; Gero & Root, 1990; Arnold, 1990). Few experimented with language as a tool for disrupting traditional archaeological practice due to the legacy of processualist thought in archaeology. In the 1960s, processualist archaeologists adopted a scientific, distanced, and sterile writing style as a way to discipline the field into being seen as a respectable scientific enterprise: a process that paralleled cultural anthropology's formation as a discipline. And like feminist anthropology, feminist archaeology, which began many years before postprocessualism emerged, often became subsumed under postprocessualism instead of being seen as a distinct field of study formed by female archaeologists.

Given the lasting legacy of androcentrism in archaeology, it is difficult to conceive how archaeologists can begin to have a conversation about managing the demands of parental and fieldwork obligations when gender archaeology still remains splintered from mainstream archaeology. Nevertheless, we must start somewhere. Feminist anthropologists likewise struggled to write under the weight of cultural anthropology's androcentric legacy; as Behar ruminated in 1995, "What kind of writing is possible for feminist anthropologists now, if to write unconventionally puts a woman in the category of untrained wife, while writing according to the conventions of the academy situates her as a textual conservative" (1995, p. 13). The first question archaeologists must ask themselves is, How can the discipline shift the narrative from seeing fieldwork as the defining characteristic of archaeology?

This leads us to a second and equally critical question: does shifting the narrative also require a shift in archaeological praxis? What if, for instance, we choose to see parenting as a site of scholastic creativity and inspiration rather than an obstacle preventing archaeologists from pursuing an academic trajectory? Might we realign our tenure and promotion standards to reward qualitative writing on archaeological fieldwork, laboratory work, and parenting given the dearth of narratives? Certainly cultural anthropologists have found value in reflecting upon their own experiences in relationship to the discipline and their informants. Are these narratives preventing certain groups of historically marginalized individuals from entering the discipline of archaeology? Ward and Wolf-Wendel documented the preponderance of negative stories found in literature on female faculty members managing their careers and parenthood during their qualitative and quantitative study of academic mothers (2012, p. 9). Ward and Wolf-Wendel sought to interrogate the veracity of these accounts by conducting a longitudinal study of mother academics and in the process uncovered a very different story of mother academics who made the institution work in their favor. In a recent study of female academics in archaeology, the authors similarly found that while the women surveyed faced challenges with "family responsibilities and scheduling fieldwork," they managed to carry out archaeological fieldwork "through a combination of supportive partners and creative childcare" (Goldstein, Mills, Burkholder, Herr, 2017).

What would an archaeology that encompasses its practitioners' daily praxis look like, and could it too pave the way for new definitions of what archaeology entails and who is an archaeologist? Archaeological storytelling can create richer, more engaging interpretations of the past, as can sharing reflexive accounts of one's experience in archaeology. This form of reflexive writing is uncommon in the discipline (Franklin, in Battle-Baptiste, 2011, p. 7). We see snippets of this kind of scholarship buried in archaeological monographs' epilogues, forewords, and dedications. In a rare exception, Wilkie (2003) sees pregnancy and parenthood as fertile ground. She observed in her historical archaeological work an African American midwife living in late nineteenth- and early twentieth-century Alabama: "When I was pregnant . . . I found myself more intrigued by the birthing aspect of midwifery practice. I became fascinated by the ways that midwives were able to combine traditional and new medical practices and products into the birth experience in ways that would have been reassuring to the different generations of women attending a particular birth. . . . I developed these ideas through October 1997, when the birth of my daughter pretty much slammed the brakes on further writing for a time" (2003, pp. xvii–xix).

Battle-Baptiste (2011) similarly finds inspiration in her family, who encouraged her to correct scholarly assumptions about the archaeological record of African American enslavement and emancipation. An archaeology that acknowledges the minutiae of *our* daily lives can help us understand the past, as Wilkie and Battle-Baptiste have demonstrated. A reflexive archaeology can also make room for those who have traditionally felt excluded by the discipline.

Conclusion

It is the fall of 2012. A graduate student and I took a trip to visit my ongoing archaeological project as a prospective M.A. project. My nearly 1-year-old son is still nursing and refuses to take a bottle, so he is along for the ride. Half of the one-way three-hour trip involves intermittent screams from a child who has always expressed his disdain for the restraint modern car seats require. The site is approximately three hours from my university; cell phone and internet service cease about 30 minutes into the drive due to the remoteness of it.

About an hour into the drive, smoke fills the air: though dissipating, fires had ravaged the landscapes that bookend my site. As soon as we arrive on site, we quickly jump out of the car and plan to make the survey quick due to air quality. I plunk a pacifier in my son's mouth and gently place him on my back in a baby carrier. He is quiet, comfortable with our snug, bodily embrace—at least for now—and we cross a creek on foot and visit the archaeological site. As soon as the visit is done and we have forged the creek once again, my son starts crying out: the pacifier has been lost, and it is going to be a long, loud drive home.

A year and a half later, I return to the site, childless, with a team of students, volunteers, and staff for four weeks. My heart is once again heavy with the knowledge that I am out in the middle of nowhere, out of cell phone range if an emergency comes up with my children who are 3 hours away. I fight feelings of helplessness, mother-guilt, and worry and focus on the work that needs to be done. Tunnel vision is essential to my survival. On our first day of the project, I cross the same creek, now icy-cold from snow melt and knee-deep in height. I follow the same path I took in 2012 with my son on my back. My eyes fixate on the ground to examine how the landscape has changed over the past year, how weather and associated erosion have unearthed previously unseen archaeological deposits. My attention is immediately drawn to a bright blue object sticking halfway out of the dirt. I pick it up and lo and behold there is the lost pacifier: a painful reminder of the absences fieldwork involves. Despite my field's best attempts to make children invisible, they are there: in the archaeological record and forever haunting my mind when they are left behind.

In 1994, Soafer Derevenski asked, "Where are the children" in the archaeological record? Children, she and others argued (Lillehammer, 1989; Baxter, 2005, 2008; Kamp, 2001), were marginalized in archaeology because "like women, children are categorized at the weaker end of the male/female and adult/child dimensions and are therefore feminized (other than male) and exist in a category of the disempowered" (Baxter, 2008, p. 162). Writing in 2007, Engelstad also lamented the waning "critical feminist and theoretical edge" of the archaeology of gender and children, attributing it to "a dwindling understanding of what it is to do archaeology as a feminist as well as to institutional contexts and a discipline that 'still rewards androcentrism in so many ways'" (2007, p. 219). And now, twenty-three years since Soafer Derevenski's seminal work, I want to return to her question and reframe it by asking, Where are discussions of children and parenting *in* archaeologists' lives? The same question was asked of archaeology when feminists first began to question how the culture and climate of the discipline can be changed to welcome women. We forget that there are often children playing in the back dirt, cleaning and sorting artifacts, and that there are partners silently toiling behind the scenes. If we want to aim for a truly inclusive archaeology, we must begin to share our narratives of these silent players in the drama that is archaeological practice.

The first step forward is to investigate current work conditions in the United States for parent-archaeologists, which expands upon feminist archaeology's focus on the gendered dynamics of the archaeological workplace. This project can start with questions that have been explored in sociological literature on the status of mothers in academia (Mason, Wolfinger, & Goulden, 2013; Ward & Wolf-Wendel, 2012; Ward, Wolf-Wendel, & Marco, present volume) but will likewise require serious attention to the "disciplinary culture" of archaeology (Wylie, 2007). The former literature has identified a number of commonly held misconceptions about academics, such as the notion that "women with children do not get work done" and "pregnancy any time prior to tenure is . . . evidence that" a women "is not seriously dedicated to her career" (Mason, Wolfinger, & Goulden, 2013, p. 13). Archaeology's unique tradition of ongoing fieldwork and heritage of gender inequality requires that we ask these questions at the disciplinary level. For instance, what are the unique barriers for women and parents in general to achieving tenure in archaeology? How are these obstacles complicated by other vectors of identity, such as race, age, ability, or class? How are other professional archaeologists and academic archaeologists managing their familial and professional commitments? Are parents opting out of archaeology altogether given the difficulties that arise in managing these often conflicting responsibilities? Does fieldwork prevent certain groups of people from entering the discipline, especially given how fieldwork has been gendered masculine (Moser, 2007, p. 259)? Are archaeologists continuing to gender their interactions with students in a way where "domains of theory" are deemed "more acceptable/'suitable' for female archaeologists, such as style, households, gender, and feminism," setting women up for failure in a field that champions certain forms of theory and archaeological labor (fieldwork) over others (such as "pink collar theory"; Conkey, 2007, p. 291)?

The task of feminism is to examine how gender ideologies and other intersecting ideologies about race, class, and age among many other variables determine the social and professional possibilities of historically marginalized groups pursuing archaeology. A feminist framework allows us to begin "questioning theory" (Conkey, 2007, p. 305), investigating deeply embedded assumptions about what it means to be an archaeologist and how archaeology is practiced in the twenty-first century. It requires that those of us occupying positions of privilege in higher education, such as tenured professors, advocate for social change within the institution. New generations of feminist archaeologists must pick up where feminist archaeology has left off; conducting longitudinal studies of archaeologist parents in academia, for instance, will help reveal the barriers specific to the field. We can provide parental support by pushing for grants to accommodate summer funding stipends to pay for faculty summer salaries and summer childcare stipends at our institutions. Some universities support entire families traveling together for conferences or offer to assist with nanny or au pair travel with a parent faculty member. The funding agency Wenner-Gren provides a model of this. As with the archaeology of gender and the archaeology of childhood—two fields that were initially dismissed as tangential and difficult to study—placing the study of parenting in archaeology's foreground will generate new understandings of how our discipline can move forward in the present, become a more diversified field, and perhaps open windows into parenting in the past.

Practical Tips

- For parents working in the field with babies, consider requesting funding from your home institution, university, or granting agency (if permitted) for a nanny who can assist with childcare.
- As I've argued in this chapter, archaeological collections research is another avenue of research for parents of infants and toddlers, one that does not require traveling or digging. Consider running a laboratory field school in lieu of an "archaeological field school" to train students in archaeological curation and digitization standards.

References

Arnold, B. (1990). The past as propaganda: Totalitarian archaeology in Nazi Germany. *Antiquity*, *64*(244), 464–478.

Bardolph, D. N. (2014). A critical evaluation of recent gendered publication trends in American archaeology. *American Antiquity*, *79*(3), 522–540.

Battle-Baptiste, W. (2010). An archaeologist finds her voice: A commentary. In J. Lydon & U. Rizvi (Eds.), *Handbook of postcolonial archaeology* (pp. 387–392). World Archaeological Congress Research Handbooks in Archaeology, Volume 3. Walnut Creek, CA: Left Coast Press.

Battle-Baptiste, W. (2011). *Black feminist archaeology*. Walnut Creek, CA: Left Coast Press.

Baxter, J. E. (2005). *The archaeology of childhood: Children, gender, and material culture*. Walnut Creek: AltaMira Press.

Baxter, J. E. (2008). The archaeology of childhood. *Annual Review of Anthropology*, *37*, 159–175.

Behar, R. (1995). Introduction: Out of exile. In R. Behar & D. A. Gordon (Eds.), *Women writing culture* (pp. 1–29). Berkeley, CA: University of California Press.

Beaudry, M., & White, J. (1994). Cowgirls with the blues? A study of women's publication and the citation of women's work in historical archaeology. In Cheryl Claassen (Ed.), *Women in archaeology* (pp. 138–158). Philadelphia, PA: University of Pennsylvania.

Bohannon, J. (2013). Survey finds sexual harassment in anthropology. *Science*. Retrieved from http://www.sciencemag.org/news/2013/04/survey-finds-sexual-harassment -anthropology

Casella, E. C. (2000a). Bulldaggers and gentle ladies: Archaeological approaches to female homosexuality in convict-era Australia. In R. A. Schmidt & B. L. Voss (Eds.), *Archaeologies of sexuality* (pp. 143–159). London, UK: Routledge.

Casella, E. C. (2000b). "Doing trade": A sexual economy of nineteenth-century Australian female convict prisons. *World Archaeology, 32*(2), 209–221.

Chester, H., Rothschild, N. A., & diZerega Wall, D. (1994). Women in historical archaeology: The SHA survey. In M. C. Nelson, S. M. Nelson, & A. Wylie (Eds.), *Equity issues for women in archaeology* (pp. 213–218). Archaeological Papers of the American Anthropological Association Number 5. Washington, D.C.: American Anthropological Association.

Claassen, C. (1994). Introduction. In Cheryl Claassen (Ed.), *Women in archaeology* (p. 18). Philadelphia, PA: University of Pennsylvania Press.

Claassen, C. (Ed.). (1994). *Women in archaeology*. Philadelphia, PA: University of Pennsylvania Press.

Claassen, C. (2000). Homophobia and women archaeologists. *World Archaeology, 32*(2), 173–179.

Conkey, M. W. (2007). Questioning theory: Is there a gender of theory in archaeology? *Journal of Archaeological Method and Theory, 14*(3), 285–310.

Conkey, M. W., & Gero, J. M. (1991). Tensions, pluralities, and engendering archaeology: An introduction to women and prehistory. In M. W. Conkey & J. M. Gero (Eds.), *Engendering archaeology: Women and prehistory* (pp. 3–30). Oxford, UK: Blackwell.

Conkey, M. W., & Gero, J. M. (1997). Programme to practice: Gender and feminism in archaeology. *Annual Review of Anthropology, 26*, 411–437.

Conkey, M. W., & Spector, J. D. (1984). Archaeology and the study of gender. In Michael Schiffer (Ed.), *Advances in archaeological method and theory*, Vol. 7 (pp. 1–38). New York, NY: Academic Press.

Derevenski, J. S. (1994). Where are the children? Accessing children in the past. *Archaeological Review from Cambridge, 13*(2), 7–20.

Engelstad, E. (2007). Much more than gender. *Journal of Archaeological Method and Theory, 14*, 217–234.

Gathercole, P., & Lowenthal, D. (Eds.). (1990). *The politics of the past*. London, UK: Unwin Hyman.

Gero, J. M. (1985). Socio-politics and the woman-at-home ideology. *American Antiquity, 50*(2), 342–350.

Gero, J. M., & Conkey, M. W. (Eds.). (1991). *Engendering archaeology: Women and prehistory*. Oxford, UK: Blackwell.

Gero, J., & Root, D. (1990). Public presentations and private concerns: Archaeology in the pages of National Geographic. In P. Gathercole & D. Lowenthal (Eds.), *The politics of the past* (pp. 19–37). London, UK: Unwin Hyman.

Gilchrist, R. (1998). Women's archaeology? Political feminism, gender theory and historical revision. In K. Hays-Gilpin & D. S. Whitley (Eds.), *Reader in gender archaeology* (pp. 47–56). London, UK: Routledge.

Gilchrist, R. (1999). *Gender and archaeology: Contesting the past*. London, UK: Routledge.

Goldstein, L., Mills, B., Burkholder, J. E., & Herr, S. (2017). *SAA task force on gender disparities in archaeological grant submissions*. Retrieved from http://saa-gender.anthropology.msu.edu/

Hays-Gilpin, K., & Whitley, D.S., (Eds.). (1998). *Reader in gender archaeology*. New York, NY: Routledge.

Hodder, I. (1986). *Reading the past*. Cambridge, UK: Cambridge University Press.

Hutson, S. R. (2002). Gendered citation practices in American Antiquity and other archaeology journals. *American Antiquity, 67*(2), 331–342.

Irwin-Williams, C. (1990). Women in the field: The role of women in archaeology before 1960. In G. Kass-Simon & P. Farnes (Eds.), *Women of science: Righting the record* (pp. 1–41). Bloomington, IN: Indiana University Press.

Joyce, R. A. (2008). *Ancient bodies, ancient lives: Sex, gender, and archaeology*. New York, NY: Thames & Hudson.

Kamp, K. A. (2001). Where have all the children gone? The archaeology of childhood. *Journal of Archaeological Method and Theory, 8*(1), 1–34.

La Roche, C. J., & Blakey, M. L. (1997). Seizing intellectual power: The dialogue at the New York African Burial Ground. *Historical Archaeology, 31*(3), 84–106.

Leone, M. P., Potter, P. B., Jr., & Shackel, P. A. (1987). Toward a critical archaeology. *Current Anthropology, 28*(3), 283–302.

Levine, M. A. (1994). Creating their own niches: Career styles among women in Americanist archaeology between the wars. In Cheryl Claassen (Ed.), *Women in archaeology* (pp. 9–50). Philadelphia, PA: University of Pennsylvania Press.

Lillehammer, G. (1989). A child is born: The child's world in an archaeological perspective. *Norwegian Archaeological Review, 22*(2), 89–105.

Lipe, W. D. (1974). A conservation model for American archaeology. *The Kiva, 39*(3–4), 213–245.

Little, B. J., & Shackel, P. A. (Eds.) (2007). *Archaeology as a tool of civic engagement*. Lanham, MD: AltaMira Press.

Lucas, G. (2001). *Critical approaches to fieldwork: Contemporary and historical archaeological practice*. London, UK: Routledge.

Marquardt, W. H., Montet-White, A., & Scholtz, S. (1982). Resolving the crisis in archaeological collections curation. *Antiquity, 47*(2), 409–418.

Marwick, B. (2010). Self-image, the long view and archaeological engagement with film: An animated case study. *World Archaeology, 42*(3), 394–404.

Mascia-Lees, F. E., Sharpe, P., & Cohen, C. B. (1989). The postmodernist turn in anthropology: Cautions from a feminist perspective. *Signs, 15*(1), 7–33.

Mason, M. A., Wolfinger, N. H., & Goulden, M. (2013). *Do babies matter? Gender and family in the ivory tower*. New Brunswick, NJ: Rutgers University Press.

McDavid, C. (1997). Descendants, decisions, and power: The public interpretation of the archaeology of the Levi Jordan plantation. *Historical Archaeology, 31*(3), 114–131.

Meskell, L. M., & Joyce, R. A. (2003). *Embodied lives: Figuring ancient Maya and Egyptian experience*. London, UK: Routledge.

Moser, S. (2007). On disciplinary culture: Archaeology as fieldwork and its gendered associations. *Journal of Archaeological Method and Theory, 14*(3), 235–263.

Root, M. C. (2006). Introduction: Women of the field, defining the gendered experience. In G. M. Cohen & M. S. Joukowsky (Eds.), *Breaking ground: Pioneering women archaeologists* (pp. 1–33). Ann Arbor, MI: University of Michigan Press.

Schmidt, R. A., & Voss, B. L. (Eds.). (2000). *Archaeologies of sexuality*. London, UK: Routledge.

Shanks, M., & Tilley, C. (1987). *Social theory and archaeology*. Cambridge, UK: Polity.

Tomášková, S. (2007). Mapping a future: Archaeology, feminism, and scientific practice. *Journal of Archaeological Method and Theory, 14*, 264–284.

Trigger, B. G. (1989). *A history of archaeological thought*. Cambridge, UK: Cambridge University Press.

Visweswaran, K. (1994). *Fictions of feminist ethnography*. Minneapolis, MN: University of Minnesota Press.

Voss, B. L. (2012). Curation as research: A case study in orphaned and underreported archaeological collections. *Archaeological Dialogues, 19*(2), 145–169.

Ward, Kelly & Wolf-Wendel, L. (2012). *Academic motherhood: How faculty manage work and family*. New Brunswick, NJ: Rutgers University Press.

Wilkie, L. (2003). *The archaeology of mothering: An African-American midwife's tale*. New York, NY: Routledge.

Woodall, J. N., & Perricone, P. J. (1981). The archeologist as cowboy: The consequence of professional stereotype. *Journal of Field Archaeology, 8*, 506–509.

Wylie, A. (1991). Gender theory and the archaeological record: Why is there no archaeology of gender? In J. K. Gero & M. W. Conkey (Eds.), *Engendering archaeology: Women and prehistory* (pp. 31–54). Oxford, UK: Blackwell.

Wylie, A. (2007). Doing archaeology as a feminist: Introduction. *Journal of Archaeological Method and Theory, 14*, 209–216.

Part II

The Truth Is,
It Will Be Hard

● ● ● ● ● ● ● ● ● ● ● ● ● ● ● ● ● ● ● ●

The Difficulties of Doing
Field Research for Mothers

BAHIYYAH MIALLAH MUHAMMAD

With field research come many challenges. While we are all proof that mothering from the field can be done, it would be unrealistic for us to pretend as though it were easy. Far from being a simple endeavor, field research takes a lot of courage and determination to see through, especially when dealing with the unexpected and unknown. In the face of adversity, the authors in this chapter take the field on, singlehandedly and oftentimes without the comfort of having family nearby. Although we hope that mothers conducting field research face as few difficulties as possible, this will not always be the case. In this section, we introduce a recurring theme to come: how mothers conducting field research embody perseverance as a means of working through field challenges.

Being a mother in and of itself can be the cause of various hardships. Here we discuss the particular ways in which motherhood shapes our fieldwork. This is important because of two main reasons. First, one's motherhood may negatively impact how seriously one is taken as a scholar. Mothers have historically struggled in academia. In chapter 4, Dixon reminds us that "motherhood has not been explicitly held up as a legitimate lens through which to produce knowledge about the world" (p. 103). Second, those of us doing the work of mothering while doing fieldwork are often doing the second shift as well—whether we are single mothers or not.

Therefore, the political implications of recognizing the validity of motherhood as a lens through which to produce knowledge are such that there is a potential to shift how mothers are viewed. In her chapter, Dixon reminds us, "Instead of distracted, mothers are capable. Instead of divided in their loyalties, mothers are strong" (p. 104). As such, knowledge produced through mothering must be seen as important and unique.

In this section, Kelley Sams, Lydia Dixon, and Cecilia Vindrola-Padros introduce readers to the hardships and heartaches that field research can all too often entail for women with children. But far from using their narratives as cautionary tales, we embrace them as part of a full and complex life, allowing us to start stepping away from an often oversimplified and masculine-dominant narrative of success achieved through self-reliance and self-determination.

Approaching the field as single mothers, Sams and Dixon face many added difficulties compared to the other contributors in this volume. Their analyses reflect those, as well as the context-specific events that shaped how their individual experiences unfolded. Vindrola-Padros, in her contribution, shows us that adversity can strike field researchers, whether they travel far or stay close to home and whether they are single mothers or with a supportive partner. Specifically, both Sams and Vindrola-Padros share how they overcame a field researcher's worst nightmare—that of having a gravely ill child in the field. Because every field experience is unique, Dixon's focus differs, instead giving insight into the tangible, intangible, and theoretical contributions motherhood makes to fieldwork and vice versa. Her contribution provides an interesting pendant to Vindrola-Padros's experience on both sides of her research study: as a researcher, as well as living through events similar to those of her participants. All three contributors show us that even amid those experiences we hope to forget are reminders of why we embarked upon this work in the first place.

Section-Specific Takeaways

- Having to travel into the field alone with your child should never become your excuse for not conducting site-based research.
- Create a research plan that is realistic for you. Take the extra time needed to fully think through each component of your site-based project. It is never too early to begin this process of planning.
- Take time during fieldwork to begin transcribing, reflecting, and analyzing your data. Remember that when you return home from fieldwork, it may take some time to transition back into the swing of things. Prepare for your return in advance.

- When you feel like your head might explode from juggling all your duties, remember that it takes time to find balance between mothering and fieldwork. Be patient with yourself.
- On a softer note, no matter how important you feel your research is, there is an entire world out there that is more important than academia. Let your child remind you of this.

3

Malaria and Spider-Man

• •

Conducting Ethnographic Research in Niger with a Three-Year-Old

KELLEY SAMS

The heat comes from inside and out.
You shake.
Your eyes open and you start to say
    something.
Then the fevered sleep comes again and
    makes you silent and smaller.
The blue cup sits on the ground beside
    the mattress and a fly circles it with
    interest.
Tonight the clouds are making noise, and
    so are your lips.
The air rattles in and out of your
    mouth.
The heat stays.
For four days I give you pills, small ones
    at first, and then bigger.
Blue, white, and yellow, like the colors of
    a faraway flag.

A nation looking for allegiance from new
    citizens, for soldiers.
I tell you to stay here with the dirty
    sheets.
To fight on our side.
I promise that I will smooth them down
    with my hands.
Brush off the wrinkles and the sand.
I promise that the heat is running out,
    but I don't say it out loud.
You shake.
—November 2010, Zinder, Niger

Introduction

In this chapter, I reflect upon the year that I spent in Niger with my three-year-old son, Jibril, as I conducted fieldwork for my PhD in medical anthropology. In this reflection, I focus specifically on two events: when my son became very sick with a difficult-to-identify fever, and when he was with me during a near-robbery. However, Jibril's reading of these events is different. This chapter is written based on my memories, notes, and emails sent from the field as well as Jibril's own memories of this period of his life six years ago. This chapter addresses how returning with my son to a field site where I previously worked as a Peace Corps volunteer (before having my son) helped me develop (1) additional layers of understanding of local representations of health and disease, (2) experiential knowledge of the complexity of accessing curative care and the diversity of treatment options, and (3) a self-reflexive view on the fixed nature of the cultural expectations that Jibril and I both carried with us to the field.

Having a child with me as I collected ethnographic data for my study on trachoma elimination added value and additional struggles, and his presence contributed to how I framed and understood my research findings. The benefits of bringing Jibril with me into the field were often revealed during the most difficult moments and highlighted by collisions of contrasting cultural expectations.

Methods

In order to write about these two events with as much detail and honesty as possible, I use my notes from the detailed notebooks that I kept during the twelve months of my fieldwork. Taking notes is an important part of ethnographic research, especially for social scientists aiming to produce "thick description" (Geertz, 1994). Each day that I spent in the field, I recorded the details of the many interviews and ethnographic observations that I conducted as a part of my study. The stack of black notebooks that now sits on my university office shelf contains descriptions of how respondents interacted with their environment: for example, describing how a nurse transferred pills into small paper envelopes with his hand protected by a black plastic bag or how a volunteer had nailed the posters developed to support community health education about sanitation and hygiene over the window of her living room to block the heat of the sun.

In between these pages of academic and anthropological field notes, and on their margins, are my writing and drawings describing my personal experience in Niger. On some pages, the rows of block letters change to looped cursive stream-of-consciousness prose; lines of my musings or grocery lists appear beside interview notes.

In the years since I finished my PhD fieldwork, I have looked at these notebooks, but always selectively, never considering these more personal and less "academic" entries, always going straight for the notes that I could use for chapters of my thesis or articles. However, these informal entries, engaged here, show a lot about what I saw and experienced in the field. The line between "personal" and "professional" life as a researcher is blurry, if it exists at all. In the social sciences, our topics of study are also often very closely related to our daily lives.

Context

My PhD research in Niger analyzed the impact and representations of a global health program that aimed to eliminate trachoma, an infectious eye disease that can lead to blindness if left untreated. I studied how the staff and volunteers trained by this program spoke and thought about the disease, as well as how their interventions were interpreted in one village where the program worked. The village that I selected as my research site was Kawari, a small, ethnically Hausa village where I spent two years working as a Peace Corps volunteer nine years earlier. During the time I spent in the village as a volunteer, I was impressed at the freedom and confidence given to very small children. As a volunteer, I imagined returning one day with a child of my own so that he or she could experience village life and the simplicity and generosity that impacted me so greatly during my time there. My friends from the village fostered this dream; each phone conversation during my nine years away was filled with pressure: first questions about when I was going to get married and have a child, and then when I was going to bring my child to Niger.

When Jibril and I arrived in the field, I had just attained PhD candidacy and ended my relationship with Jibril's father. I chose to rent a house in Zinder, the regional capital city that is a one-hour drive from the village. Zinder had many things that Kawari did not—most importantly, electricity that worked most of the time and running water that came on only at night during the hot season but was present for the other nine months of the year. The conveniences offered by the city, including stores that sold canned tuna and butter, stands with grilled chicken, and a preschool run by the French Cultural Center, provided some of the comforts that my son had been used to during the first three years of his life in Florida. It also allowed me to have time with Jibril alone, something that was difficult in the village where curious people constantly surrounded us. For twelve months, I regularly made the drive from Zinder to Kawari. Sometimes Jibril came with me, and we would spend a few nights in the hut where I had lived as a volunteer.

Hurting but Not Hurting: Reflecting on Different Social Strategies

When I ask ten-year-old Jibril what he remembers about his experience in Niger, he remembers it fondly:

> My first impression of Niger was, whoa, this is pretty. There was a lot of space, of sand and stuff. And then afterwards I sort of felt like I lived there. Like I was born there and stuff. There weren't any electronics. I could run around a lot. I had a big house. I had dogs. A big space.... We took cold showers and I'd dance to stay warm and I almost fell out of the shower a lot. I could play by myself. Not like Florida where we had to be indoors all the time.... It was beautiful, and people gave me candy whenever I wanted. You didn't even have to pay.

While I was worried about how Jibril would adapt to our new living situation, he did not share my same concerns. For him, having access to candy, the pets that came with our rented house, and space meant happiness. Or at least that's how he remembers it now. While three-year-old Jibril did receive a lot of free candy and attention during our year in Niger, there were also difficult times as well, many that he seems to have forgotten.

However, I remember these frustrating events. For example, there were times when, before learning Hausa, Jibril would ask questions in English that would be met enthusiastically with "yes!" even though the person on the other end of the question had not understood the meaning of the request. "I'm hungry!" Jibril complained one morning, and I offered him what we had to eat: grilled peanuts, drinking yogurt in a bag, and bread. None of these options pleased him, and he demanded his favorite snack that we had brought with us from the United States but had finished within our first week in the country: Pepperidge Farm Goldfish Crackers. "Goldfish! Goldfish!" Jibril demanded, exploding into angry tears and refusing to believe my answer that the goldfish were no longer an option.

The friends who witnessed this scene were confused. In a place like Niger, where food is often scarce and children receive what is left over after the adults have eaten, it was unusual for a child to have such a dramatic reaction or even to insist on a particular food in the first place. Several people rushed in to intervene: offering Jibril small packs of cookies or pieces of candy, which he refused. My longtime friend Ali, whom I had met as a Peace Corps volunteer, took Jibril's hand and led him away from the crowd to a shady spot underneath a tree. I could not hear the conversation between them, but when they came back to join us, Jibril was smiling, and his tears had disappeared. "Ali is going to give me goldfish!" he announced happily, looking at me like he knew he deserved this snack that I had unjustly refused him.

I had a choice at this point: I could frustrate and disappoint Jibril by telling him the truth and position myself again as the bearer of bad news, or I could go along with Ali's false promise. "What does he want?" Ali asked me. "What are 'goldfish'? He wants to eat fish?" In his effort to be kind and to calm Jibril, in his very limited English, Ali had made the promise to respond to a request that he had not understood. I do not recall how this exact situation ended—perhaps I told Jibril the truth and he was angry, or perhaps he forgot about the goldfish in his new state of happiness and moved on to something else, but I do remember being very disappointed that, for a few minutes at least, he was being made happy by a lie.

This scenario is representative of a cultural strategy that I found difficult to accept, especially when it involved Jibril. While I value telling the truth over protecting feelings, it was the opposite in Niger. Rather than saying, "No, I cannot give this to you, I cannot do this for you," and causing immediate disappointment, people made promises that did not materialize. I had learned to navigate this while I was in Niger as a Peace Corps volunteer, to understand that even some of my best, most trustworthy friends would sometimes say yes instead of no, knowing quite well that the final answer was negative but believing that the initial positive answer would temper my reaction. Beyond learning to doubt every positive answer, I had never tried to analyze the reasons behind this behavior.

Often, when Jibril would cry for one reason or another, friends would promise candy, toys, or rides on motorcycles. Once Jibril started to understand and speak Hausa, these promises became more elaborate—anything to make him happy. As someone who valued truth even when it hurt, I was worried about the damage that this could do to him. Could these unfulfilled promises damage the trust that he gave so freely to people? When I discussed this with Jibril at the time, he explained that he found it kind. He explained to me that protecting someone's feelings showed that you care about that person. This perspective gave me insight to the interactions between the trachoma program and the population that I was studying in Niger. From both ends—from the program side and the side of the population—I often saw false agreements and false promises. Rather than analyzing these as simply going against the truth, I began to think of the relationships that these interactions were striving to protect and nurture.

When a community outreach agent made a promise to the population of one of the trachoma program's target villages that he would return tomorrow with medication, for example, this promise had great social value, regardless of whether it was actually kept. From the opposite side, members of these target communities also provided the answers to questions that the trachoma program hoped to hear even if they were untrue. I often saw my interlocutors reporting to the program that all eye infections were treated using the exact strategies promoted by health education activities, or that the behaviors advised by the program were being engaged to prevent eye infections, while my observation and informal conversations showed that this was not the case. Although Jibril helped make me aware of the social value in delivering words that another person wants to hear, I also wondered about how this strategy shaped the data I was collecting through my research interviews.

"Maybe It's Just His Time": Getting Sick and Navigating Care in a Place Where Sick Kids Do Not Always Get Well

Toward the end of our year in Niger, Jibril became sick with a very high fever. The poem at the beginning of this chapter is scrawled in the middle of a page of one of my field notebooks from this time, surrounded by sketches of objects in our bedroom drawn in the same blue pen: the metal trunk containing our clothes, the ceiling fan, boxes of pills, a digital thermometer. In between driving Jibril to different doctors, health clinics, pharmacies, and laboratories, I spent hours sitting by the bed that we shared—a mattress on the floor—watching him sleep and making marks in my notebook.

Because my research in Niger focused on health and illness, I had discussed and witnessed many parents treating their children's sicknesses. I knew that there were often no simple solutions, that multiple sources were navigated for treatment: government and private biomedical clinics, traditional medicine providers, pharmacies, spiritual healers. I studied these treatment trajectories with the objective distance of an academic researcher, but my own son getting sick quickly brought out my own cultural beliefs about how illness should be treated and expectations about how this treatment should work.

With my experience living in and studying areas in sub-Saharan Africa where malaria is common, I knew that high fevers were often indicative of the disease. At the first sign of fever, I took Jibril to have his blood tested for malaria at a small private laboratory that was near our house in Zinder. The test came back positive, and the laboratory technician recommended Coartem for treatment, a popular artemisinin-based combination therapy that I had often seen in the homes of my interlocutors. As we drove away from the laboratory, my PhD and my fieldwork obligations were far from my mind; I was solely focused on doing whatever I could to make my son feel better.

Jibril was asleep in his car seat in the back of my car by the time we arrived at the pharmacy, his head leaning heavily toward his chest and beads of sweat from the fever and the heat outside collecting on his forehead and nose. I unstrapped him from his car seat and carried him into the pharmacy with me, still sleeping. I explained to the pharmacist who stood behind the white tile counter in front of shelves filled with boxes of medication that my son had malaria and that I wanted to buy Coartem as well as a medicine to reduce his fever. Instead of handing me the blister pack of Coartem with the drawing of a boy taking a pill with a glass of water that my friends and neighbors used to treat their children, he showed an unfamiliar white box with the name *Coartem* written on the front. "This one is for people with money or foreigners," the pharmacist told me.

Although I knew that my son's malaria was biologically identical to the malaria of other children his age—and from reading the package of medication, the medication was also identical to the cheaper version used by others in the area—I felt pressured into buying this box of the "premium version" of the medication that the pharmacist felt better corresponded to who my son was. During the next three days of treatment, I spent most of my time in the bedroom watching Jibril sleep as I wrote in my field notebook and did internet searches about malaria on my iPhone. However, after his treatment course was completed, Jibril's fever was still high, and he was still sick.

As I had seen many of my interlocutors do for their children, I sought other sources of treatment, searching for, as Byron Good describes, efficacy rather than meaning (Good, 1994, p. 164). My only child having a fever high enough to make him scream when I touched a wet washcloth to his skin to cool it down made me panic. I brought Jibril, falling in and out of sleep, to be examined by the team of Cuban doctors who lived down the street from me, and then later to the public hospital, and then to the private clinic. Everyone seemed to agree that he needed to be treated with stronger malaria medication, but knowing how strong the recommended drugs were, as well as the side effects they could provoke, I was hesitant. I would listen to the health-care worker's advice and then go see another provider, hoping for a different answer.

Several of my neighbors, upon hearing how sick Jibril was, came to visit and brought gifts of boxes of juice and packs of cookies. After watching him wake up, begin talking, and then fall asleep in the middle of a sentence, one neighbor, a woman with three children of her own, turned to me and said, "If it's his time, it's his time. There's nothing you can do if God wants to call him." The possibility that Jibril's illness could be fatal had not really registered in my mind as a reality before this time, and I realized that I come from a place where it is unthinkable that *our* children die.

While losing a child hurts a Nigerien woman just as much as an American, unfortunately, this is a reality in Niger. I recognize that it is my social status, more than my refusal of the mortality of my child, that facilitated his recovery. My neighbor explained that, in addition to her three living children, she had three other children who had passed away when they were around Jibril's age. One had eaten paint that was left in the yard, and the two others had become sick with illnesses "that had no cure."

This phrase reminded me of many interviews that I had conducted for my fieldwork. Interlocutors from my research site explained that despite trying many different sources of treatment for their illnesses, sometimes they just had to accept that there was no medication that would work. The Trachoma Elimination Program, founded on the biomedical model of disease, took a very different approach to treatment. Those working for the program explained with certainty to individuals living in the villages where the program intervened that there were certain steps everyone could follow to stay well and certain substances that were guaranteed to work to treat trachoma.

Jibril was severely ill for almost one week. During this time, I began to think about leaving Zinder and going to the capital, which was a difficult twelve-hour car ride away. I did not call my family, who had spent the previous year trying to convince me that bringing a three-year-old to Niger was dangerous. I had hope that eventually Jibril would receive the care that he needed in Zinder, which he did. When I heard that the city's best pediatrician had finally returned from a trip, I immediately called him on his cell phone and begged him to come to our house. When Dr. Daouda arrived at our house, he was the only health-care professional who looked at Jibril's throat. The pediatrician explained that Jibril was sick from malaria and severe strep throat. Although the Coartem had eliminated the malaria, Jibril would continue to test positive for several weeks and needed to immediately begin antibiotic treatment for the strep throat. After Jibril's first day of antibiotics, his fever disappeared. Dr. Daouda refused payment for this house visit. After Jibril was feeling better, I visited the doctor in his office with a gift of fruit juice and cookies but still have the feeling that it was not enough.

I learned many things from the experience of Jibril's illness in Niger: practical, personal, and related to my work as a medical anthropologist. I learned that fever reducers do not bring high fevers down to normal but only reduce them a few degrees. I also discovered that despite my interest in treating myself and my son with natural, plant-based medications, I was culturally attached to biomedicine and immediately turned to biomedical intervention when presented with a serious health problem. This experience also revealed my belief in the control that I had over my son's health and existence of a biomedical solution.

Like others struggling to navigate a weak health-care system, with a plurality of incomplete treatment sources, I drew upon the resources that were available to me to address my son's illness. However, unlike many people living in Niger, I had the social and material capital that facilitated this process. Because I was a foreigner working in Zinder, the Cuban doctors welcomed me into their home, the pediatrician made a house call immediately after arriving in town, and the hospital did not make me wait in line. I was even able to read about malaria online using the 3G internet connection on my iPhone. For others living in Niger, seeking care is complicated by social and financial barriers. Although my search for treatment for Jibril's fever seemed complicated and frustrating, I knew that it was much easier than what many of my interlocutors experienced when seeking care for their children.

During the interviews that I conducted, many mothers reported that to treat their children's eye infections, the best medications were found at the hospital or the pharmacy near the market. However, due to time constraints, long waiting times, and disrespectful treatment by hospital and pharmacy staff, they often decided to buy the inferior, but more easily procured, medicine from the informal vendors at the village center. While seeking care and effective medication for Jibril had not been easy for me, access to transportation, free time, and my social status made it much easier than it would have been without these things.

My Superhero: Seeking Justice

During our time in Niger, I witnessed Jibril's growing fascination with Spider-Man and his understanding of justice. Seeing how many people lived lives and experienced struggles that were very different than ours reinforced these early questions of what was right and wrong yet were expressed in his self-focused concerns with experiences that he believed should have happened differently.

When I told Jibril that I was writing about our experience in Niger and asked him to tell me some stories about things that happened during our stay in the country, he focused on things that seemed unjust in his mind yet often had a just conclusion:

One time I went on a taxi motorcycle, and I was really tired that day. So I started to fall asleep. After, I completely fell asleep, and I was sleeping really well. And that day I had flip-flops on. And so those flip flops, while I was sleeping, one of them fell off. So at the end, when I got off the taxi motorcycle, I only had one shoe. And so I had to go to a market to buy some boots. And so I had those boots. Spiderman boots.

And the first day I went to school in Niger, I went to my classroom and I recognized a game called Candyland that I really liked in the United States, so I really wanted to play with it, so I tried to take it to play with it. But the teacher said "No, No, No," but I really wanted to play with it, so I continued touching it. And the teacher took me by the hand and hit me. It hurt. And I was surprised, because I was 3 or 4 and I just wanted to play with a board game. After, my mom talked to the principal of the school, not about me being hit, about something else, and in the middle of the conversation I brought up that one of the teachers hit me. She was surprised too, and she already fired this woman. And that teacher couldn't teach anymore for the rest of her life.

The first day at my second school I didn't want to go there. And I was crying, crying, crying, because of my experience at the first school. And when I went to the second school, I really didn't want to. When my mom brought me there I really didn't want to. I was crying, crying, crying, because of my experience at the old school. After, I ended up going there, and after a few days, I really liked it. I learned the alphabet, and we used to eat bread with margarine. I used to call the margarine "yucky butter," but I liked it, or no. Did I like it? I think I did. Anyways, at the second school, just in front of the school, there was this crazy naked woman. And that crazy naked woman used to throw big rocks at me. At everybody, I think. I guess I was scared. And I was weirded out by it. A crazy naked woman throwing rocks!

Many of the things that at first seemed strange to Jibril and that he was unable to fight became accepted as a part of his daily life and integrated into his strategies of negotiation. Together we developed our own logic to mitigate the negative effects of the seemingly unjust actions of others. For example, the mentally unstable woman who slept in a fort made from sticks and plastic bags near the entrance of his school became an expected part of our mornings. Like Jibril's classmates and their parents, he and I would calculate her presence and walk quickly through the entrance gates in order to avoid the rocks that she occasionally threw.

In the village, Jibril was an excellent research assistant. After learning very quickly how to speak Hausa, he would spend hours with children from the village, running in the fields, playing games in the sand, while I conducted interviews. When he came back from these periods of time alone, he would report back about the things he saw and spoke about with his friends. These reports were often grounded in his sense of right and wrong—for example, stories of how certain children would or would not share toys or food or analyzing hygiene practices that he found abnormal. This insight into the world of children, a place that I was not able to directly access myself, was very useful to my understanding of health-related practices in the village that I analyzed in my PhD thesis.

Jibril reported to me about how he would accompany the boys who became his friends to the millet fields to "go poo" and wondered how these children felt so free to collectively perform this activity that he, even at this very young age, thought of as very private. He told me about how sometimes he and the boys would sneak into the compounds of other families to drink water or eat leftover food. Sometimes Jibril would listen to the interviews that I conducted in the research households, but usually at some point, a child would catch his eye, and he would quickly peel himself away from me and go back into his own world of boys.

Jibril describes,

> I don't remember learning Hausa. I just learned it by speaking it. I would tell you things that the kids did or said. And you said it helped you with your thesis.
>
> The thesis was about malaria and stuff like that. Oh, no, trachoma. Whatever. I think it was about sickness. But I was more into catching crickets and running around. I wasn't listening. I know you interviewed people about sickness.

My Superhero: Fighting for My Social Status as a Mother

The two years that I spent in Kawari as a Peace Corps volunteer in the late 90s contributed greatly to my understanding of how to parent. In a country where women give birth to an average of seven children during their lives (Institut National de la Statistique and Macro International Inc., 2007), I was often surrounding by women who were raising multiple young children. I continually thought back on my experiences in Kawari during the first years of Jibril's life in Florida; in Miami, letting him crawl on the sidewalk in front of my apartment made me reminisce about life in the village, even though my Miami neighbors watched the scene with criticism. When I tied Jibril to my back and walked to the laundromat carrying a heavy basket of dirty clothes, I reminded myself that women in Kawari carried much heavier jerry cans of water to their households every day. I even attributed my easy, successful breastfeeding to what I had seen in the two years that I lived in Kawari; I had been convinced that breastfeeding was easy and natural. Whenever Jibril cried, I would take out my breast and, like I had seen so many times in Niger, swing him around from my back to my chest for comfort.

Returning to Niger with Jibril, I realized that becoming a parent had changed my social status from what it had been when I was a childless Peace Corps volunteer. It was no longer acceptable for me to play cards and drink tea under the shade of a tree with the men in the village, something I was able to get away with during my previous stay without much reproach. Instead, I was expected to join the other mothers in preparing food and spending time with the children. Women also opened up to me in ways that they had not during my first stay in the country. We discussed our health problems, our struggles with our children.

Although Jibril never understood the power that his presence added to my social status, one experience did validate his feelings of being a superhero and my protector. One night, much later than expected, we arrived by bus to Niamey, the country's capital city; the taxi that was taking us to our destination was cut off from the road by four motorcycles that suddenly surrounded it. The taxi driver shut off his engine and started talking loudly in Zarma with one of the eight men pressed against the four sides of the car. The largest man, dressed in a stained polo shirt and jeans, came around to my window and looked at me angrily. "Tu as une cigarette?" he asked me in French before violently grabbing a lit cigarette from my hand through the open window.

This is it, I thought. *After more than ten years of working in Africa, of hearing warnings from my friends and family in the United States that my presence in these developing countries was risky, something bad is really going to happen.* My body went limp, my common reaction to stress that is disappointingly neither flight nor fight, and the polo-shirted man reached his head and hand through the window to grab my bag, which was strapped across my chest. Since it was so late at night, no one was in the street, and the driver had stopped protesting and was looking apathetically at the road in front of him. It seemed unlikely that anyone would step in to help.

As his hand touched the strap of my bag, Jibril, who had been asleep on the seat beside me, sat up and leaned toward the man. They looked at one another, with my body between them, and the man quickly released his grip on the strap and moved out of the window and away from the car. He spoke again in Zarma to the other men surrounding the car, and they remounted the motorcycles, and drove away quickly.

I will never know why discovering Jibril's presence made this group of men decide against robbing me. Was it respect for my status as a mother? The idea that I possibly had a (partly) African son? When I discussed what happened with Jibril, he was confident that he understood why the situation had ended the way that it did. "I scared away the bad guys, Mama, like Spider-Man!" he told me, before falling back asleep on the seat. Although he no longer remembers this incident, Jibril often referred to it when we were in Niger and immediately following our return to the United States. In his telling of the story, he was always the hero and intentionally protected me with his actions.

Conclusion

In the six years that have passed since our time in Niger, Jibril has forgotten how to speak Hausa but remembers our time in the field as a mainly idyllic twelve months. Conducting fieldwork and negotiating life in West Africa with a young child was not as easy as I had imagined when I was a Peace Corps volunteer but greatly helped me gain additional cultural insight. As a mother, not only a researcher, in the field, caring for a sick child allowed me to develop experiential knowledge of the challenges involved in accessing quality health care as well as local representations of health and illness. As I parented and Jibril grew in the Nigerien context, I saw how both of our fixed cultural expectations sometimes collided and usually adapted.

Jibril and I now live in France, where I work at a research institution as a medical anthropologist and he continues to negotiate a culture that is different from his own. Seeking medical care when Jibril experiences illness in France, and listening to how friends speak about his health, continues to highlight the complexity of the cultural representations of health and illness. Even in a culture that, at first glance, seems very similar to that of my home culture in the United States, culturally bound beliefs concerning the treatment and causes of illness are often very different. I have learned, from example, of the importance of always keeping my neck covered in windy weather and never drinking cold water when sick. Having Jibril here with me in France has allowed me again to develop an additional layer of experiential and empirical knowledge about the cultural complexities of staying well that addresses both my personal and professional interests.

While I worried about Jibril's physical health or the possible negative effects that could result from living in such a resource-poor and culturally different place like Niger, I rarely questioned my decision to bring my son with me to the field. Niger was a part of Jibril's life since he was born, even if he did not realize this, and I wanted him to experience the society that had been so important in transforming me when I was a Peace Corps volunteer. My previous experience in Kawari greatly impacted how I mothered my child from the time that he was born. It was very important to me to share this place that had changed my understanding of the world with my son. What I did not realize before spending twelve months in the field with him is how much he would contribute to changing and deepening the way that I understood life in Niger. My experience as a mother in Niger was very different than my life as a young Peace Corps volunteer. Although many of Jibril's memories of our time in the field have begun to fade away, I know that he was changed profoundly by this experience and that he will never completely lose the strategies and knowledge gathered during our time in the field. Even if he does not want to admit it, I think this experience, combined with his intense interest in different ways of being, and his data collection and analysis skills, could even lead him toward a career in the social sciences when he gets older. I am thankful that he made it through all our adventures thus far safely, courageously, and better than he began. Like Spider-Man.

Practical Tips

- Try to do one thing every day, and do not feel guilty about not doing more. When my friend was leaving to do fieldwork, her PhD advisor told her, "Just try to do one thing each day." I thought of this often during my year in Niger. With this approach, my research moved slowly, but it did move. Sometimes the one "thing" that I was able to achieve was not even related to research—sometimes it was related to parenting, and I allowed myself to count that too.

- Get to know people. Fieldwork may be your "work," but the time you spend in the field is also the minutes, days, and years of your life. You and your child need to share this time and these experiences with the people you will meet in the field. These people can provide your child with different perspectives and insight to the larger world that you are both part of. If you are in the social sciences, these relationships can also deepen your understanding of your research context. No matter what discipline you come from, these relationships will at least help you find where the best doctors and snacks are.

- No matter how important your research is, there is a world out there that is more important than academia. Let your child remind you of this. We become researchers because we are interested in discovering surprising things. Let yourself be surprised without searching for

FIGURE 3.1 Kelley carrying Jibril during a marriage celebration in Kawari, Niger, in 2010

it. Follow him when he calls you away from your computer screen to show you what he's seen.

References

Geertz, C. (1994). Thick description: Toward an interpretive theory of culture. In M. Martin & L. C. McIntyre (Eds.), *Readings in the philosophy of social science* (pp. 213–231). Cambridge, MA: MIT Press.

Good, B. (1994). *Medicine, rationality and experience: An anthropological perspective*: Cambridge, UK: Cambridge University Press.

Institut National de la Statistique and Macro International Inc. (2007). *Demographic and health survey Niger 2006*. Retrieved from Calverton, MD.

4

Birthing in the Field

• •

LYDIA ZACHER DIXON

"The problem we are facing is that there just aren't enough births here," sighed Antonia as she gave me a tour of their revamped birthing center. It was July 9, 2009, and my first day officially "in the field" conducting ethnographic research for my dissertation on midwifery education across three states in Mexico. I was back at the CASA (Centro para los Adolescentes de San Miguel de Allende) midwifery school and clinic in the picturesque colonial town of San Miguel de Allende, Guanajuato—a place where I worked as an intern after college but had not seen in the years since I had moved back to California to begin graduate school studies in anthropology. Entering the field was feeling more like coming home to old friends. I hugged midwives and greeted the physicians we passed in CASA's hallways. There had been many improvements to the clinic during my absence, including updated paint jobs and a new water-birthing room, but Antonia lamented that business was down despite the more colorful and contemporary look. She began to describe the impacts of the new national free health insurance program, how women would come to CASA for prenatal care but ultimately go to public hospitals to deliver because of financial incentives. The tension this was causing would later become a central theme in my research, but at the time I let the topic go when Antonia paused at the doorway to one of the birthing rooms.

"Aquí nació tu hija—your daughter was born here," she said, turning to me with a smile. I looked up from my notebook and saw that she was hold-ing open the door to room ten. The room was tidy and orange and smelled of disinfectant. One wall was taken up by a glass door that led out to a patio, and sunlight filled the room. She motioned for me to sit on the bench at the foot of the bed, and my eyes darted around, observing all the details. This was indeed where my daughter, who I will refer to as J, had been born three years before, although I had not been in the room since. I immediately felt a wave of emotion break over me as I closed my notebook. I didn't need to write down what Antonia said next, although it mesmerized me to hear it from her, this woman who had helped birth my child into this world and who had also helped so many others before and since. "You were one of the screamers," she began, and we both laughed a little.

> Most of my women don't scream, but you sure did! When we had to transfer you from home to the center, that whole car ride you were just screaming in my ears. I know you think I don't know what you were saying in English, but I know those bad words—they don't really need translating. Anyway, I knew you didn't really need to come here, I could have delivered your baby at home. But your doula was getting nervous about how long it was taking, and no one wants nervous people at a birth. Once we got here, all those students barged in to observe us, remember? And then your daughter was born after just a few pushes . . . and a lot more screaming. Right here in this room. (A. Cordova, personal communication, June 2009)

As my research project developed, Antonia continued to be a central informant to whom I returned repeatedly to discuss the changing face of midwifery and midwifery education in Mexico. She was the cofounder of the CASA school and knew its history better than anyone. Her calm demeanor and easy humor made her a joy to talk to, and she wasn't afraid to give her opinion on topics related to health care in Mexico. Also, she continued to be a comforting presence for me—this seemingly ageless woman who had coaxed my child out of me so calmly, even as I screamed profanities into her ear. Similarly, my birth story continued to be present throughout my fieldwork; it became a story that at once tied me to my field site and changed how I was perceived there.

In this chapter, I discuss my experiences studying birth in Mexico after giving birth in Mexico and studying maternal health there while being a mother there. I draw on these experiences to make two broader arguments about what it means to mother in the field. First, when mothering and fieldwork coincide, they have the potential to make one another stronger. I offer this as a counter-narrative to the abundance of literature on the difficulties of parenting and working and more specifically of mothering in academia (Schlehofer, 2012; Graybill Ellis & Smartt Gullion, 2015). Second, I argue that the lessons taken from mothering in the field should make us rethink knowledge production more generally. By considering the productive possibilities of motherhood as an ally of knowledge production, we can begin to think more seriously about inclusivity and diversity of perspectives in all kinds of ways. Thus the bulk of this chapter emphasizes the tangible, intangible, and theoretical contributions motherhood makes to fieldwork and fieldwork makes to motherhood in a way that is informed by—and has informed—my understanding of a feminist research methodology. This perspective has taken me a decade to come to, on both a personal and academic level, as I look back on my first forays into the preliminary fieldwork of early graduate school. I begin where many of my fieldwork journeys as a mother began: in chaos, in an airport.

Arrivals and Homemaking in the Field: Finding a Practical Balance

As I held up my drowsy five-year-old with one arm and tried to wrangle my carry-on bag with the other, I wondered absently why I kept booking us red-eye flights to Mexico. It was our third time taking the 1 a.m. flight departing from Los Angeles, California. I already knew from previous experience that the flight would be just short enough to assure that we would only get a couple of hours of sleep before landing. At that point, we would have to navigate customs, collect our luggage, and take an hour-long shuttle ride to San Miguel de Allende, a quaint colonial city in central Mexico. We would inevitably arrive at our little rented apartment bleary-eyed but hyper, in that wild sort of way that young children and mothers can both relate to. Although we had done this before, it was not getting easier.

We journeyed this way because it was cheaper. As a single mother supporting myself and J on teaching assistantships and external grant funds—all of which seemed to be designed for individual students or perhaps parents who had partners with incomes of their own—frugality was key. While many things in graduate school helped with the costs of single motherhood—subsidized housing and on-campus preschool, for example—there was not much to be done about the extra costs of fieldwork with a child. School fees, dance lessons, food, and travel all added up.

When we arrived at our apartment, after haphazardly unpacking and collapsing in a heap together for a long siesta, we began the earnest work of homemaking. For me, as J's sole care provider, creating a home meant weaving a tight net of support through friends, school, classes, library cards, activities, and plans. We could make a home anywhere if I could arrange those things. I was lucky that we had lived in this town prior to beginning graduate school, and so such support was more a matter of renewing old connections—indeed, this was a major reason that I had chosen to make San Miguel de Allende my home base—yet setting up our home life still took a couple of weeks. And once I felt like our home was set, I could begin my work.

My work entailed ethnographic fieldwork with midwives and midwifery students. I had designed a project that would examine the diverse models of midwifery education being developed and taught at three very different schools: CASA's professional midwifery school, Nueve Lunas traditional midwifery school in Oaxaca, and Mujeres Aliadas professional midwifery school for nurses in Michoacán. I conducted participant observation in classrooms and administrative meetings and with students and teachers outside of class at each location and interviewed midwives, students, administrators, physicians, and politicians involved in women's health care in Mexico. Overall, I was interested in the tensions between midwifery schools and between midwives and the Mexican state about what midwives needed to know, how they should be taught, and what their roles should be in the existing health-care system. Because I was focusing on established educational centers, I was able to easily secure Institutional Review Board (IRB) approval despite working in the sensitive field of reproductive health care abroad. While J did not figure into my official research plans or IRB application, I had planned my research with her needs in mind. For example, the majority of my research design centered on the educational model of CASA. That the central location for my research was the same CASA midwifery clinic where J was born was not accidental; my personal ties to CASA gave me a sense of the stakes involved for those who worked there and also eased my way into the field.

I also chose to make CASA's city of San Miguel de Allende our home base because of its educational options; I would need J to be enrolled in school while I worked, and San Miguel de Allende offered many great options, from a Waldorf program to a Montessori school. I decided to enroll J in the Montessori school, which was affordable, bilingual, and small enough to make me feel that she would get help transitioning into speaking more Spanish at school. Based on recommendations from friends and teachers, I also signed J up for gymnastics, dance, and piano lessons, all of which were within walking distance from our apartment. Once I got her settled into a school and extracurricular schedule, I set up a fieldwork schedule for myself.

On Mondays, Wednesdays, and Fridays I would spend the entire day observing at the CASA midwifery school and clinic, from the time I dropped J off at 8 a.m. until I picked her up at 2 p.m. Most families at her school followed the traditional schedule of preparing and eating a large *comida* (midday meal) right after school. This cultural norm meant that the idea of after-school care did not make sense to the majority of the population and therefore did not exist; for those of her classmates whose parents worked all day and could not take the midday *comida* break, often a nanny or family member would come for the child. Initially, I worried that stopping fieldwork at 2 p.m. would limit my data, but I soon realized that keeping pace with my local friends and neighbors, and enjoying the occasional after-school *comida* with them, was more valuable for our quality of life and sense of belonging. Over quesadillas and instant coffee, we would chat while our children played. The other parents were interested in my fieldwork topics of childbirth and health care and had plenty to say about their own experiences with the doctors or midwives in town. Discussions about birth resonate among groups of parents in a way that other topics might not. Through these leisurely afternoon lunches, while my child was entertained and well fed, I nurtured both my social connections and my research. This was a helpful reminder that "the field" was bigger than I originally assumed and knowledge gained outside of hours spent with a notebook in hand, vigorously observing clinical procedures, could be equally valid. Once I realized this, I brought up my research everywhere that I could, gathering perspectives from unexpected sources such as taxi drivers, hair stylists, and market vendors.

On Tuesdays and Thursdays, I would install myself in a coffee shop in the town square. There, I would transcribe my hastily scratched, handwritten notes from the day before as well as any audio recordings of interviews with midwives and students. Occasionally I would write myself what I called "memos"—brief think pieces on topics that I had a hunch might become something bigger later on. Many of these memos ultimately became chapters or paper ideas. This time in the café was completely necessary, although sometimes I worried that I was not spending enough time "in the field" by missing days that I could have been at the clinic or school. Yet I had learned through the years as a single parent in graduate school that the value of time management and planning ahead are not to be underestimated. I needed that time writing and processing because I knew that I would not have evenings or weekends to do it. Further, I knew that when I got back from the field, I would have to hit the ground running—working as a teaching assistant, writing my dissertation, searching for jobs, and caring for my child. By building in time to transcribe and reflect, I bought time for myself in the future. I saw this process—and continue to see this process—as if I am throwing breadcrumbs out onto the path ahead of myself. Knowing that there is some sustenance to come keeps me calmer when the stresses of motherhood and academia bog me down. A lesson for both motherhood and academia has been that you must think three steps ahead and recognize that the things you are working on (collecting data or raising children) may be long-term investments.

While my schedule of fieldwork and transcription worked well while we were in San Miguel de Allende, we spent a fair amount of time traveling to two other midwifery schools I had set out to study as well as to conferences and meetings around Mexico. This meant that we rode lots of buses and stayed in many interesting places. For two weeks, for example, we stayed in a commune in the mountain town of Malinalco, just outside of Mexico City, attending a traditional midwifery training workshop with midwives from around

FIGURE 4.1 Much of Lydia Zacher Dixon's fieldwork was carried out with her daughter J in a pack on her back. In this photo, taken in 2009, Lydia and J are on a hike with a group of midwives outside the town of Malinalco, Mexico, during a midwifery retreat.

the country. Wherever we went, I packed careful bags of activities for J, but often she would end up curled on my lap, quietly listening to talks about birth and bodies. Presentations about birth fascinated her, as did the demonstrations that traditional midwives would do. This was mystical, interesting stuff to a young girl—carried out by passionate women. I would look down at J and then up at the woman demonstrating prenatal massage techniques and think about how lucky I was. Having J—especially having had her with a traditional midwife in Mexico—gave me insight and personal connection to the material I was studying; and studying this material let me offer an exciting and enriching life for J. Of course, the daily logistics and financial strain were difficult and real, but they did not—and do not—define my experience of mothering in the field.

What Doesn't Kill You Makes You Stronger:
Growing from Struggles in Fieldwork and Motherhood

While having a natural childbirth in a tiny midwifery clinic in central Mexico, I was pretty sure that I was going to die. I think I probably screamed that exact sentiment to Antonia, my midwife, many times during the last hour or so of labor. A year later, when I became a single mother, I also felt like things could not get harder. Being alone and in charge of this precious and energetic toddler while trying to get into graduate school felt as if I was drowning. What kept me afloat was the idea that I wanted to be a model of strength for my daughter. I had to keep moving forward even as I struggled. I applied to schools and took my GREs in a haze as I simultaneously dealt with the aftermath of a volatile relationship, worked, and adjusted to life back in the United States. Graduate school represented a chance to grow professionally while providing stability for J for at least the five years it might take me to complete a PhD. Friends and family expressed concern about my plan to go back to school full time as a single mother; I understood what they meant, but I pushed their concerns away because I could not imagine a different path. It came as a surprise, then, that my life substantially improved once I started graduate school.

So much writing about academia and motherhood—as well as about motherhood and working in general—focuses on negative aspects. Women experience graduate school and the tenure track differently, especially when it comes to having children (Mason, Wolfinger, & Goulden, 2013), students treat women faculty differently (Young, Rush, & Shaw, 2009), schedules do not allow for the dual pressures of motherhood and the tenure track (Moran Craft & Maseberg-Tomlinson, 2015), and women are paid less than men in similar academic positions and institutions (West & Curtis, 2006). For women of color, these experiences can be amplified (Kachchaf, Ko, Hodari, & Ong, 2015; Turner, González, & Wong, 2011), and the impacts may be measured differently among, for example, the STEM fields versus the social sciences and humanities (Hill, Corbett, & St. Rose, 2010). These are real and valid concerns, and the stories behind them are hopefully bringing about necessary changes in the academy as in the broader workforce.

Yet for me, joining the academic world as a single mother was a huge relief, and I think that it is important to discuss the ways that academia—and fieldwork specifically—has the potential to be uniquely compatible with motherhood (and single motherhood in particular). Here was a lifestyle with a flexible schedule, where I could attend J's school functions or take time to stay home with her if she was sick. It was a lifestyle that offered advantages of time above pay, such as through summers and holidays off, which allowed me to spend more time with my family. While not much, the stipend from my teaching assistantship provided just enough for us to live frugally in subsidized housing. In addition, the excellent university childcare center (also nearly fully subsidized) was across the street. Health insurance was included, and health care was easily accessible on campus. We had a rich social life and could walk to all our friends' homes in the campus family housing development, which was full of diverse students from all over the world. I knew where we would be for the next several years, and I was able to establish a home and community for my daughter. As a single mother, these elements were doubly important—I needed this support network and flexibility because I didn't have a partner or any family nearby to help.

Academic life made me a better mother and allowed me to provide a better life for my daughter. I could be there for her when she needed me, and I could raise her in a safe and nurturing environment. I was stimulated intellectually, had easy access to a gym (with childcare!) on campus, and thus felt like I was taking care of myself enough to be strong and stable for her. I realize that this is not the experience that all mothers have in graduate school (Graybill Ellis & Smartt Gullion, 2015), and I do not mean to say that there were not real and daily difficulties involved; however, I want to recognize the ways that mothering in graduate school provides potential lifestyle advantages.

Fieldwork also made me a stronger mother. In some ways, this was literal; without wide sidewalks for strollers, I carried J in a backpack all over Mexico while lugging our suitcases and my books and notebooks too. I felt that I could go anywhere as long as I could carry her and all our stuff. This was a powerful and liberating realization. I know that it has impacted our relationship, and I hope that it continues to inspire her to be strong, to travel, and to know that she can do anything her heart desires. That sounds corny, I know, but recently, I complained about not being able to do something well, and she actually told me in surprise, "But you do everything well, mama!" Her earliest memories are from the vantage point of being on my back, looking out at the world as we moved through it.

My fieldwork helped me become a better mother because I felt freer. I was no longer afraid to try new things with J while we were traveling. We ate exciting foods (crickets, freshly made chocolate, cactus fruits), went to all the parades (J accidentally ended up leading one during a *Posada* during the Mexican Christmas festivities), signed up for dance classes, stayed out late to attend community festivals, and socialized nearly every night. I became more relaxed about schedules, sugar, loud music, and bed times. Life felt colorful, exciting, and full, and this in turn made motherhood colorful, exciting and full. I could not have offered all of this to J back at home.

Stronger Motherhood, Stronger Fieldwork: How Motherhood and Fieldwork Can Be Mutually Beneficial

Being a mother also improved my fieldwork. It did so in a number of ways, ways that I usually don't talk about with people because they seem too detailed or too personal—the kind of thing that just gets rolled into the mundane and quiet stories we keep to ourselves about how we get through things as mothers. Yet I increasingly realize these things need to be talked about because the ways that motherhood improved my fieldwork were through things that could be helpful to anyone conducting fieldwork. Also, recognizing the contributions of motherhood to fieldwork legitimizes motherhood in a world where it seems that motherhood often still needs to defend itself.

A very tangible way that my fieldwork was improved through motherhood had to do with time management. As I previously explained, I followed a generally regular working schedule that entailed three days of observations and interviews and two days of reflection and writing per week. This ultimately saved me time once I got home and kept me from burning out while in the field. The daily clock of motherhood—getting up early, having regular meals—also ensured that I was consistently showing up for work. Sleeping in was not an option. I planned our side trips carefully, and well in advance, because there was school and other extracurricular activities to consider—all these microdecisions meant that things did not get overlooked and tickets did not sell out.

On a more substantial level, my fieldwork was improved because being a mother gave me access. I cannot know the full extent of this access or what my research would have looked like without it, but I came to recognize when it was happening; when brief mentions of my child, my birth, or my personal connection to Mexican midwifery opened doors, smoothed conversations, or sparked others to share their own experiences. While this could sound calculated, it was no less important to my fieldwork than other ways that researchers use personal details to gain access; gender, class, language, friendships, and affiliations all smooth the way for researchers in ways that we usually don't disclose or deeply examine (although with the reflexive turn in anthropology, this is changing to some degree). In my case, the fact of and daily displays of my motherhood allowed me to establish rapport in a world where motherhood itself was at stake.

My project was largely an investigation of how Mexican midwifery education was gaining traction with politicians because of its promised ability to lower maternal mortality for the country (Dixon, 2015). At the time of my fieldwork, from 2011 to 2012, Mexico was racing to meet the United Nations' Millennial Development Goal to reduce maternal mortality ratios by 75 percent between 1990 and 2015 (United Nations, 2000). While they had made great strides in some regions of the country, too many women continued to die during or shortly after pregnancy, especially in the more marginalized poor regions of the country (Fernández Cantón, Gutierrez Trujillo, & Viguri Uribe, 2012; Gómez Dantés et al., 2011). The target date in 2015 came and went, and Mexico did not meet its goal; reducing maternal deaths and improving reproductive health care more generally continue to be vital projects of the state.

Additionally, my project tackled the quality of women's health care in Mexico and the ways that midwives there were protesting what they referred to as the obstetric violence that many women faced in hospital births (Zacher Dixon, 2015). The movement against obstetric violence was shaping how midwives were learning and practicing. Midwifery was entangled with activism, as students and practitioners argued that the humane treatment of women in birth should be a human right.

Coming into the field as a mother allowed me to participate in conversations about these risks to birth and mothers in a way that was clearly personal as well as academic. While my academic credentials and knowledge of the history and breadth of these issues lent me some level of acceptance with those midwives who saw me as a peer and colleague in the push to change birth policy in Mexico, it was my position as a mother that seemed to convey to people that my investment was honest. I had given birth, had understood the vulnerability a woman experiences in that moment. Furthermore, I had worked as a doula in hospitals in the United States and had experienced firsthand the range of ways women are treated during that vulnerable time.

An important part of fieldwork, therefore, was establishing this personal connection. I told my birth story, and shared stories from those births I had attended as a doula, with many of the midwives and their students. In turn, they shared their own birth stories and discussed the births they had attended. We commented on each other's experiences, found commonalities, shared outrages, and felt a connection. We came to trust each other because baring the realities of birth, with all its dangers and fears and pain and joy, brought us closer. This didn't make me one of them—I was still the *Americana* with the notebook, I lived in an apartment in town instead of in their dormitory, I could travel freely across borders—but it made us friends in a genuine and deep way that came from this connection and trust. This kind of trust enabled a rapport that shaped the kinds of data I collected and the kind of work that it has produced.

Because my data emerged from the rapport that I generated through my connections as a mother, I reflected often on how personal my project had become. Later, after analyzing the data and writing the dissertation, I thought about how specific my work is to my experience, how the voices that emerged in my work said things to *me* because of our relationship and often because of the connections we forged over parenthood. Motherhood and fieldwork were not separable in my experience but rather informed each other. As Allison Antink-Meyer (2015) states, "To the mother, they are less two separate worlds and more two different multidimensional contexts which play off of one another to shape how she views the world and how the world understands her contribution" (p. 148). Through the process of designing and carrying out a research project as a mother, I came to see how who we are when we go into the field matters. As the feminist reflexive turn in anthropology has argued, women's experiences necessarily shape their understanding and critique of social processes (Behar & Gordon, 1995; Haraway, 1998; Harding, 1991). The experience of motherhood is itself a filter through which women approach their research, as it can be central to who many of us are. Recognizing the unique value of knowledge produced by mothers in the field is one more way to recognize the importance of multiple voices and multiple perspectives in research across disciplines.

Conclusion: Making Mothers' Voices Matter in Research

There are not finite stories to be told in the world. I learned this lesson early on in my fieldwork, when I realized that there was another anthropologist in my field site, seemingly studying the same things. Initially, I was concerned—every graduate student is groomed to imagine her project as being unique—but I came to realize that it would be impossible for us to gather the same data and interpret it in the same ways. Further, having both of our perspectives on the topic could only add depth to the bank of knowledge about women's health issues in Mexico. More recently, I have collaborated and written with other women (some of them mothers) working on similar topics in Mexico. Through these processes, it is often our motherhood that helps us connect—even as we discuss how it also shaped our fieldwork. Thus our positions as mothers influence us at every stage of fieldwork, from planning where we will go to conducting the work to writing and collaborating years later.

I also wanted to know how mothering has shaped the work I read. Sometimes there are hints of it; authors sometimes mention their children in the introduction. Yet this is almost always done to humanize the author. The motherhood is checked at the end of the introduction, when the real data begins at chapter one. I am not saying that motherhood needs to be discussed throughout a book or an article. I just want a more explicit acknowledgment of the specific ways that our knowledge emerges through—not in spite of—our motherhood.

Of course, I don't think that it is only motherhood that should be recognized as impacting the knowledge we produce through our fieldwork. It's clear that who we are and where we come from shapes what we see, say, ask, and write. But calling out the particular ways that motherhood shapes our fieldwork is important because of two main reasons. First, one's motherhood may not be disclosed because of concerns of being taken less seriously as a scholar. Mothers have historically struggled in academia, and so motherhood has not been explicitly held up as a legitimate lens through which to produce knowledge about the world.

Second, those of us doing the work of mothering while doing fieldwork are often doing the second shift as well—whether we are single mothers or not. Therefore, the political implications of recognizing the validity of motherhood as a lens through which to produce knowledge are such that there is a potential to shift how mothers are viewed. Instead of distracted, mothers are capable. Instead of divided in their loyalties, mothers are strong. Knowledge produced through mothering must be seen as important and unique.

Practical Tips

- Be realistic about what you can achieve in the field. Parenting takes a lot of energy, and children's needs change over time. Set yourself up for success by not designing a research program that is not achievable or is achievable only at the expense of your health and sanity. As a single mother in particular, I had to come to peace with the fact that I would not be working endless hours. However, by planning out a structured fieldwork schedule, I was able to balance parenting and research in a way that worked most of the time.
- Schools and childcare options matter. Select a field site where you have quality childcare so that you can have peace of mind while conducting your research. Before going into the field, do as much research as you can on childcare in the area, and know ahead of time what paperwork you may need to enroll in schools. Some schools require notarized copies, which may be easier to complete before going into the field.
- Spend a little more money if necessary to live in a place where you feel safe and comfortable with your children. You don't want to have to worry about safety while trying to get research done. Conduct as much research as possible before going into the field to determine an appropriate neighborhood. For me, being close to some of the people I already knew and public transportation was important.
- When traveling for fieldwork with children, build in extra time for recreation so that you—and your children—don't burn out. I took my daughter on many long bus trips to visit sites around Mexico. Wherever we went, I was sure to limit my research time so that we were able to explore new cities, try new foods, and visit markets or museums.
- Pack strategically for children. Sometimes children have to come along to meetings, interviews, or other research activities, so having a bag full

of distracting and engaging items is vital. For my daughter, tiny dolls with clothing and accessories, coloring supplies, and endless snacks were essential. For times when she had to be entertained longer, such as during a conference session, movies on my computer came in handy as well.

- Build time into your fieldwork schedule to periodically transcribe, reflect, and analyze data. This will save you time later on and will allow you to capture your reflections while they are still fresh. I found it helpful to start "memos" as I typed up my notes and transcribed interviews in the field. These were short pieces or collections of ideas that I thought might be important later on; indeed, many of my memos went on to become chapter sections or seeds for articles later on.

References

Antink-Meyer, A. (2015). Cultural border crossings between science, science pedagogy, and parenting. In A. Young (Ed.), *Teacher, scholar, mother: Re-envisioning motherhood in the academy* (pp. 141–150). Lanham, MD: Lexington Books.

Behar, R., & Gordon, D. A. (1995). *Women writing culture*. Berkeley, CA: University of California Press.

Dixon, L. Z. (2015). *Delivering health: In search of an appropriate model for institutionalized midwifery in Mexico* (Doctoral dissertation). University of California Irvine.

Fernández Cantón, S. B., Gutierrez Trujillo, G., & Viguri Uribe, R. (2012). Maternal mortality and abortion in Mexico. *Boletín Médico del Hospital Infantil de México, 69*(1), 73–76.

Gómez Dantés, O., Sesma, S., Becerril, V. M., Felicia, M., Knaul, F. M., Hector, A., & Frenk, J. (2011). Sistema de Salud de México. *Salud Pública de México, 53*(2), S2220–S232.

Graybill Ellis, E., & Smartt Gullion, J. (2015). "You must be Superwoman!" How graduate student mothers negotiate conflicting roles. In A. M. Young (Ed.), *Teacher, scholar, mother: Re-envisioning motherhood in the academy* (pp. 151–166). Lanham, MD: Lexington Books.

Haraway, D. (1988). Situated knowledges: The science question in feminism and the privilege of partial perspectives. *Feminist Studies, 14*(3), 575–599.

Harding, S. (1991). *Whose science? Whose knowledge? Thinking from women's lives*. Milton Keynes, UK: Open University Press.

Hill, C., Corbett, C., St. Rose, A., & American Association of University Women. (2010). *Why so few? Women in science, technology, engineering, and mathematics*. Washington, D.C.: AAUW.

Kachchaf, R., Ko, L., Hodari, A., & Ong, M. (2015). Career–life balance for women of color: Experiences in science and engineering academia. *Journal of Diversity in Higher Education, 8*(3), 175–191.

Mason, M., Wolfinger, N., & Goulden, M. (2013). *Do babies matter? Gender and family in the ivory tower*. New Brunswick, NJ: Rutgers University Press.

Moran Craft, C., & Maseberg-Tomlinson, J. (2015). Challenges experienced by one academic mother transitioning from maternity leave back to academia. *NASPA Journal about Women in Higher Education, 8*(1), 66–81.

Schlehofer, M. (2012). Practicing what we teach? An autobiographical reflection on navigating academia as a single mother. *Journal of Community Psychology, 40*(1), 112–128.

Turner, C. S. V., González, J. C., and Wong (Lau), K. (2011). Faculty women of color: The critical nexus of race and gender. *Journal of Diversity in Higher Education, 4*(4), 199–211.

United Nations. (2000). Resolution adopted by the General Assembly; United Nations Millennium Declaration. Retrieved from http://www.un.org/millennium/declaration/ares552e.htm

West, M. S., & Curtis, J. W. (2006*). AAUP faculty gender equity indicators 2006*. Washington, D.C.: American Association of University Professors.

Young, S., Rush, L., & Shaw, D. (2009). Evaluating gender bias in ratings of university instructors' teaching effectiveness. *International Journal of Scholarship of Teaching and Learning, 3*, 1–14.

Zacher Dixon, L. (2015). Obstetrics in a time of violence: Mexican midwives critique routine hospital practices. *Medical Anthropology Quarterly, 29* (4), 437–454.

5

Looking at the Field
from Afar and Bringing It
Closer to Home

● ●

CECILIA VINDROLA-PADROS

> Fieldwork is the central activity of
> anthropology. . . . It is fieldwork, more
> than the distinctive content of the
> material, that produces the uniqueness
> of anthropology and that entitles the
> anthropologist to professional status.
> —Howell, 1990, 4

Our immersion in the lives of "others," their everydayness, is what gives anthropology its disciplinary identity (Coleman & Collins, 2006). Traditionally in anthropology, the field was conceptualized as something "out there," immutable, waiting for the ethnographer to "discover" it (Coleman & Collins, 2006). However, several authors have problematized this notion of bounded field sites in faraway lands and have proposed, instead, to consider fields as processes that are made and unmade, never natural nor static (Coleman & Von Hellermann, 2011, 3; Faubion & Marcus, 2009). Attention has also been paid to the ways in which these fields are constituted, highlighting the role of the anthropologist's social origins, affiliations, dispositions, gender, and previous field experiences (Bourdieu, 2003). This chapter seeks to expand this line of work by exploring how one characteristic of the field researcher, her role as a mother, influences the conceptualization and constitution of shifting fields, the fieldwork itself, and the practices associated with mothering and motherwork.

We don't always get a glimpse of personal aspects of the anthropologist's life in the ethnographies we read. How do anthropologists balance the demands of fieldwork and parenthood? How do they experience fieldwork when traveling with a baby or leaving one back home? One potential explanation for this omission of the researcher's life could be its lack of recognition as a relevant aspect of the research. However, by failing to include this information, an important component of the anthropologist's identity is overlooked, an identity that plays an important role in defining the field(s) and conducting fieldwork.

Carolyn and Richard Lobban (1987) describe their experiences carrying out fieldwork in Sudan and Egypt before and after having children. They indicate that after they had children and carried out fieldwork as a family, their social status in these encounters was "enhanced." Their roles were accepted and legitimized as they were seen to conform to local cultural norms where married couples have children shortly after marriage. Traveling with their children also allowed them to obtain additional knowledge on local parenting practices; "it opened up new areas of Sudanese reality" (Fluehr-Lobban & Lobban, 1987, p. 246).

New challenges emerge when carrying out fieldwork as a parent and even more so when bringing children to the field as in the case of the Lobbans. In an edited volume titled *Children in the Field* (Cassell, 1987), anthropologists and their families reflected on their experiences during fieldwork. The chapters highlight the stress, anxiety, joy, and surprise field research with children offers and the particular effects it can have on daily life. Reflecting on the ten field narratives presented in the book, Cassell argues that through the act of parenting and bringing one's family to the field, "the relationship between those who study and those who are studied becomes less interrogative, more dialogic," and can lead to "more profound understanding and, consequently, to better social science" (1987, p. 259).

Anthropologists have always worked in different ways, and many anthropologists work outside of academia (or with one foot in academia and the other one somewhere else) in corporations, NGOs, transnational organizations, schools, hospitals, and so on. Their field site is not a distant community, but the boardroom of a company, the bathroom of a private academy, or the operating room in an acute hospital. Many anthropologists live permanently in their field site, obtain services or care in their field site, and take their field site with them as they travel. If, as Appadurai (1988) has argued, we never leave the field site in our interconnected world, how do we create conceptual distinctions between what we deem "researchable" and what is not part of the study? How do we disentangle field research from daily life? Should we disentangle field research from daily life?

These questions draw attention to the ways in which the anthropologist's life influences how the field is constructed, studied, and experienced and how particular events in life, such as motherhood, play a role in these (re)conceptualizations. In this chapter, I focus on my own work and life as a mother of two and medical anthropologist interested in health service delivery in acute hospitals. I present an overview of my engagement with field research as a childless researcher, during two pregnancies, and while caring for a baby and toddler. I explore the ways in which motherhood and field research have intertwined and shaped each other throughout these years.

In this chapter, I argue in favor of revisiting notions of "the field," field research, and parenting. I include field notes from the past ten years that I have collected in the form of conversations with collaborators and participants I remember from fieldwork as well as communication I had with my husband, friends, and other family members. These conversations pointed to the porosity and blurriness of the lines that divided fieldwork and family life and my transformation as both field researcher and mother. The chapter also includes the voice of my husband due to the active role he has played in helping me think about my work, motherhood, and mothering. His voice appears in the form of comments he made after reading the first draft of the chapter. I have inscribed them in the same location where he made them and have not altered them in any way. They complement, expand, refute, critique, and praise the original description of my life experience (I would say they go in tune with our daily dynamic as a couple). Even though they might appear secondary in their narration, these comments provide a window into his experience as my partner and cocreator of this journey.

Creating My "Original" Field Site

You will see when you have children of your own, then you will really understand.
—Mother I interviewed during the beginning of my doctoral fieldwork in Argentina

I heard this phrase frequently as I was carrying out fieldwork for my doctoral thesis in Buenos Aires, Argentina. I guess you could call this my original field site, as it was my first experience with long-term fieldwork. My doctoral dissertation, entitled *Life and Death Journeys: Medical Travel, Cancer, and Children in Argentina*, focused on exploring the experiences of children seeking oncology treatment in Buenos Aires and their parents. I wanted to understand how children with cancer and their families thought about and lived with and through cancer treatment. I was particularly interested in the cases of families who had to travel from distant areas of the country to the capital in order to access care. Their journeys of leaving their home and traveling hundreds of miles to obtain what they considered to be the best care highlighted that experiences of cancer treatment need to be studied both within and outside of the hospital, as they are influenced by travel needs, financial difficulties, loss of parental employment, interruption of schooling, and family separation.

From an emotional standpoint, this was not an easy topic to study. Many of the children I got to know over those years were very ill. Some of them died during the fieldwork or shortly after. I witnessed the pain of parents who knew their children would eventually pass away. Despite encountering what would probably be one of the most difficult moments in their lives, parents were very kind to me during my fieldwork as they took the time to share their stories. When writing about their experiences, I made a direct effort to portray their feelings as I witnessed them. Even though I did not have children at the time and could not grasp the inexplicable pain of losing a child, I could try to relate to other quite raw emotions (anger, sadness, despair, and still some moments of happiness and hope) expressed by these parents. There will always be a partiality to the experiences I was able to describe; not having children at the time is only one of many reasons the stories I narrated in my ethnography are (and always will be) incomplete.

For many of the parents I interviewed, the fact that I was a married and childless researcher meant that they needed to explain to me what parenting was like. I think several of them thought I would have children soon, so they saw our conversations as a way to "prepare me." In a way, my naivete was an excellent way to collect rich data on their views of parenting, but it also meant I needed to be equally open about my personal life and the decisions I was making in relation to future parenting. Kanaaneh, an anthropologist who conducted fieldwork on the family planning strategies of Palestinian women in Israel, describes a similar situation in the field. She writes, "Inasmuch as I had been married for 3 years and did not yet have any children, my going around asking people why and when they had babies was just begging for the questions to be turned back on me. Ethnographic attention was often focused on me" (Kanaaneh, 2002, p. 14). In the case of my fieldwork, in addition to the multiplicity and shifting roles performed by interviewer and interviewees that Kanaaneh points to, I think the mothers I interviewed relied on their views of parenting as a way to make sense of what they were going through. For them, facing harsh realities, such as the potential loss of their child, was a part of motherhood, and strong mothers found ways to fight and move forward.

Even though I returned to the United States to write my dissertation, I continued to maintain a relationship with my field site—returning to Argentina on several occasions after the fieldwork and becoming involved in similar studies. When he was reading this section of the chapter, my husband said, "I

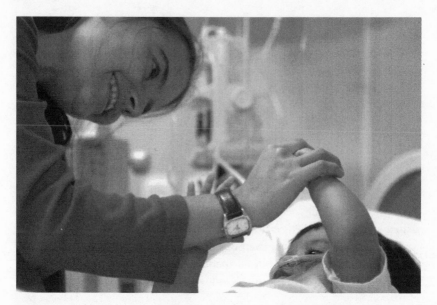

FIGURE 5.1 Fieldwork in Argentina in 2010 (photograph courtesy of Lucas Cannistraci)

don't understand why you don't mention your background and family connections in this section. Your family is from Argentina and you lived there for a
long time. These might have been the reasons why you went back to Argentina
to carry out fieldwork. Your insider knowledge of the culture, language, and
ways in which people socialize with each other probably made this a richer
field experience than the ones you've had in other countries." His comment
made me think about Gallo's (2011) argument that the distinction between
"insider" and "outsider" is complex, blurry, and highly contextual. I agree
with him that there was a lot about Argentinean culture that I did not have to
"learn," and I could grasp nuances from the language that could have probably been missed by a nonnative speaker. However, I was also an outsider in
many ways: I did not have children, I had never experienced cancer treatment
myself or had a family member with cancer, I was not a medical specialist, I
had never worked in these hospitals, I had not lived in Argentina for a while,
and my Argentinean Spanish accent was a bit off in some words (due to my
time living in Mexico, perhaps). Nevertheless, the concept of insider/outsider
in fieldwork is good to think with, as it allows us to explore how aspects of the
anthropologist's or field researcher's life might frame their coconstruction of
the field with research participants. Would being a mother at the time have
made me more of an "insider"?

Bringing the Field Closer to Home

The boundaries between formal research and the everyday are fuzzy.
—Kanaaneh, 2002, p. 8

From the United States, my husband and I moved to the United Kingdom, where I carried out a postdoc on the development of specialized cancer services for young people in England and young cancer patients' experiences of care. I was pregnant when I interviewed for this post. Needless to say, I didn't think I would get the job. Contrary to this expectation, I was offered the research post, was given the chance to participate in the design of the study, and began working six months into pregnancy (there was no hiding it by then). My field site had now moved considerably closer to home, about forty-five minutes away by the underground. Our growing family was certainly one of the reasons I decided to search for a nearby field, but I was also interested in learning about the experiences of parents and children in other countries. I worked almost until my due date.

My labor was relatively straightforward. I didn't experience any major complications, and baby and I were back at home twelve hours after his arrival. Getting used to motherhood was a different issue. Everyone tells you that raising children is hard, and when you don't have children you agree with them, but deep down you think they are probably exaggerating. It can't be *that* hard; everyone does it. Well, for me it felt like the hardest thing I ever did. This new sense of responsibility over this little life felt so heavy. I started to think that maybe this was what the mothers who shared their stories with me in Argentina were trying to communicate when they said I would *really* understand when I had children of my own. I found myself constantly worrying and wondering what I would do if something happened to my child.

There is one anthropologist who very eloquently examines her new relationship with the field when she became a mother. Alma Gottlieb (2004) presents an insightful narration of how her field experiences made her question her own preconceptions of motherhood and cultural norms of parenting maintained in her country of origin. She also describes how the process of becoming a mother allowed her to see children and parents in her field site in a different way (Gottlieb, 2004). I read Alma's book for a doctoral course on the anthropology of childhood and practically glossed over this part. I read it again a few years ago after my oldest son was born, and her words resonated with me in multiple ways. I saw myself incorporating some aspects of the experiences of motherhood of the women I interviewed in Argentina (their strength, their desire to do everything they could for the well-being of their children), but I questioned other ideas they maintained, such as their belief that only mothers could be strong and had to face everything alone.

I had not even begun to get my head around motherhood when it was time to get back to work. Motherhood and the workplace started to interact at a very tangible level, a negotiation Bailey has explored using the concept of interspatiality (Bailey, 2000). Some days, I felt relieved I could get out of the house and think about something else. Other days, I felt guilty. I saw myself constantly thinking about the baby. Was he all right? Would he eat if I weren't there? I had a short maternity leave by UK standards (six weeks), so I was dealing with a lot of the physical aspects of motherhood (like breastfeeding and sleep deprivation) while going back to the field. My first baby didn't sleep through the night until my second baby was born, so sleep deprivation was a close companion over these years.

At this time, I was carrying out interviews and observations in hospitals providing specialized services for young cancer patients. I was able to visit some sites close to home in London, but on several occasions, the work still required full days away from my newborn. My husband reminded me of what it was like at home when I left for work. He said, "This newborn would cry from the moment mommy left the house, to the moment she came back." We tried breastmilk in a bottle, but on several occasions, my husband still needed to travel to the hospital with the baby so I could feed him in between interviews. Sometimes we were able to find a separate room for the three of us, but usually I would end up feeding baby in the hallway or hospital café. This meant that research participants and colleagues would come by to say hello and meet the baby. I think this showed them a different side of me; it made "the researcher" more human. Even though we lacked "privacy," I cherished these moments with my husband and baby. I missed them like crazy.

On other occasions, I traveled on my own and spent the day away. I remember texting my husband several times: "My boobs hurt so much, I can't wait to get home." Managing breastfeeding and fieldwork was harder than I had anticipated. I had a constant fear that my breasts would start leaking in the middle of an interview and the interviewees would notice. I couldn't pump at work like some of my colleagues suggested because I had nowhere to pump and nowhere to store the milk. When the fieldwork required even longer travel, the three of us traveled together. It was manageable for us then, as we only had one child and my husband was studying. Packing for fieldwork in these cases also meant packing diapers and toys. The field and life with baby were feeling quite close to each other.

Reencountering the field as a mom was not easy, but I had so many new things to discuss with my research participants. Some of them knew me from when I was pregnant, so they anxiously asked me about the new baby and how I was coping. Others gave me brilliant advice on how to deal with teething (using teething biscuits) and when to start toilet training (follow their cues and let them guide the process; don't pressure them). The daily practices of parenting became a great way to socialize with participants as well as my colleagues in the hospital and the university. I became part of a wider community of moms who could ask for and share advice with other moms.

Becoming a Part of "the Field"

I was hospitalized for days. How do they do it for months or years?
—Question I asked my husband

When that postdoc ended, I applied for a post in another university to expand my work on acute hospitals. This time, I worked across multiple diseases and populations (not only with children). During my second postdoc year, I had another baby boy (about two and a half years after my first son was born). This time the labor was not straightforward, and we had complications. My baby had breathing irregularities, and the doctors suspected an infection. Our plans to be home the next day suddenly vanished as we were moved to an eight-bed bay in the postnatal ward.

My baby slept pleasantly that night, but I couldn't get any rest. Even though I was exhausted, the uncertainty surrounding my baby's health wouldn't let me fall asleep. Doctors and nurses came to monitor his breathing through the night. They wouldn't say anything to us. They counted the number of times he would breathe in one minute, wrote the number on a piece of paper, and walked away. When my husband and I asked them for more information, they said we could speak to the doctor in the morning. The morning ward round took forever to arrive, and even after the doctor came, all he could tell us was that they needed to draw blood from the baby to run tests to rule out an infection. His breathing wasn't normal, and they needed to monitor it regularly.

One day turned into two, and by the third day, we were told he could have meningitis. They moved us to our own room, which was a relief in the sense that we could get some sleep at night but also worried us, as it highlighted the gravity of the situation. These nights in hospital brought back memories from my fieldwork in Argentina, where mothers described a different environment in the wards at night. They complained about the noise on the ward, the lack of privacy in shared bays, and on nights when they were able to get over the perverse ward feeling, their worries wouldn't let them fall asleep. I felt like I hadn't slept for years by the time we were on our fourth day of hospitalization.

In order to rule out or confirm meningitis, the doctor needed to perform a lumbar puncture. We needed to consent to the procedure. The doctor highlighted the reasons this procedure was required but also pointed to the possible complications that could arise as a result. I remember thinking we would have time to discuss the pros and cons once the doctor left the room, but after giving us the explanation, he stood there waiting for our answer. My husband

and I looked at each other and agreed to the procedure. The doctor then proceeded to wheel our baby out of the room in his little crib. "Wait," I said. "You are doing this now?" The doctor indicated that it needed to be done as soon as possible to make a decision regarding his treatment. I thought we would have more time to process the news. My husband has often said, "After the doctor said lumbar puncture, my mind and everything around me became silent. I was completely paralyzed." Even though we were both there, we experienced this situation in completely different ways. It made me wonder about other ways in which our perceptions of our son's hospitalization might have differed.

My son was wheeled out of our room. We weren't allowed to accompany him or see the procedure. The procedure would take about one hour. All we could do was wait. I couldn't think straight; I didn't know what to do with myself. I couldn't bear to think of such a small baby undergoing such an invasive procedure. I cleaned and straightened out the room. I refolded my sons' tiny clothes three different times. I had to keep busy. I remembered all the times I sat with parents and waited with them while their children were getting lumbar punctures (a common procedure in cases of leukemia). Sometimes they were so nervous they couldn't talk, so we sat silently in the room until the doctor came back in. I remember hearing them say that they didn't mind if I stayed, that my presence helped them think about something else.

When he was brought back to our room he was asleep, covered in a green blanket and wearing the light blue hat we put on him that morning. When I changed his nappy, I didn't want to see the plaster that covered the wound. Fortunately, the lumbar puncture helped the doctor rule out meningitis, and no other source of infection was found. We had to stay in hospital for five more days so they could administer precautionary antibiotics.

I wanted my baby to be well and cared for, but I longed to go home. I missed my other son terribly. He had gone to sleep one night and woken up to find that his mom and dad were gone, and he had to stay home with grandma and his aunt and uncle. He was only two at the time, so I don't know if he understood the explanations they gave him. I got to see him after three days of being in the hospital. He got to meet his brother for the first time. I saw him for one hour that day, and when he left to go back home, it was so hard to say good-bye. How did other people do this?

I had worked with parents who had to be hospitalized with their children for months, leaving their partners and other children behind. They traveled hundreds of miles to the hospital not knowing when they would be able to return home. I remembered the case of one mother who burst into tears during our interview as she told me, "My other children grew up without me." I had only stayed apart from my son for ten days; she did it for two years. I definitely saw my old field experiences in new light.

My interactions with my current field site have also changed. As I talk to patients who complain about the noise at night, having to share a bathroom, or not having privacy, I remember the way I felt. As family members struggle to make sense of the information thrown at them and are forced to decide on the spot that will determine the care their loved ones receive, I remember how hard it was to keep a clear head in such stressful moments. I can also see now that small gestures, like the nurse who smiles at you, a hot cup of tea, or someone who is willing to listen, are actually grand acts of kindness.

Looking at the Field from Afar

Even though I have a close relationship with my field sites in the UK, I look at my "original" field site from afar. Some days, when nostalgia hits, I tend to miss witnessing the everydayness of patients' and caregivers' struggle to obtain services and the ways in which hospital staff negotiate barriers to deliver the best care they can. This is probably due to the emphasis anthropological research places on the importance of "being there." As Sobo has argued, "On-site presence enables us to experience a given location, sometimes allowing us to participate in activities, sounds, smells, sights, and so on that constitute that sociocultural arena" (2009, p. 211). There is a certain texture that you are able to capture as a field researcher that you cannot capture any other way.

My current responsibilities (both at work and at home) don't allow me to travel to Argentina for extended periods of time, but it still remains a long-distance field site in practice and memory. When I am able to travel, my children enter the field with me. My long-term relationships with collaborators in this country mean that family life cannot be disentangled from work. My friends from the field site want to see how much my boys have grown since they last saw them, and close friends of my parents or husband will want to know how they are doing. We will discuss our ongoing projects over coffee or *mate* (a popular national beverage) and interlace conversations on data collection and analysis with the challenges of finding a good nursery or raising my children in a bilingual environment. As a "native" anthropologist, the field is a part of me, and consequently, it is a part of my children as well.

Revisiting Field Research, Motherhood, and Mothering

Fieldwork is a profound and emotional experience. Reaching out to "the other," we move deep within ourselves; learning foreign ways, we illuminate our native culture; studying strange assumptions, we confront our unexamined preconceptions.
—Cassell, 1987, p. 257

We don't need to travel to new and exotic lands to "move deep within ourselves," as Cassell (1987) points out in the quote above. There are life experiences such as motherhood that move us closer to our field site, make us question ourselves, and help us rewrite the stories we tell. Even if we carry out fieldwork in a distant place, the field is never far away. We bring it with us in our imaginations and visit it often as a source of inspiration, learning, admiration, and regret.

Our relationship with and understanding of the field changes as we move through life. There are events such as becoming a parent that create particular reconfigurations of both the anthropologist and field site(s). In the same way that the field can be packed in our back pocket to travel with us as we go, our identities as mothers or fathers are close companions during fieldwork. I do not attempt to argue that one needs to become a parent and bring children to the field to conduct proper fieldwork—I think the key message that the anthropologists cited in this chapter transmit when they reflect on their field experiences as parents is the importance of reflecting.

A key component of contemporary anthropological fieldwork is reflexivity. Reflexivity entails the conscious exercise of understanding how our background, personal life, and characteristics influence our perception of and relationship with the people we meet in our field site. It is a critical examination of the ways in which others might understand our role in the field but also a deep look into how our own identity and life experiences act as the lens through which we document and live in our field sites. Reflexivity needs to be an iterative process throughout fieldwork but also throughout our careers.

Practical Tips

Thanks to this process of critical reflection, there are some practical lessons I learned that I hope can be useful for other field researchers and mothers in similar situations.

- Instead of trying to separate motherhood from field research, we need to make a conscious attempt to bring them together even more, to use motherhood as a tool in field research and capture lessons from our field experiences that can be applied to our daily lives. For a long time, I struggled to deal with the messiness of life and work, but I learned how useful it is to embrace the messiness, to see it as an intrinsic part of daily life. In doing so, I think I ended up feeling happier and calmer and able to do better work.
- In this chapter, I have presented a more "traditional" concept of "the mother," but I think mothering from the field needs to go beyond this idea of the female mother who is responsible for labor, caring, and

raising her children. Considerable work has been carried out to unpack the concept of motherhood, critically examining what constitutes a mother and understanding who is deemed suitable to mother (Taylor, Layne, & Wozniak, 2004). A multidimensional interpretation of motherhood surfaces in the concept of motherwork proposed by Badruddoja and Motanpanyane (2016) as they explore the "invisible labor of care giving" by "wo/men," thus including mothers, fathers, and other forms of caretakers.

As can be seen in this chapter, my husband has done quite a bit of mothering too. Other family members and friends have also played a role in the mothering of my children, either during visits when they lived nearby or at a distance through video chats or emails. My mothering has also been shaped by the many books I have read on parenting (some helpful, others not so much) and my own intuition and experience as a daughter.

- Mothering has also been informed by my field sites, both far away and close to home. The many parents who shared their experiences with me and "trained me" to become a "good" mother have certainly influenced the way in which I approach the relationships with my children. The courage and humility with which they faced their children's life-threatening illnesses have certainly given me a new outlook on the important things in life; where daily dramas lose their severity, as there are worse things people have to go through. There are still days—when the children need to be bathed, fed, and put to bed and field notes need to be typed up, papers need to be written, and deadlines are looming—when it is still easy to get lost in our everyday routine. Nonetheless, I make it a conscious exercise to focus on the grander scheme of things. As one mother I met during fieldwork said to me, "I used to complain about and reprimand my children for the tiniest things, but now I see that they really were tiny things and I have learned to enjoy life and enjoy my children." This chapter presents a brief overview of my field experiences before and after having children, focusing on highlighting the ways in which fieldwork and motherhood have shaped each other. As we move forward with our exploration of mothering from the field, we need to consider the changing nature of our field sites, the fieldwork we carry out, and our roles in research and in life.

References

Appadurai, A. (1988). Putting hierarchy in its place. *Cultural Anthropology, 3*(1), 36–49.

Badruddoja, R., & Motanpanyane, M. 2016. *New maternalisms: Tales of motherwork (dislodging the unthinkable)*. Bradford, OR: Demeter Press.

Bailey, L. (2000). Bridging home and work in the transition to motherhood: A discursive study. *European Journal of Women's Studies*, 7(1), 53–70.

Bourdieu, P. (2003). Participant objectivation. *Journal of the Royal Anthropological Association*, 9(2), 281–294.

Cassell, J. (1987). *Children in the field: Anthropological experiences*. Philadelphia, PA: Temple University Press.

Coleman, S., & Collins, P. (2006). "Being . . . where?" Performing fields on shifting grounds. In S. Coleman & P. Collins (Eds.), *Locating the Field: Space, Place and Context in Anthropology* (pp. 1–21). Oxford, UK: Berg.

Coleman, S., & von Hellermann, P. (2011). Introduction: Queries, collaborations, calibrations. In S. Coleman & P. von Hellermann (Eds.), *Multi-sited ethnography: Problems and possibilities in the translocation of research methods* (pp. 1–15). New York, NY: Routledge.

Faubion, J., & Marcus, G. (2009). *Fieldwork is not what it used to be: Learning Anthropology's method in a time of transition*. New York, NY: Cornell University Press.

Fluehr-Lobban, C., & Lobban, R. (1987). "Drink from the Nile and you shall return": Children and fieldwork in Egypt and the Sudan. In Joan Cassell (Ed.), *Children in the field: Anthropological experiences* (pp. 237–255). Philadelphia, PA: Temple University Press.

Gallo, E. (2011). The unwelcome ethnographer, or what "our" people (may) think of multi-sited research. In S. Coleman & P. von Hellermann (Eds.), *Multi-sited ethnography: Problems and possibilities in the translocation of research methods* (pp. 54–72). New York, NY: Routledge.

Gottlieb, A. (2004). *The afterlife is where we come from: The culture of infancy in West Africa*. Chicago, IL: University of Chicago Press.

Howell, N. (1990). *Surviving fieldwork: A report of the advisory panel on health and safety in fieldwork*. Washington, D.C.: American Anthropological Association.

Kanaaneh, R. (2002). *Birthing the nation: Strategies of Palestinian women in Israel*. Berkeley, CA: University of California Press.

Taylor, J., Layne, L., & Wozniak, D. (Eds.). (2004). *Consuming motherhood*. New Brunswick, NJ: Rutgers University Press.

Sobo, E. (2009). *Culture and meaning in health services research: A practical field guide*. Walnut Creek, CA: Left Coast Press.

Part III

Teamwork Makes
the Dream Work

• • • • • • • • • • • • • • • • • • • •

The Importance of Networks
and Family Support

BAHIYYAH MIALLAH MUHAMMAD

In the previous section, authors shared their challenges with conducting field-work. This is often the side of stories told, albeit behind closed doors when discussing the merger of fieldwork and mothering. To balance this perspective, we discuss the flipside: successful strategies used during fieldwork experiences to keep the ball rolling.

We start by introducing some of the key feminist concepts that make mothering from the field successful. We put the emphasis on networks of support, whatever shape they may take. By doing so, we build on the difficult experiences discussed in section two and refine our alternative narrative—one that is often polyphonic. Indeed, in this section, we see voices other than mothers' emerge and weave into the complexity of the argument. Because we know not everyone will be privileged to travel with a family support group or be given any support at all, we situate all three contributions by incorporating their privilege into the narrative and allowing it to shape the story.

My husband, Muntaquim, and I, in sharing our various strategies for traveling with two young children, exemplify this section's title. Furthermore,

I speak to my family role in the field as resistance to a system that works to detach the Black woman from her child.

Following is a contribution from Grace Stephenson, John Stephenson, and Joanne Karram—a mother researcher, her husband, and mother, respectively. The focus in this chapter, revolves around the disconnect between Grace's emotional turmoil as per her seemingly contradictory roles of field researcher and mother and her husband's and mother's narratives. She illustrates how much of mother-researchers' internal conflicts are self-imposed and how much our loved ones truly can support us.

Finally, Brian Wolf shares his perspective as a fathering field researcher and scholar who shelves his privilege and research for the trials and tribulations of being the lead parent during Mélanie's fieldwork at a morgue in France. Brian shares the unadulterated truth about his nursing daughter, who seemed at times to want nothing to do with him. Still, in the end, he joins John Stephenson and Muntaquim Muhammad in finding the satisfaction that comes from ensuring that strong family bonds are woven.

Section-Specific Takeaways

- Working as a family team is a learning process. It's OK to learn through trial and error, but this should include agreeing on roles and expectations and a clear and open communication process.
- Try your best to not burn yourself out. Don't be shy about asking for help when you need it. Use your network of support to balance your load and maintain a healthy mental state.
- Even when traveling with a family, make an effort to meet and get to know other people.
- Incorporate "time off" for yourself, especially for those who are traveling in the field alongside researchers.
- Being a father requires you to make sacrifices. Accompanying your partner into the field should be one of those sacrifices.
- It's OK to break the old mold of what is "expected" of a father. Pave a new path!

6

Parenting through the Field

· ·

Criminal Justice Ethnography,
Cinematography, and Field
Photography in Africa with
Our Babies

BAHIYYAH MIALLAH MUHAMMAD

AND MUNTAQUIM MUHAMMAD

Introduction

Thinking back, the beginning phases of our international site-based research
experiences were informative and exciting. We have definitely come a long way
and learned a great deal. Currently under our belts are short- and long-term field
projects in Malaysia, Thailand, Cambodia, Vietnam, Edinburgh, Dubai, Abu
Dhabi, St. Croix, Kenya, Uganda, and various locations in the United States
with our children in tow. In addition, we are currently planning a semester-
long research trip to Cali, Colombia, to explore their juvenile justice system
and conduct an ethnographic study on Afro-Colombian children of incarcerated parents. For the purposes of this chapter, we focus on our individual experiences during our shared summer research trip that took place from May to
August in the summer of 2014. Drawing from this three-month experience in

Uganda and Kenya, we highlight our predeparture preparation and challenges, unique field experiences, and how faith, physical and mental strength, and our planning processes brought us across the finish line with an infant and toddler in tow.

First, we discuss the criminal justice ethnographic project that I (Bahiyyah) conducted and the field photography and cinematography that my husband (Muntaquim) completed during our stay mostly in Uganda and briefly in Kenya. Second, we examine how we continuously worked to balance our family bonding time with fieldwork. In concluding, we provide practical tips for anyone considering site-based fieldwork or individuals seeking advice on how to support researchers with children who accompany them and those who do not. It is our hope that this chapter serves as motivation for mothers, husbands, and families to dream big and plan long term when considering site-based research with children.

Criminal Justice Ethnography and Field Photography in Uganda and Kenya

Bahiyyah

I have been conducting criminal justice ethnographic work with families affected by incarceration since 2005 (Muhammad, 2009; Muhammad, 2011). When I first began this work, I was without children. I conducted ethnographic fieldwork in prisons, jails, and detention centers mostly in New Jersey, the state in which I was residing at the time. During the five years prior to the birth of my first child, I traveled to various cities, including East Orange, Irvington, Newark, South Orange, Orange, and Jersey City to interview children who were experiencing or had experienced the incarceration of one or both of their parents. The farthest I traveled to interview research subjects was South Jersey. During that phase of the study, I lived in a hotel in Cumberland County for a month. I share this to highlight the evolution of my site-based research that eventually grew into traveling and living in hotels for months at a time in locations far and wide.

The majority of my research portfolio includes work that highlights the experiences among children of incarcerated parents (Muhammad, 2018). The project I discuss here is part of a global exploration into various countries to complete a comparative analysis. It is my vision to turn this global study into a book. Although this project is ongoing, the visit to Uganda and Kenya served as a framing pilot study (Muhammad, 2014b). In other words, this field experience has served as the foundation for all my subsequent site-based work. While in Uganda and Kenya, my exploration consisted of interviews with incarcerated parents, families affected by incarceration, community members, program coordinators who provided services to the population, and children of incarcerated parents. In addition, observations were conducted at male and female prisons during family visitation sessions and prison tours.

Muntaquim

I served as documentary director of Bahiyyah's exploratory research project in Uganda and Kenya. In other words, I spent the summer working for my wife. As Bahiyyah worked to capture the narrative of her research subjects, I captured photos and videos in support of her project. In this position, I oversaw an undergraduate research photographer and graduate cinematographer (Thorne, 2014). I spent the summer in Uganda and Kenya leading the media team in capturing the lived experiences of families affected by incarceration. This component of the project served to supplement the ethnographic inquiry and rich narratives of the overall study. Project photography consisted of candid shots and behind-the-scenes documentation of personal experiences (Cole & Ross, 1985) to be included in future publications and aid in recall during comparative analyses (Wolcott, 2001). In addition, Bahiyyah used some of my photographs to promote her fieldwork on her department website (COAS Howard University, n.d.). Lastly, I used video footage to produce a documentary short entitled "*Iron Kids around the World: Mothering in the Field*" (Muhammad, 2015). This short highlights the site-based project discussed in this chapter and provides an inside look at motherhood and fieldwork. Because this was Bahiyyah's first ninety-day international study, she was adamant about capturing every minute of it. Outside of my role as lead photographer/videographer, I also served as lead caregiver for our girls during the entire three months in the field.

Generations of Fieldworking Parents

Although neither of our parents were conducting research, we both grew up in families that exposed us to their fields of work.

Muntaquim

Growing up, I remember going to work with my mother and aunt. They both worked at the post office and would be at their sites for very long hours. Often nights turned into early mornings and consisted of heavy lifting, sorting, and taking notes of things that needed to be addressed during the next shift. While in the field with my mother, I met her colleagues, learned postal duties, and gained a long-lived respect for how hard she and my aunt worked. I also accompanied my grandfather to his construction sites. He introduced me to heavy machinery and taught me about forklifts, excavators, and the importance of staying alert when working around such high-powered equipment. I remember having to get eight hours of sleep before going into the field with him. This serves as a pro-tip that I currently use. I really enjoyed the seriousness of fieldwork with my late grandfather and think he would be proud that I learned the importance of exposing children to your work.

Bahiyyah

Muntaquim and I share the fact that a deceased loved one exposed us to fieldwork. My late mother introduced me to the field. For me, being homeschooled meant that I would learn from going into work every day with my mother and sometimes with my father. I remember the commute consisting of a lot of time being spent in the car. We traveled from New Jersey into New York daily to serve the customers at *Muhammad's Oasis*, our vegetarian restaurant in Harlem and later to *The Gift Horses*, a chain of gift shops in the Bronx. Alongside my parents—mostly my mother—I was never allowed to just play. My homeschool curriculum required that I complete tasks in the store, help with management and operations, and sell products to adult customers. I remember filling bottles, bagging orders, greeting customers, and collecting money from sales and providing change to customers. Not only did I learn the ins and outs of running a family business; I also gained immense social skills, interacting with individuals of various ages, races, and genders. This field-based homeschooling taught me everything I know. For example, I learned math from handling cash transactions at the store and calculating what my pay would be at the end of the night. The advantages of growing up in the field are evident in my life today.

The skills learned through fieldwork at my parents' stores were cultivated and expanded by going to work with my grandmother. She owned *Kay's Karizma*, which was a beauty salon also in Harlem. In fact, it was right next door to *Muhammad's Oasis*. I loved going to my grandmother's shop because I didn't have to work there. I could just chill and eat snacks. Her customers would give me dollars, and I would use them to buy candy, chips, and very sweet juices. While at *Kay's Karizma*, I got to engage with the elderly women getting their hair done. They were friendly and would talk to me for hours at a time. When I think back to those times spent with my grandmother and mother, the field was always like a second home. We spent so many hours working, it was like we lived in there. Although we went home most nights, it was mostly just to sleep. Overall, I felt comfortable in the field, but there were some scary times. Having my father and brothers around helped ease the tension during those times.

In retrospect, the field taught me more than I realized before writing this chapter. I grew up watching my mother and grandmother maneuver in and through the field with children—in my mother's case, with nine children and my father nearby. This taught me that it was OK to do the same. While in the field, I was free to talk to adults, learn my environment, and most importantly, dream. It was a feeling I wanted to one day incorporate into my future family.

Muntaquim and I consciously desired a family life inclusive of parenting in the field. It was what we both grew up around. We were raised around site-based work and wanted our children to become exposed in similar ways. Initially the comfort of our early field experiences with parents and grandparents gave us motivation, but we began to think about the many differences between our childhood years and today. We wondered if our early experiences would fit into a contemporary lifestyle because there were so many differences. In the end, our plan was to put everything in God's hands.

Everything Is in God's Hands: *Bismillah Ir-Rahman Ir-Rahim*[1]

Prior to our first international trip into the field with Jaelah and Jian, we spent many late nights at the kitchen table with cups of tea, talking and planning for what started our global field research and field photography as a family. Oftentimes, our conversations ended around four in the morning, when we were required to pray *Fajr*.[2] During this first prayer of the day, we put all trust in God and felt assured that our affairs would be set straight. Praying together helped ease our nerves.

Muntaquim

I felt intense anxiety about my religious role as protector, a role I have taken very seriously since the day I married Bahiyyah. Although I did anticipate this role expanding and taking on new forms in the field, I really couldn't imagine the ins and outs of what would be required of me. One thing I knew for sure was that I had to persevere—especially because the Islamic faith dictates a husband's requirement to accompany his wife on extended trips of three or more days.

For example, *Sayyiduna Abu Sa'id al-Khudri* (Allah be pleased with him) narrates that the messenger of Allah (Allah bless him and give him peace) said, "Let no woman travel for more than three days unless her husband or a Mahram [unmarriageable kin] is with her" (Muslim, 2009, p. 22). With this in mind, our faith served as the foundational motivation for prioritizing our movement into the field as one.

Bahiyyah

I am grateful for our belief system, my husband's *iman*,[3] and family support. Islam is a lifestyle. Therefore, it provides direction on anything that an individual has encountered or will encounter. The Koran provides answers to anything and everything—it even covers what is required of a wife, husband, family, and *ummah* (community) when mothering from the field. From a religious perspective, this made things easier. Although having a strong belief system was helpful, it was still hard to imagine going into another country away from my child, nursing infant, and husband—it was especially difficult to consider being away for an entire summer. Luckily, I didn't need to imagine this because we would be spending our summer in the field as one "happily family," as Jaelah would often say in her younger days.

The summertime is strategically good for completing research projects and catching up on what wasn't completed during a busy academic year. During the summer, we catch up on family bonding and enjoy taking things slow. This wouldn't necessarily be the case while we were in Uganda and Kenya, but either way, we preferred being together rather than apart. Personally, when my spiritual beliefs, family, and work goals are in order, I am at peace. This helped me remain productive and focused.

Predeparture Obstacles for International Travel with a Child and Infant

Taking young children into the field is no easy feat. The obstacles and challenges that one must consider and overcome are tremendous (Starrs, Starrs, Starrs, & Huntsinger, 2001). Therefore, planning for our three-month summer project in Africa began approximately one year in advance. Working as a team from the start allowed us to use our time wisely. In fact, we went as far as splitting our duties in half. Each of us was responsible for those things we had the most experience with. This was our way of trying to make things easiest for us both. Muntaquim immediately began researching accommodations for our stay, focusing on communities near the research site as well as child-friendly activities that could be enjoyed during our down time. I was responsible for all the administrative work for the trip. This included completing proper travel authorizations, researching travel requirements (i.e., vaccines, prescription medicines, visas, and information on travel advisories), and identifying local resources available for international travel. As a new faculty member, this presented a large learning curve for me. As time went on, these duties evolved and changed. During this predeparture planning phase, we learned to be patient with ourselves and the process. Eventually, we became comfortable and understood that it is impossible to plan for everything, and there is nothing wrong with that. Although this shared understanding did not stop us from discussing and strategizing all components of the trip, this pre-preparation dialogue helped balance our initial overexcitement about everything.

One of the most important planning components of this trip included preparing our eldest child, Jaelah Millah (four years old), to have realistic expectations. We started by connecting this flight experience to other shorter flights we had taken. In addition, we walked her through the full travel process from beginning to end. Using *National Geographic* magazines and picture books, we explored landscapes, cultural practices, food, wildlife, birds, flowers, and fun things for families to do. In terms of our youngest child, Jian Alaa (one year old), there was not much prep needed. We expected that she would be in Bahiyyah's lap or arms most of the time. It would be the children's first time in a country that required immunizations, malaria pills, and no brushing or rinsing their teeth with faucet water.

Bahiyyah

The idea of our kids taking malaria pills was a nightmare. This requirement brought flashbacks of my undergraduate study abroad experience in South Africa. Knowing firsthand the side effects of malaria pills, I was very concerned, to say the least. I was not alone, as many traveling parents worry about the effects of these medications on children (Coll & International Herald Tribune, 1996). This is one of the reasons families refuse to travel to Africa, especially with young children. For me, however, it was not a deal breaker because going to the "Motherland" as a family outweighed the challenges it took to get there.

To keep Jaelah focused on what was manageable for her, we childproofed our pre-preparation by restructuring her bedtime routine. About a month prior to departure, we began brushing with bottled water and micromanaging bath time to explain to a four-year-old that while in Uganda and Kenya, there would be no playing in the tub as she was accustomed to. These small changes in our eyes, big in hers, led to many questions and bath-time conversations that helped her understand that our lives would be different in Uganda and Kenya. Although this didn't shrink her interest and excitement in going, she continued to ask questions, and we continued to answer them. We supplemented her trip preparation with books[4] and age-appropriate YouTube Kids[5] videos that explained water contamination and what to expect while abroad. Jaelah took this trip as seriously as a four-year-old could and maintained her eagerness to meet new children.

Muntaquim

After getting our travel vaccines, we had to secure temporary visas. We visited the Uganda embassy numerous times to ask questions and submit paperwork. They required a host letter from the research site, accommodation information, and immunization records, specifically the yellow-fever travel booklet with signatures and dates. At the embassy, we received lots of booklets and pamphlets. Some highlighted the beauty of the country, while others were outright scary. They discussed Zika risk in Uganda, Malaria concerns, sick children, and contaminated villages. As if we weren't already a bit nervous, this put the icing on the cake. Yet again, we continue to proceed.

Unique Field Experiences

Bahiyyah

When conducting research among global populations affected by incarceration, typical site-based work becomes unique, to say the least. I am often asked how and why I bring my children into the field, especially as a criminologist. I answer by sharing a story about one of my dissertation advisors who conducted all her international research on incarceration with her family in tow. She traveled with her husband and three children. She also was a criminologist and spent much of her time abroad inside prisons and jails. She stated that it was the only way she could do it. I remember that day in her office when she told me, "You never let your work come between you and your family. You include them in it." This to me was a unique perspective. It reinforced what I learned from my mother and grandmother in the field and let me know that sometimes you just have to do things your way.

In a research study she conducted with incarcerated mothers and their children, she wrote about using pictures of her own children to share with child participants during the assent process (Henriques, 1982). When conducting a pilot study in 2005 and a dissertation study, *Exploring the Silence Among Children of Prisoners*, from 2006 to 2009, I used this same concept with pictures of my nieces and nephews during my assent process with child participants (Muhammad, 2011). Since I didn't have children of my own at the time, I used this method to connect with child interview participants. When the child participants viewed the photos of my nieces and nephews, they opened up and began to communicate with me in deeper ways. By the time I had a child of my own, I began bringing her instead of photos to my interviews. This was my unique way of showing children that I could relate to them. Immediately, my interviews got better. There was one family interview that I conducted in a local park. During the assent process, I introduced my eldest daughter to the child participants and their families. The children played together in the park while I interviewed their caregivers. During the interview, Muntaquim took pictures of the entire process. These photos became an important part of the recall-and-analysis phase.

Everyone has their own reasons for conducting fieldwork while parenting. We work hard to balance what works for our family and what benefits the overall project—not just during the data collection phase but analysis through study completion.

Playdates and Research Sites

A Boarding School for Children of Incarcerated Parents

The research site in Uganda was at a boarding school for children of incarcerated parents. At the time, there were more than sixty children residing at the boarding school. Our daughters thoroughly enjoyed the research site being a school full of children. When we first arrived, Jian and Jaelah were surprised by all the children who were lined up, singing a beautiful greeting song. Jian was in a baby backpack–style carrier, sitting high up on my back, and Jaelah walked in herself with a big smile, taking each step with a strong sense of pride. We had arrived, and our children and the children there were excited. Immediately, one of the girls from the school grabbed Jaelah's hand, and they proceeded to walk hand in hand the rest of the way. Every so often, Jian would shyly peek down from her seat to admire her sister moving around so freely. The first day was long and packed with events, beginning with a detailed tour of the facility.

Muntaquim

During the walk around the facility, I began taking pictures. The camera was fascinating to the children, and every flash made them eager to get closer. Some of the children who were not shy actually ran my way to learn more about me and the camera. I took some time to speak with them and show them the camera. I pointed to Bahiyyah and told them that she was my wife and that Jaelah and Jian were my daughters. I also told them that we would be there for a while and I would come back with the camera and let them take a few pictures of their own. They were very happy to hear that.

Usually a big camera with a bright flash makes people, especially children, nervous and shy. It was the opposite in this case. The children lined up for what turned into an impromptu photoshoot. By this time, Jaelah was comfortable and parading around the place with different groups of kids. I was able to capture some amazing photos and make great memories. The rest of my day consisted of taking pictures and videos. After the tour, there were performances by the children. This included dancing, singing, praising, and storytelling.

Bahiyyah

I conducted my observations with Jian on my back the entire time. I was very cognizant of how comfortable children were around me because I was a mother and wife and not just some creepy lady who watched everyone and everything, took notes, and asked lots of questions. Kids began coming up to me to request Jian's freedom. In other words, they wanted her down and within their reach—they wanted to play with her. After a quick walk back to the truck, I changed Jian's diaper and put peppermint and eucalyptus oils all over both children. This was our natural way of keeping mosquitos away.

Family Tracing Interviews in Remote Villages

Although the entire summer research project was full of interesting observations and interviews, traveling to remote villages to conduct family tracing is the process that was most memorable. During family tracings, we were able to learn more about community life in the villages. With our host organization, we visited families to bring them messages from their incarcerated family members.

Bahiyyah

Village interviews were a stark difference from field days at the boarding school. Interview days began extremely early and ended unbearably late. In a typical case scenario, the drive into the village was mapped out on a piece of paper from an incarcerated individual who sent us to inform the family of their whereabouts. There were no GPS systems, and I can't recall ever seeing any street signs. In one particular case, it was a six-hour drive (one way), with an indefinite arrival time. This would not pose a problem if we were childless, but with kids, the "I'm not sure" arrival time was more problematic. Luckily, there were many stops along the way. We had to stop for bathroom breaks, and we stopped to pick up items to be donated to families, such as soap, beans, rice, bread, sugar, tea, and other small items. These items would serve as compensation for their participation. We also stopped a few times for gas. This meant that we could purchase snacks from the small store to keep the kids occupied for the rest of the ride.

Muntaquim

I packed extra fruit because I knew Bahiyyah would pack lunch bags for the kids. I tried to keep extra power foods in my stash to make sure that we all maintained energy levels of at least 50 percent. When conducting fieldwork with family and children, putting the children's needs first comes almost automatically. Therefore, it is important to be strategic about what you decide to bring into the field so that everyone can benefit. I mostly packed items that were nonperishable because they lasted longer. I also considered weight. Two children are heavy when you have to lug them around. Having extra bags of food on top of that can be problematic. For us, nourishment in the field was important. It was something we always planned the night before. We couldn't stop randomly on the side of the road for food because there were health warnings; therefore, we packed an entire day's worth of food to feed four individuals.

Bahiyyah

I was so grateful that Muntaquim stashed extra food. I really needed it. He also packed ice cold water, a few mangos, and some walnuts, pistachios, and raisins. He even brought a veggie burger sandwich. I ate most of it and fell asleep for the rest of the ride. I woke up to the driver blowing the horn and stepping on the brakes so abruptly that I thought for a second that we had gotten into an accident, only to find out that this was his attempt to awake us. We had finally arrived. I nursed Jian, covered myself back up, and jumped out of the car. I was eager to meet families and begin interviews.

After making our way to the front of the village, I saw a few families waiting for us. As we got closer, more family members came out. They were smiling and looking at Jaelah and Jian in amazement. It was as if I was an afterthought—everyone was more interested in the children. I was told later that our babies were the first Black children to visit from America. The ladies and elders in the village took turns hugging the girls. After greeting everyone, my kids were left alone to play with the village children and baby chickens that roamed freely. As I conducted interviews, I could see Muntaquim capturing pictures in the periphery. I could also hear my children's enjoyment through their laughter and the swiftness in their feet hitting the ground as they ran around my interview mats.

Every so often, Jian would interrupt my interviews for milk. I nursed her on the spot and covered us both with a piece of the *Khimar*[6] wrapped around my head. Everyone knew what I was doing, and they respected it. To the African women, it promoted a sense of pride to be in the company of a nursing mother. It was something that the elders honored. In their eyes, it distinguished one as having closeness to God. I continued to nurse as I sat on the ground conducting the interview. When Jian was full, I burped her, and she remained in my lap almost falling asleep for a few minutes before running back into the field. My interview continued.

I was in the Motherland, and to be back with my children and husband was a true blessing. Our souls were at peace, and the feeling was mutual throughout the entire village. There was no code-switching. There was no trying to fit it. There was no worrying about what was right or wrong. It was all good. We felt at home in Africa.

Wakanda Forever: United We Stand, Divided We Fall

We never could have imagined that parenting in the field on a research trip in Africa would be the focus of our family movie night to see *Black Panther*. An entire four years later, Jaelah (8 years old) and Jian (5 years old) were in the back seat of the car making connections between our trip to Africa and scenes

FIGURE 6.1 Jian Muhammad sitting on Bahiyyah Miallah Muhammad's lap during a field interview with a grandmother living in the Butalyia village in Uganda. Jaelah Muhammad (not depicted here) is playing in the background with a few village children. This photo was taken by Muntaquim Muhammad in July 2014.

from the movie. Jaelah yelled over the music, "Can you please tell Jian that we went to Wakanda? She was too small to remember." Without answering, Muntaquim and I looked at each other and smiled. We hoped to hear more of the children's conversation, to gain insight into what their experience means now. They continued to talk, and we continued to feel that sense of love that filled our hearts. In the field or in the car driving home from a movie night, we always feel stronger together.

Muntaquim

Every field experience has strengthened our bonds as a family. It has reminded us of what is truly important in life. Specifically, it has helped me gain a detailed and descriptive understanding of Bahiyyah's research portfolio and qualitative skills in the field. It has empowered my desire to remain helpful and beneficial to her process. In many ways, it has united us and allowed me to gain understanding of creative ways of balancing work and family by embracing the parenting perspective. Seeing Bahiyyah as a mother and researcher in the field was natural. Actually, I was impressed to see her use mothering as a method for connecting with families and children of incarcerated parents.

Bahiyyah

Mothering in the field has allowed me to make deep connections with research families around the world. Working alongside my husband and bringing our children along humanized the entire research experience and facilitated open rapport with interview subjects. At the same time, it allowed me to thrive within my family, in the ivory tower, and within global communities. Most importantly, it has empowered me to maintain dignity and integrity without losing my soul in the process (Rockquemore & Laszloffy, 2008; Reifman, Biernat, & Lang, 1991). Site-based research has allowed me to successfully collect data in ways that keep me progressing on the tenure track and respected within my family and community. The thought of achieving tenure and promotion at the expense of family (Martin, Harrison, & Dinitto 1983) is depressing (Young & Wright, 2001). It is a choice that no one should be forced to make. This is something that I have strategically worked to avoid.

As a Black mother in academia, I use my field methodology as a mode of resistance to institutional oppression and persistence toward upward mobility in the ivory tower (Simmons, 1983). This conscious decision to not leave my family behind has helped maintain my sanity. Thus I have been able to triangulate my work, family, and career in a balanced approach. Although conducting site-based research with family and children can be a challenge, it is not impossible. When planned properly, it can be a way of generating rich data, building rapport within global communities, and bonding with your family in unforeseen ways.

The final section of this chapter provides practical tips for traveling to conduct site-based research with a family and children. The list is not exhaustive. Instead, it serves as a framework for getting readers to think deeply and critically about creating their own personal strategies for engaging family with fieldwork.

Practical Tips

These tips are broken into the following categories: (1) administrators, (2) field helpers, and (3) site-based researchers. Each of these groups are loosely defined, and individuals may fit into multiple categories. Administrators consist of those individuals in leadership roles—specifically, those who supervise faculty researchers or administer funding for university or departmental budgets. Field helpers can be anyone who accompanies the researcher into the field or stays at the home location to be of service to the fieldworker during their time away (i.e., family members, family friends, babysitters/nannies, pet sitters, house sitters, landlords, research assistants, hired experts, etc.). The site-based researcher is the individual who is responsible for data collection (i.e., the principle investigator [PI], co-PI, research consultant, etc.). This section ends with extra tips for travelers with babies, advice for the traveling father, and a few tips for field photographers.

ADMINISTRATORS
- Allow new researchers the ability to supplement start-up packages with family funds—this will include funds to support family in the field or at home.
- Allow "equipment funds" to be loosely defined. For site-based researchers, this may include items needed to accommodate a family in the field and other nontraditional items, such as international phones and plans, travel strollers, body carriers for babies, and items required for special-needs children.
- Allow flexible timelines in the use of funds, especially for mother researchers, who may only be able to conduct research during summers. Such schedules would require more time to complete an actual study.

EXTRA TIPS FOR TRAVELING WITH BABIES AND INFANTS
- When selecting accommodations, read reviews and speak with individuals who have stayed there. Prior to leaving, connect with locals prior to gain an "on-the ground-perspective" of how things really are.
- Be reminded that nursing mothers are at an advantage when researching in a country where the water is unsafe. Being able to nurse on demand without worrying about clean water and formula may ease some stress.
- Get comfortable with a "dirty/sloppy/imperfect" baby. While in the field, you may not be able to change soiled clothes as quickly as you may like. Be OK with a field baby who is not always picture perfect. It is OK, and it's not the end of the world.
- Be patient with your child's transition into new places. Anticipate that they may not be comfortable at first, and this may take them more time than you wish.
- Visit a local park or playground on the first day. This can be very comforting for the child/children. No matter how jet-lagged you may be, your child will appreciate a few minutes in a space that brings comfort.
- Make sure to pack the child's favorite snacks, especially for the first few days. It may take some time to find favorites among local selections.
- Check in often with your child/children to incorporate their perspectives into your decision-making process.

EXTRA TIPS FOR TRAVELING DADS

- Be confident and remain resilient no matter what you are faced with. Naturally, you will be looked to as a problem solver by members outside of your family.
- Begin your exercise regimen way in advance of the trip. This will come in handy throughout the entire travel experience. I carried babies, camera equipment, and extra bags for team members who became fatigued.
- Pack of few pairs of cargo pants. They really come in handy with all the pocket space they provide. Having numerous pockets with zippers will assure that you have enough room for yourself and others.
- Research natural remedies for insect repellant. We used natural peppermint oil and citronella oil on our children and ourselves. The smell was very strong and worked to keep all kinds of bugs away.
- Keep a journal. Even if you aren't the writing type, it's a great way to reflect on your experiences and contextualize things for yourself.
- Travel with local currency and American dollars. Small currency comes in handy when making bathroom or food stops in random towns.
- Create a travel playlist. This will help you relax in times when you need to put on a pair of headphones and disconnect.
- Don't be shy about including "me" time into the schedule. It may actually work as an advantage for the family. It can allow you time to get to know the area and identify places to possibly bring the family back to.
- Have daddy-baby time often. This will give your partner some quiet time to catch up on things or simply sleep without interruption.
- Pay attention to nonverbal communication from your partner and others. Be proactive rather than reactive.
- When things don't seem right, don't be shy about speaking up. Remember that your safety and that of your family come first.

TIPS FOR FIELD PHOTOGRAPHERS

- Take lots of pictures and have others take pictures of you. As part of a camera crew, have others capture you in candid moments in the field. You will appreciate this footage in the long run.
- Photograph something the first time you encounter it. Do not procrastinate.
- Never leave the camera behind. You never know what you will see.
- If you promise to send or bring a picture back to a participant, follow through.
- Always bring extra memory cards and batteries. Don't assume that you will have access to electricity for charging purposes.

- Pack a camera strap and use it often. After long days of shooting, equipment gets heavy, and you don't want unsteady footage.
- Get insurance on your equipment. It is always safer to be covered.

Notes

1   In the Arabic language, this phrase is commonly translated as "In the name of God, most Gracious, most Compassionate." It has been said that this phrase contains the true essence of the entire Quran as well as the true essence of all religions. This expression is so magnificent and so concise that all but one chapter of the Quran begins with these words.

2   *Fajr* means "dawn" in the Arabic language, refers to the dawn prayer offered by practicing Muslims, and usually applies to the first daily obligatory prayer, whose time extends from dawn until sunrise.

3   The belief in the six articles of faith, known as *arkan al-iman*.

4   A few of the books include *The Water Princess* by Susan Verde, *A Is for Africa* by Ifeoma Onyefulu, *Africa Is Not a Country* by Margy Burns Knight and Mark Melnicove, *Africa Is My Home: A Child of the Amistad* by Monica Edinger, *When Africa Was Home* by Karen Lynn Williams, *I Am Africa* by Carl R. Sams II and Jean Stoick, *Ugo's Fantastic African Voyage* by Chris Woodard, and *Children's Travel Activity Book and Journal: My Trip to Africa* by Travel Journal Books

5   YouTube Kids is an app that we download on Jaelah's iPad. YouTube Kids is a family-friendly version of YouTube for younger children of various ages.

6   A head covering or veil worn in public by some Muslim women, typically covering the head, neck, and shoulders.

References

Brown, A., & Peers, L. (2006). *Pictures bring us messages*. Toronto, ON: University of Toronto Press.

Brown, T. M., & Masi de Casanova, E. (2009). Mothers in the field: How motherhood shapes fieldwork and researcher-subject relations. *Women's Studies Quarterly, 37*(3/4), 42–57.

COAS Howard University. (n.d.). *Dr. Bahiyyah M. Muhammad visits Uganda, Africa to conduct research and empower families of incarcerated individuals*. Retrieved from http://www.coas.howard.edu/sociology-criminology/news-events/2014summer-bahiyyah-muhammad-uganda.html

Cole, H. M., & Ross, D. H. (1985). The art and technology of field photography. *African Arts, 18*(4), 46–55.

Coll, S. K., & International Herald Tribune. (1996, October 18). Kids: Anti-malaria drugs pose hard choice for parents. *The New York Times*. Retrieved from http://www.newyorktimes.com

Haney, E. (2010). *Photography and Africa*. London, UK: Reaktion.

Henriques, Z. W. (1982). *Imprisoned mothers and their children: A descriptive and analytical study*. Lanham, MD: University Press of America.

Martin, P., Harrison, D., & Dinitto, D. (1983). Advancement for women in hierarchical organizations: A multilinear analysis of problems and prospects. *Journal of Applied Behavioral Science, 19*(1), 19–33.

Muhammad, B. M. (2009). Counting children of incarcerated parents: A methodological critique of past and present literature. In Muraskin, R., & Roberts, A. R. (Eds.), *Visions for change: Crime and justice in the twenty-first century* (5th ed.). New York, NY: Pearson Prentice Hall.

Muhammad, B. M. (2011). *Exploring the silence among children of prisoners: A descriptive study*. Retrieved from Rutgers University Electronic Theses and Dissertations. (Accession Order No. EID.00061087)

Muhammad, B. M. (2014, July 10). *Iron kids—the Uganda project* [Video file]. Retrieved from http://m.youtube.com/watch?vzMGP5qD

Muhammad, B. M. (2015, May 27). *Iron kids around the world: Mothering in the field* [Video file]. Retrieved from http://m.youtube.com/watch?feature=youtu.be&v=TgRdN1oxtBE

Muhammad, B. M. (2018). Against all odds: Resilient children of incarcerated parents. In Gordon, L. (Eds.), *Contemporary research and analysis on the children of prisoners*. Newcastle, UK: Cambridge Scholars.

Muhammad, B., & Muhammad, M. (2014a). I don't understand: Questions among children of incarcerated parents. *Corrections Today*. Boston, MA: Pearson Learning Solutions.

Muhammad, B., & Muhammad, M. (2014b). *The prison alphabet: An educational coloring book for children of incarcerated parents*. Atlanta, GA: Goldest Karat.

Muslim, S. (2009). *English translation of Sahih Muslim*. Riyadh: Dar-us-Salam.

Mustafa Al-Jibaly, M. (2005). *The fragile vessels: Rights and obligations between the spouses in Islam*. Arlington, TX: Al-Kitaab & As-Sunnah.

Reifman, A., Biernat, M., & Lang, E. L. (1991). Stress, social support, and health in married professional women with small children. *Psychology of Women Quarterly, 15*(3), 431–445.

Rockquemore, K. A., & Laszloffy, T. (2008). *The black academic's guide to winning tenure without losing your soul*. Boulder, CO: Lynne Rienner.

Rose, G. (2010). *Doing family photography*. Farnham, UK: Ashgate.

Smith, A. T. L. (1983). The black woman—Overcoming the odds. *The Crisis, 90*(6), 14–15.

Starrs, P. F., Starrs, C. F., Starrs, G. I., & Huntsinger, L. (2001). Fieldwork . . . with family. *Geographical Review, 91*(1/2), 74–87.

Thomas, S. S., Smith, V. C., & Muhammad, B. M. (2016). Mass incarceration: Perpetuating the "habits of survival" and race identities of black women caregivers to children of incarcerated parents. Special topic: Revolutionary criminology. *Journal of Criminal Justice and Law Review, 5*(1–2), 95–115.

Thorne, Kevin. (2014, July 21). *Iron kids* [Video file]. Retrieved from http://m.youtube.com/watch?feature=youtu.be&v=b6eJeQtxy6k

Wolcott, H. F. (2001). *Writing up qualitative research*. Thousand Oaks, CA: Sage.

Young, D. S., & Wright, E. M. (2001). Mothers making tenure. *Journal of Social Work Education, 37*(3), 555–568.

7

Privilege, (In)Competence, and Worth

• •

Conflicting Emotions of the Student-Mom and Her Support Community

GRACE KARRAM STEPHENSON,
JOHN STEPHENSON, AND
JOANNE FLORENCE KARRAM

In my most anxious dreams I relive my commute to Knowledge Village along Dubai's highway 57. I can see the waves of heat rising from the desert. Driving past camels as they stand still on the dunes. They calmly watch our constant motion of cars, trucks, buses. The crux of the chaos is the round-about at Sheikh Mohammed Bin Zayed Road. I sense the centrifugal pull of the traffic before I see it. The approach is slow as cars await their turn. I hold my breath, a moment of stillness, and then dart forward, filling a small gap in the swirling mass. A four-lane, three-kilometer circle. A five-minute panic. Drive aggressively, drive defensively. Then off the circle and onward to my fieldwork. (Excerpt from Grace's reflective field journal, January 29, 2014, Dubai)[1]

It had been a long night adjusting to a new time zone. The time difference from Dubai to Kuala Lumpur is only 4 hours, but for little kids, it takes more than a week to adjust. I was tired. Now, it was 10:30am, 35 degrees Celsius outside, and I was pushing Maëlle in the stroller to find a kids play group in a section of the city we hadn't yet been to. As we walked along, I tried to think about the great time we had had in Dubai and all the really amazing friends we had made in only 2.5 months there. I was sure it would be the same here in Kuala Lumpur . . . but this first week was hard. (Excerpt from John's reflective field journal, March 17, 2014, Kuala Lumpur)

At first there was a lot of mommy stuff going on—baby holding, cooking and a little cleaning while mommy napped, emailed, blogged. Sometimes I even went to her academic institution to keep baby near so she could nurse when needed. There were lots of walks around the neighbourhood to give mommy time alone to concentrate on her studies for a few precious hours. All in all, it was pretty sweet (for me). (Excerpt from Joanne's reflective field journal, June 15, 2015, Toronto)

Introduction

The following chapter is written with two aims: (a) to validate and explain the emotional discord mothers experience as they embark on their fieldwork and care for their children and (b) to identify and affirm the broad range of supports that are necessary for these women to succeed. This chapter is cowritten by me, Grace, with contributions from my husband John and mother Joanne. I am the one who will receive the degree, but over the past five years, John and my mother have given 100 percent, continually rearranging their schedules to care for our children and advise on my research. This chapter grapples with three lingering questions that have been at the heart of my emotional discord throughout my PhD program: Am I privileged? Am I competent? Has this been worth the effort? By writing this chapter as a team of three, it became clear that many of my anxieties were not shared by John and my mother, and the process of sharing our hearts lessened my burden significantly.

Chapter Overview and Methodology

This chapter uses a comparative essay methodology to situate me (Grace), the student-mom, amid the two main agents who supported my studies (John, my husband and father of my children, and Joanne, my mother and care provider to my children) to illuminate the many layers of support that were necessary for the successful completion of my PhD. This methodology is rooted in the epistemological perspective that each person has the "impulse to narrate" (White, 1980, p. 5) and that we gain intersubjective understanding through the stories we tell of our own lived experiences.

For data collection, each of us wrote our own reflective field journals independently during or after fieldwork. After we had all written our pieces, I brought them together in this chapter, highlighting the different perspectives and responses we created. It was fascinating to realize that John and my mom did not share the anxieties that were so central and defining for me. They never kept count of what they gave or questioned whether it had all been worth the effort. Instead, they both highlight the amazing components of our journey and attest to their gratitude for having been part of such an experience.

Research Questions: The Paradox of Graduate Studies

Completing my PhD and having children has been an ongoing paradox. I have struggled with the busy, competitive, relentless pace of graduate studies. Yet there have been many precious days: heartfelt conversations with other student-moms, energizing debates about theories and ethics, and research that actually makes a difference for the participants. Through it all, I have been embedded in the nurturing haven of my family: my parents, my husband, my sister, and my brother—all of whom have watched my children, edited my chapters, and attended my research talks. Throughout the journey, I continually found myself asking these questions: Am I privileged? Am I competent? Has it been worth it? I have asked so much of so many people, and I am unable to answer a definitive yes or no to any of these questions. I attribute my ambivalence to three conflicting processes.

First, completing my PhD was a longtime desire of mine. When I received my acceptance letter, informing me that I would be paid to study for four years, I felt like I had won the lottery. I get to think deep thoughts for four years. Awesome. Furthermore, my husband John and I had always lived on a small, fixed income. Even the humble offer of a graduate stipend was a new level of financial stability. Thus my first emotion and self-perception upon entering graduate studies was a sense of privilege. Throughout the ensuing four years, my sense of privilege has also been connected to the excellent support people in my life. While my peers slogged on alone, I have a husband and two sets of grandparents nearby and ready to help.

Paradoxically, this privilege has also been linked in my mind to a deep sense of incompetence. I have none of the PhD vibrato that people ascribe to me at parties ("Wow, you're doing a PhD!"). Rather, every time I receive help from my husband or mother, every time I call in a favor because I have children, I feel deeply incompetent and a little distrustful of myself. Many of the student-moms I know have little support, working each day to balance children, research, work, and household responsibilities. They have few people they can call to for help. Surely I should be able to do more on my own without depending so heavily on those around me.

The final emotion or self-perception that has been paradoxically linked to my privilege is a continual questioning of whether it has been worth it. Perhaps it is a bit decadent to sit around and debate new forms of education, to still be a student at thirty-four years old. Others have put their own money, time, and energy into supporting my studies, going significantly out of their way to help me. I feel very anxious, wondering if all this effort has been worth the cost.

My Story: Grace's Background

It is the summer of 2016. I am thirty-four years old and scheduled to defend my dissertation in September. In November 2011, three months into my doctoral program, I realized I was pregnant. Conflicting emotions arose immediately. My husband John and I were thrilled. We had been trying to get pregnant and had lost hope. On the other hand, I was full of dread. I had started the journey toward obtaining a PhD because, after two years of trying unsuccessfully to have a baby, that was the open door. At a time when most mothers are taking in the joy of becoming a mom, I was bombarded with so many of my own questions. I had many questions: How I would tell my supervisor and the professors I worked for? What would they think about me taking maternity leave? Was I being fair by trying to juggle both motherhood and higher education? Was it possible to do both?

As a new mother, I continued to face my limits as I missed conferences, speaking opportunities, and paper deadlines. I struggled with deep feelings of incompetence as I compared myself to my friends who managed to work multiple research contracts, publish with professors, and teach courses. In January 2013, following my four-month maternity leave, I returned to school and began the monumental task of writing my proposal and preparing for fieldwork. One of my committee members had casually suggested that I examine university branch campuses in the United Arab Emirates and Malaysia for my research. I took the suggestion to heart and planned my research around those two sites, literally a world apart. The paradox, however, was that I could not escape the feeling that I was privileged. Only the generous flexibility of those in our lives allowed me to complete my proposal. During that time, John was working for a church as a community organizer, supporting low-income tenants in the neighborhood's public housing. His boss, the local priest, was also behind my studies 100 percent and generously gave him five months of unpaid leave to travel with me and watch Maëlle.

The Beauty of Traveling with a Child

We left for Dubai in January 2014, exactly one year after I started writing my proposal. My daughter Maëlle was like a magical portal into a new world of travel. John and I had traveled extensively in our early twenties, but in contrast to our fieldwork experiences, those past travels were merely consumptive, quick movements across new locations to see, hear, and touch but not connect. A decade later, when we landed in Dubai, it was clear something was different. The friends of friends who offered to pick us up from Dubai's international airport were so excited about our visit because we came with a baby. They gushed over the chubby, cuddly, giggly one-year-old. Thankfully, our daughter's presence made this fifty-something, professional couple eager to help us. And we desperately needed the help to survive those first weeks on the ground. The time difference was almost impossible to push through with a child, and our friends kindly took her for morning walks while we caught up on sleep. Amazingly, in receiving their help, we deepened our connection as we shared life together with these new friends. They become invested in us, and we in them. Our child made us needy, and in receiving help, we became emotionally accessible. John noted the following in his field journal:

> There are two well-known methods of making friends quickly anywhere in the world. The first is to eat whatever your hosts put in front of you and tell them you love it. The second is to wander around with cute kids. As a dad supporting my wife on the journey of completing her field work, I did both well and we ended up making friends quickly. (Excerpt from John's reflective field journal, April 2, 2014, Kuala Lumpur)

I even suspect that I received access to one institutional research site because of our daughter. While we were preparing to travel, I had posted a picture on my blog of Maëlle sitting in our suitcase as we attempted to pack our bags. Then in Malaysia, when I went to meet the director of an institution where I hoped to interview students, the director was more eager to talk about my family than my ethical protocol, having seen Maëlle's picture on my blog. The director was also a mother and an academic who planned on completing a PhD. She and I formed a mutual attachment as we discussed the difficulties of balancing our professional, academic, and family lives.

The beauty of traveling with a child is a common theme John and I both explore in our reflective field journals. Although I struggled with feelings of guilt over my white privilege and John and I had many conversations about traveling the world as "expert researchers," things were different with a child. Whether it was because the family unit is stronger in other countries or because we slowed down and traveled less consumptively, we were entering into authentic and meaningful relationships with those around us.

Seeing the world through the eyes of children is an amazing way to travel. I admit there were times when I wished I could just sit at a street side café by myself sipping Turkish coffee in the morning, while Grace interviewed

FIGURE 7.1 John, Grace, and Maëlle visiting friends in Bahrain in February 2014

students. But being there as a dad was really the best thing ever. Maëlle and I discovered incredible parks, met other families, played with sandcastles on the beach, fell asleep riding an old dhow, wandered down narrow pathways that caught Maëlle's attention . . . the list is infinite. If it had just been me, I could have said that I visited all the tourist sites, but children slow you down, in a good way. (Excerpt from John's reflective field journal, April 2, 2014, Kuala Lumpur)

Privilege: Four Main Themes

Although the ongoing needs we experienced while traveling lessened my sense of privilege during our fieldwork travels, I still find that an overwhelming sense of privilege pervades my life. Yet there has been a noticeable shift away from seeing privilege as only economic in nature. Rather, the most important areas of privilege in my life are those areas of personal support, rooted in the relationships that guide my life and enable me to complete my studies. As I analyzed my reflective journals, the most common recurring theme relates to my disquiet about my privilege. However, in reading our field journals, four main themes of privilege are shown, offering a framework to supporting mothers who are studying and writing.

The Finances and Freedom of Fieldwork

People's reactions are rather distressing when they realize my husband John and I are raising two children in a condo that is only 670 square feet. But we own it. And in Toronto, a city with the fourth highest housing costs in North America, this is a huge privilege. (Excerpt from Grace's reflective field journal, June 2, 2016, Toronto)

The first theme that was clearly demarcated in my field journal was financial support. This, however, was more complex than merely receiving adequate funding. The stability of owning our condominium was as important as the monthly income we received and allowed us to leave on fieldwork and seamlessly return home. In Toronto's inflated housing market, many students do not want to leave their secure rentals to travel because of the risk that they may not find reasonably priced housing when they return.

I am often asked how we survive financially with my husband's non-profit salary and my small graduate stipend. But I was fortunate to receive a federal scholarship that provided two paid maternity leaves. This meant that I earned more money than most of my kid-less peers. I also have my husband's income to provide for our daily needs. Our small income would likely be a shock to many of our neighbours, but a steady income is still a huge gift. (Excerpt from Grace's reflective field journal, June 2, 2016, Toronto)

Despite a strong and growing student support field across North American universities, the conversation about student support still seems too dominated by economic concerns (Burdman, 2005; Cooke et al., 2004). It is certainly true that student debt has risen exponentially, greatly hindering job prospects and personal landmarks. There is also a need to advocate for more funding for PhD students and lengthy paid family leave. However, for graduate student mothers, financial support is just the starting point for the many factors that need to be in place for successful completion of meaningful fieldwork and matriculation through doctoral programs.

Spousal Support and Job Stability

I also receive a lot of pity when people realize I am doing a PhD and having children. However, my husband has taken more than 14 months off work at different times and we spent five months as a family going to Dubai and Malaysia for my fieldwork. When I see the burden of many of my colleagues, how their studies are entirely on their own shoulders, I realize that my husband's support is a big privilege. (Excerpt from Grace's reflective field journal, June 2, 2016, Toronto)

The stability of John's job was another theme that emerged in my writing. This was largely due to the kindness of his employer, who allowed him to take time off without penalty. His boss was one part of our social community that made it possible for us to complete fieldwork.

Family and Grandparents

After our little grandbaby was born there were a few months of adjustment with no university work, [but then] our daughter needed to get back into the academic groove. I offered to come down one day a week to help in any way she needed. It is almost a two hour commute each way by public transit, but it was fun—so much fun. (Excerpt from Joanne's reflective field journal; July 15, 2016; Toronto).

As I analyzed the recurring mention of family in my field journal, it was clear that my family contributed to several areas of support. In particular, the contributions from my mother were central. She provided financial support by watching my children for free; she provided well-being by allowing me to nap; she edited my thesis, thereby supporting my academic success.

Figure 7.2 shows the areas of support that I found necessary to complete my PhD. None of the factors alone could have single-handedly led to my success. Mothers who are embarking on fieldwork are very aware of this. We might have unlimited financial resources (though few of us do), but we are still in need of trustworthy and reliable childcare. I felt this most acutely during my fieldwork. When we arrived in Dubai and Malaysia, John and I had enough money to pay for our accommodations, but we would have quickly burned out had we not had a community—friends of friends—who helped us learn the systems of a new city and cared for our daughter so we could get some rest. Looking back on our travels, it would have been very difficult to find trustworthy childcare in a completely new city, with cross-cultural dynamics to overcome, had we only money and no personal contacts. John was very capable being the full-time parent, but exhaustion is just a day away when there is no backup plan.

Academic Supports

Likewise, as I learned when obtaining a previous degree, money will not overcome an absentee supervisor or substandard university support. Without a supervisor to sign our ethics protocol or advise on our study plans, there will never be a fieldwork experience. My doctoral supervisor, Dr. Ruth Hayhoe, is

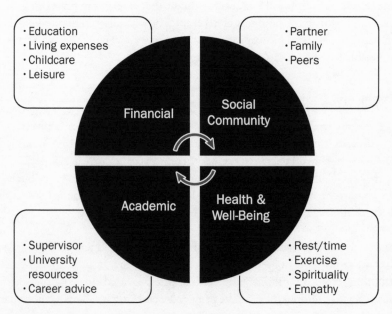

FIGURE 7.2 Factors contributing to a successful PhD experience

a beautiful example of an academic with a nontraditional pathway to parenthood. Almost twenty years into her career, she married an older man, previously widowed, who had five children. Although most of his children were well into adulthood, Dr. Hayhoe jumped right into her role as mother, grandmother, and supportive partner. She taps into this nurturing side in her support for her graduate supervisees. Chapters are returned within forty-eight hours, and my deadlines were never missed. Without her warm reception as I brought my babies to meetings or made unconventional plans that worked for my whole family, my fieldwork plans would not have materialized.

Self-Care and Life outside the PhD

Perhaps the most undervalued and unattainable area of support for PhD moms during fieldwork are the extracurricular activities—like yoga, scrabble, or novel reading—that refresh us and make us glad to be alive another day. There is just no time. And when unexpected pockets of time do emerge, we are socialized to give them back to our children and sacrifice like martyrs.

Of course, finances are still important and a central theme in my reflective field journal. I needed my federal scholarship to provide paid maternity leaves, I needed my husband's income to supplement our travel money, I needed the day care subsidy that gave me two more days of work as well as my mom's free quality care. But I have always been interested in the Polanyian concept of social embeddedness that argues that economies need to be integrated in their social context (Beckert, 2007). This is the case for moms who go abroad with their children. They need finances, but they need a social community even more.

There is a lot more that can be said about Figure 7.2. For example, the areas are linked. Money for leisure contributes to mental health and builds relationships. Peer support allows you to debrief those intense committee meetings. In the end, I would like to suggest that we should all strive for some sort of healthy balance between the areas, but this feels unrealistic. Instead, we should find the configuration of imbalance that works best for us and for our family.

Competence: New Standards for Success

Compared to many graduate student moms, I received a lot of help and was thankful to be socially embedded in a supportive community. However, all the help I received left me feeling incompetent. The debilitating myth of having to do it all is so pervasive that when we do it together, there is less applause. Yet teamwork in mothering, teamwork in parenting, is a beautiful counter-narrative to the myth of the self-made man. Feminist authors have attempted to rewrite these individualist myths for years, encouraging us to break down the hierarchy and pride that dominate academic careers. Too often, the study of women in educational settings is conducted in relation to their perceived deficits and the structures that determine their institutional positioning as "others" or the barriers they face to their career advancement (Acker, 1990; Wallace, 2009). I continually struggled against this positioning, trying to reframe my support community as an asset rather than a debt I needed to repay. Instead of feeling guilty for my need, I tried to view all of us as a team that had worked together, maintained peace amid hard situations, and lived to laugh about it all.

As I read my mother's story that follows, she seems oblivious to my concerns about competence. She was not helping because I am inept; she was helping because of her status as my mom, and that is what mothers do. Amazingly, needing my mother has deepened our relationship. My mother knew from the outset not that I am incompetent but rather that being a parent is probably the hardest thing I will ever do in my life. She knew because of her experience. Instead of watching from afar, waiting for my failure, she jumped on board. It is true that I have not done this by myself in a feat of individual strength, but the celebrations have been infinitely sweeter because they are shared together.

Grandma Joanne's Story: Nanny, Cook, Editor

They say, "Once a Mom, always a Mom." Well, it's true, at least for me. So when our youngest daughter told us she was pregnant even though she was working on her PhD, I naturally said (after the screaming and hugging subsided), "I'm here to help you if you need me." I had recently retired from a 22-year career in teaching and had some time on my hands. So, the adventure began.

Then one day when baby was 4 months old, out of the clear blue, our daughter asked us if we'd like to go to Montreal with her (a 5-hour drive) to look after baby while she attended an academic conference and led a workshop. It was a bit of a surprise but after thinking through all the logistics, Grandma, Grandpa, baby and Mommy hopped on a train together and spent 2 days and nights in Montreal. It was so much fun!

Then came the bombshell. Our daughter announced one day that to do the research for her thesis she would have to travel overseas for an extended period of time—likely 4 or 5 months. Casually, she asked one day, "So mom, how would you like to go with me to Dubai to look after Maëlle?" Right. Not likely. The subject was dropped. But like a bad penny, it came up again, and I said, "No, pet, I really can't do that." She didn't push—I think she knew it wasn't the best solution anyway. In the end, her husband was able to get a leave from his job, and they were able to find someone to sublet their condo, making it financially possible for them to go. So they stored stuff in our basement (again) and came to stay for a few weeks while the renter moved into their condo and they waited to fly out. Such fun.

Their time away was a bit anxious for us, but I volunteered in a kindergarten classroom one day a week to keep up my little kid skills and we kept them close in prayers, emails and the occasional skype. Five months later we waited impatiently at the airport with lots of family members for 4 hours while security held everyone from their flight for some unknown reason. They came to our place again for several weeks to get over jet lag and to wait for the subletter to move out. Fun again.

Then, life got really busy for her. Because I was only one day a week, she hired another babysitter for a few hours on other days. I truthfully don't know how she managed to keep up with everything. I do know she worried a lot about how she was going to manage to write a thesis and be a good mommy at the same time. One day, when this anxiety was reaching its peak, and daycare facilities in her area had long waiting lists and seemed impossible to access, an almost random phone call resulted in a spot for little M two days a week at the best and closest facility; a blessing for sure, allowing enough time for mommy to get some work done but not feel too guilty.

After baby number two arrived, which coincided closely with the writing of the final and most challenging chapters of her thesis, things became more urgent. Now she often needed two days a week from me to be able to write, attend meetings and fulfil the demands of her part time job working for a professor. I would still commute to their place one day a week and they would drive out to our house on Fridays. That way, Grandpa D could share the fun and help with the two busy little people. More fun!

One day about this time, I was sitting at our daughter's kitchen table having lunch when I started reading from a page that was sitting beside her laptop. I soon realized that this was a page of her thesis and I was somewhat horrified to see several obvious mistakes in grammar and flow. Up to that point, I had never been directly involved with her academics, and I debated whether it was my place to draw her attention to these errors or not. I timidly asked if I could show her something I'd found on the page and to my surprise she responded almost joyfully, "Are you editing my thesis? I really need someone to do that for me." So it was that I got the job of first editor of her first draft. I couldn't enter into all the academic complexities, but I could surely check for spelling, grammar, inconsistencies and organization. It was tedious work but I was excited to read about the results of all her efforts. It was fascinating. (Excerpt from Joanne's reflective field journal, July 15, 2016, Toronto)

It was important for me to read my mom's reflection. I needed to hear that she had enjoyed the journey even though I thought I had spent the last five years taking and taking from her generosity.

What I was not expecting, from her or John, were their own feelings of incompetence. They both expressed concerns that their reflective field journals weren't good enough. Mom said, "I am sure this is not what you were hoping for." However, when we all realized that the sense of insecurity was universal, we shared a laugh and rolled our eyes. Again, the experience of togetherness provided necessary strength and perspective to overcome the fears we held even with writing this chapter.

The social sciences have long been a battleground between classic methodologists who, from a positivist view of data collection, approach those in their research sample as "subjects" and those whose epistemological positioning frames those in their research sample as "participants" (Creswell & Creswell, 2017). The latter group affirms the intersubjective nature of knowledge and the importance of understanding participant's lived experiences through their own words and descriptions. This has gone a long way to expand and broaden our understanding of research methods and affirm the valuable contributions of participants. Likewise, this approach should be applied to the positioning of the researcher themselves, affirming the many contributors who make possible the success of the "experts." The feminist critique of individualism is necessary for an authentic acknowledgment of the many support people who make our research possible (Avineri & De-Shalit, 1992).

Was It Worthwhile? Evaluating a Monumental Group Effort

Despite the busy, competitive pace of academic life, there has been much about completing a PhD that has been meaningful. Through my research, I was able to highlight the experiences of students at Western branch campuses in Islamic nations—students who are split between very different worlds. They were eager to talk to me about their personal changes and the adventures and conflicts of their undergraduate degrees. Their experiences with their families featured prominently through their interviews. I was more attuned to the importance of this because I am a mom, and I viewed each of my students as precious beings with unique stories. Being able to tell their stories was worth it. It was worth the sleepless nights; it was worth the loss of income; it was worth the anxiety.

I have definitely worked hard over the past five years, and as my mother rightly says in her journal, there were times when it was a "huge burden" to complete this degree. But for me it has been worth it. And although I felt deeply anxious about whether my support team felt the same, when I read their reflections, it was as if they had never thought of that question. My mom wrote the following:

> I realize as I write this, that I have not really been entering into the huge burden our daughter's academic work has placed on her personally, and on her husband,

who has been extremely supportive from the moment she made the decision to pursue her doctorate. My little "one day a week" stints have been lovely for me, the recently retired Grandma, while she has had to slog on day after long day, despite sleepless nights and family responsibilities. For me, the only downside has been being good and tired at the end of a long commute. (Excerpt from Joanne's reflective field journal, July 15, 2016, Toronto)

I was shocked to read the final sentences in my mom's field journal: "Worth it? Of course! We always want the best for our kids! Once a parent, always a parent. Glad to be useful. We need each other." This actually made me laugh out loud. Seriously? You never worried at all? Never questioned all the long hours I was away from my children and the monumental effort it took to go on our fieldwork? We stayed at your house for weeks. No, indeed, she loved that part.

It is clear from reading John's reflection that he also never questioned whether this has been worthwhile. I seem to be the only one worried about this. John discusses whether it has been worth it here:

In the end, the benefits to our family from doing field work far outweighed the costs associated with it. We missed out on five months' worth of pay. But what we gained was truly priceless. For one, I have a new understanding and apprecia-tion of my wife's research. Without all the supports like at home, we had all been involved in small and large ways in making sure Grace recruited enough students for the interviews; developed relationships with university staff who could make connections to students; and made contingency plans if we weren't able to interview enough students.

As a family who was able to pack up and travel the world for five months, I'm fully aware of our privilege in our global world. Grace's scholarship, my salary and stable job meant that we could all experience field work together. But what this also meant is that Maëlle will hopefully have experienced what other parts of the world are like and be inspired to love and help others as she grows and matures.

Maëlle is now four years old and our new little guy—John Justice (JJ)—has just turned one. I've often wished Grace needed to do field work again. I regret that I won't be able to take 5 months off in a new country with JJ as I did with Maëlle. (Excerpt from John's reflective field journal, July 5, 2016, Toronto)

Postlude: Writing My Thesis

My fieldwork may seem grand, but there have been many, many ordinary moments since then. And some moments I never want to repeat. During my second pregnancy, my iron levels dropped dangerously, and all my regular functions—sleep, speech, hand-eye coordination—were impaired. On days when I was supposed to be writing, I found myself sleeping for hours. My dream of submitting a full draft before our son was born in June 2015 evaporated. Instead, I was still missing two chapters, substantial analysis, and discussion pieces, and this haunted me during my second maternity leave.

Oftentimes, these hard moments are my "thin places"—places where the Celtic mystics are closer to God, more aware of the divine hand in our lives. Each time I am ready to give up, something monumental plucks me off the ropes, dusts me clean, and sends me in for another round. This is what calms my heart as I ask those questions: Am I privileged? Has it been worth it? I need that divine intervention. I need my social embeddedness because existing in two worlds, mommy and academic, threatens to tear me apart.

Conclusion

I experienced graduate school as a community event. Yet in analyzing my field journal for this chapter, it is clear that I had expected to be self-sufficient, to achieve my goals alone. When I received help, I felt guilty and incompetent. Yet those who helped me appreciated having something to give. They felt valued and happy to be part of my story. It is possible that there are other graduate student mothers who feel the same turmoil, whose expectations are linked to self-sufficiency as mine were. To them, I offer this encouragement: the doctoral journey is a journey of accomplishment with high moments of praise. When our expectations of self-sufficiency are removed, we can invite others into the journey to join us in accomplishing great things.

Practical Tips

As a team, John, Joanne, and I learned many things during my PhD program and fieldwork adventures. Most of them we learned through trial and error. These are the highlights:

- Practice asking for help—don't be dejected when people say no. Ask someone else. (Grace)
- Learn to receive help—peacefully hand over your problems to those who are willing to help. (Joanne)
- Take a leave when you need to—do not wait until you are burned out. (Grace)
- Live simply and save money—savings can go a long way during fieldwork. (John)
- Do not aim for a full-time work week after maternity leave—do what fits your kids. (Grace)

- Ask other student-moms for advice—you are not the only one doing this. (Joanne)
- Pay people to do the peripheral work so you can be with your kids—pay a copy editor to perfect the final drafts rather than paying a sitter to watch your kids. (Joanne)
- Set high goals and then let them go—write down what you actually accomplish. (John)
- Make friends in the country you are going to—becoming part of a faith community (church, mosque, etc.) is a great way to meet other families. (John)
- Make weekends family time during fieldwork—ensure there is some time when you are not working. (Grace)

Note

1 The data for this chapter was collected from reflective field journals written by each of the authors during and after their fieldwork travels.

References

Acker, S. (1990). Teachers' culture in an English primary school: Continuity and change. *British Journal of Sociology of Education, 11*(3), 257–273.

Avineri, S., & De-Shalit (Eds.). (1992). *Communitarianism and individualism.* New York, NY: Oxford University Press.

Beckert, J. (2007). The great transformation of embeddedness: Karl Polanyi and the new economic sociology. *Institut für Gesellschaftsforschung. Discussion Papers, 26.*

Burdman, P. (2005). The student debt dilemma: Debt aversion as a barrier to college access. Center for Studies in Higher Education. Retrieved from https://cshe.berkeley.edu/sites/default/files/publications/rop.burdman.13.05.pdf

Cooke, R., Barkham, M., Audin, K., Bradley, M., & Davy, J. (2004). Student debt and its relation to student mental health. *Journal of Further and Higher Education, 28*(1), 53–66.

Creswell, J. W., & Creswell, J. D. (2017). *Research design: Qualitative, quantitative, and mixed methods approaches* (5th ed.). Los Angeles, CA: Sage.

King, T., & Bannon, E. (2002). The burden of borrowing: A report on the rising rates of student loan debt. *The State PIRGs' Higher Education Project.* Retrieved from https://files.eric.ed.gov/fulltext/ED470025.pdf

Wallace, P. (2009). Career stories of women professional accountants: Examining the personal narratives of career using Simone de Beauvoir's feminist existentialist philosophy as a theoretical framework. *Qualitative Research in Organizations and Management: An International Journal, 4*(1), 62–84.

White, H. (1980). The value of narrativity in the representation of reality. *Critical Inquiry, 7*(1), 5–27.

8

Fathering in Support
of Fieldwork

● ●

Lactation and Bourgeois
Feminism (and More
Privileged White
People's Problems)

BRIAN C. WOLF

Why can't I lactate? I figured that I would always understand fatherhood within the context of feminist praxis. I was not however thinking of "feminist praxis" the first time I took my four month-old daughter to the Chagall museum. Drenched in sweat and the summer grit of the more wretched parts of the otherwise lovely Cote d'Azur, I hastened to get my daughter to the museum. I had 87 more stair steps to go along a path that hugged an expressway and an elevated heavy rail line. Hauling a distinctly American sport utility stroller, with pneumatic tires and suspension, rigged to accommodate an infant car carrier. The bombast of Detroit iron in the land of impression and vogue.

Each step was a grunt and a clank. The bottom of the stroller had two tiny cans of weak French lager along with a slipshod prepared lunch—baguettes sliced lengthwise with ham and cheese packed catawampus. The cup holder had a bottle of refused formula. Strolling had briefly satiated her after an unabated cry fest, but she was ramping it up again. My daughter was screaming to get to the Chagall museum and had been for three hours—practically an eternity for an infant. At the top of the hill awaited my wife, probably working on mastitis from not feeding our infant for nearly five hours. I repeated this ritual every day for six weeks, the length of time for which my wife conducted fieldwork and during which my infant refused to take a bottle. I didn't actually get to see the inside of the Chagall museum until our last day there.

Introduction

This chapter is a reflection of my experiences as a new father providing lead parenting to our daughter during my wife's six-week-long fieldwork at a medical examiner's office in Nice, France. By "lead parenting," I simply mean taking on a central role in the care of a child while a spouse spends most of her time at work. "Lead parent" is probably not the best way to describe our situation, especially since fieldwork is a temporary transition. It is more correct to say that I was in the role as a "stay-at-home parent" while my spouse was doing her fieldwork, but she always came home to a "second shift."

My aim here is to contextualize my reflections within a broad sociological perspective, providing for a contrasting interpretation of my wife's experience as a lactating fieldworker, presented in chapter 9 of this volume. I situate my experience within the narrative of a Millsian "sociological imagination" while drawing on a critical account of liberal and radical feminist discourses concerning fatherhood and parenting. In particular, I reference the similarly contrasting perspectives that have appeared in popular media. Lastly, I conclude with a reflection on what it's like to be a stay-at-home parent while a spouse is in the field.

My wife is a comparative criminologist who spends her research time hanging out in morgues taking notes about how death is categorized in a cross-cultural context. Although I love good qualitative social science research, I am not a good fieldworker, and the thought of spending my days with corpses makes me especially queasy. I am mostly content to pore over existing texts and datasets for my academic contributions. Prior to writing this piece, I did take some time to look over my notebooks from when I was the lead parent to a four-month-old while my wife was in the field. In a way, they resemble field notes of a different type. The notes chronicle leaky diapers, failed attempts at giving a bottle, and half-finished grocery lists with some horribly Anglicized French phrases. While I was a primary parent, I did find a little bit of time to work: sixty minutes on an online French language lesson, ten minutes on some emails, or thirty minutes on a writing project (if I was lucky). I do find that my notes and memories tell an important story—one of a new parent struggling to understand the needs of an infant while trying to be a supportive husband to a wife who spends her summers hanging out with the dead.

So goes the life of a trailing partner when the other does fieldwork. We were both seasoned travelers long before we met, fell in love, and made a baby. I was comfortable getting to know a new place in a foreign land. The ability to travel for either work or pleasure is an important privilege that comes with responsibilities. My own research in conflict zones has put me in some less desirable places: the occupied West Bank, the killing fields of Cambodia, and the sewage-filled streets of Bangalore. The fact that my wife's fieldwork was in the south of France was like a dream to me. Were I childless, I would have spent the days reading, wandering the coastline, and exploring the eccentric shops that inhabit most French cities. Instead, I had to get diaper cream.

While I have been privileged to travel abroad fairly often, I do not have the "gift of tongues." Nearly half a year in India netted only a handful of words and phrases. I never even studied French until I met my wife, and this was particularly unfortunate now that I was the one charged with finding items for our household and infant. Routine tasks of cooking, shopping, and finding a toilet, suddenly made more difficult with an infant, were further compounded by a language barrier. Never quite sure how to get what I needed, simple tasks became both frustrating and totally comical at the same time—like when

FIGURE 8.1 Changing my daughter's diaper in front of the Casino Royal in Monaco during one of our weekend excursions to escape the doldrums of my wife's fieldwork in Nice, France, summer 2014

my daughter needed diaper cream, and I wasn't quite sure how to ask for it. I pondered "Crème de couche" but resolved that it translated more into "cream of diaper," which probably accounted for the strange looks I got. I tried "Mon bébé a un derrière rouge" (My baby has a red behind). Ha! I got it. Minor successes such as this would often be the highlight of my day.

Fatherhood in the Sociological Perspective

My understanding of good ethnographic research is that one should always be wary of one's social location and "reactivity" when reflecting on one's own research. That is to say, some reflexivity is necessary when trying to disentangle the emotions and "biases" that may taint field observations. Clearly my location as a father taking on the role of primary parent has some effect on my perspective. My goal here is not so much to provide the "male" or "father's" perspective, although my gender obviously shapes the lens by which I understand the experience. Rather, my goal here is to ponder the role of primary parenting from the first-person perspective of a social scientist.

As an academic married to another academic, mundane parts of life rarely escape the standard intellectualizing and deconstruction of powerful relationships and hidden meanings. As a sociologist, issues in my personal life rarely escape purposeful reflection within the analytical scope of a sociological imagination. C. Wright Mills described this imagination in his famous question, "How do personal troubles relate to public issues?" (1959). Individual decisions (personal troubles) are always mired in a larger social structure (public issues). A father's decision to take on primary parenting for any length of time may be entangled with a variety of social and political issues confronting society at large. In other words, the sociological imagination means that one cannot fully understand an individual quandary or dilemma without understanding the social structure such troubles may be immersed in. I am well aware that the quandaries my wife and I faced as new parents fall well within the scope of "first world problems." We have our struggles, but we are solidly middle class, white, and educated. Being able to "take a summer off" to parent while my wife worked in the field is a privilege few parents are able to ponder.

The Millsian postulate on the relationship between troubles and issues necessitates that we understand the individual experience of parenting in a context whereby the experience is shaped by social forces beyond the individual. Parenthood is an individual dilemma, but it is always enmeshed in the social institution of family and parenting. We live in a world where norms concerning parenting roles are changing, while ideas and discourses on parenthood are often in conflict, sometimes contradictory. All decisions, no matter how personal, feel entangled in politics, theorizing about women's bodies, and wrought via the historical material imperatives of late-stage capitalism. Do you breastfeed? Does your husband take paternity leave? You gave your six-month-old a flu vaccine? You put her in disposable diapers?

By the time my daughter was born, I had several advantages and privileges compared to a lot of new fathers. Both my wife and I have jobs at universities that have what I would call "better than what most Americans get" parental leave policies. I was in an even more advantageous place than my wife: I had earned tenure and promotion the year prior. I no longer felt the urgency of being on the publishing and research treadmill. Better yet, I was about learn the joys of a semester-long sabbatical where I could start an entirely new book and research project. For my daughter's first summer of life, I would be a full-time father while my wife completed her research. I was on the verge of turning forty, older than most new dads but still young enough to consider parasailing. So I was in a place in my life where I could put things on hold to step up into a lead parent role, but that still did not mean that I could lactate.

Enforcing interpersonal visions of egalitarianism in a sea of structural inequality is a fool's errand. Life is not fair, and Mélanie seemed to be getting the short end of the stick. I did not and do not want our marriage and family to be about "your turn, now my turn," but that is what seemed practical at first. Before our daughter was born, we always talked about the importance of equality and sharing of parenting roles. We both embraced principles of feminist parenting, and I genuinely thought I could do my part, but it didn't exactly start out well. First, I missed most of Mélanie's first trimester while I was abroad teaching the prior summer. She should have been conducting her fieldwork then, but immigration issues and a much desired but higher stress pregnancy had put her work off for more than a year. Second, of course I was not the one who was pregnant for nine months. Third, I was the one who urged Mélanie to breastfeed based on my understanding of the benefits widely affirmed in the cult of parenthood. This last one is particularly unjust to women. All I could do in return is get diaper cream.

Fatherhood in a Feminist Perspective

The beauty of the sociological imagination is in the ways that the perspective lends itself to augmenting, or complementing, other interpretive frameworks. For, instance, while it may not square perfectly with all feminist perspectives, it certainly triangulates nicely with the aims of contemporary feminist theory. For instance, feminists, especially promulgated by Angela Davis, have long argued how the personal is always political (2009). I could not possibly probe all the richness and depth of the variety of approaches of feminism in this space. At the same time, it is useful to situate the role of fatherhood in consideration of feminist discourses while drawing on my own experience (personal troubles) and popular discourses (public issues).

I married my wife in July 2012. That same month, Anne-Marie Slaughter wrote a provocative article in the *Atlantic* arguing women could not "have it all." Her reluctant thesis explained that middle-class women could not be both top professionals and mothers (or at least be any good at both) without major changes in social policy and cultural attitudes toward parenting. From Slaughter's point of view, successful women needed to have a devoted partner at home the same way successful men do. Drawing from her own accomplished career and experience as a parent, she reflected that significant changes needed to take place in American policy and culture before women could be truly equal. Slaughter discussed much-needed structural change in terms of family-friendly policies as well as enlisting underutilized male counterparts. The article drew criticism for how it framed career-oriented mothers and reified what exactly having it all entails. While my wife was in the field, I'm not sure I can say that I wanted to "have it all." I just wanted some solid sleep, my back to stop hurting, and maybe a night out without a kid.

Since this reflective section is written as a contrasting perspective to my wife's, I do find it useful to comb through our popular discourse of parents in similar roles. For example, more than three years after Slaughter's "you can't have it all" article appeared, her husband, Andrew Moravcsik (2015), wrote a supporting rejoinder about why he "put his wife's career first." Like Slaughter, he argued for the need for more family-friendly policies and for men to be more open to embracing the role of "primary parent." Like Slaughter's article, his point of view struck a chord in several areas, including that it was nauseatingly self-congratulatory. Moravcsik goes on to talk about his success as an academic while being the primary parent to their boys. He quips that women are just as reluctant as men to have fathers in a primary parenting role. In short, men can "have it all" through simple changes in attitudes.

"Having it all" is a long-standing, if simplistic, critique of second-wave feminism, which is rightfully criticized as being bourgeois and exclusive of minorities and women without college educations. On this, bell hooks's *Feminist Theory: From Margin to Center* (1984) always resonated strongly with me. I read it as a graduate student more than a decade and a half before I even considered parenthood. The book offers a critique of white, bourgeois feminism, suggesting ways the feminist movement can be more inclusive of minorities and men as comrades in the struggle against sexist oppression. hooks notes that while the women's movement was marked by white women entering the male world of work and careers, Black women were lamenting how they wish they had more time to spend with family.

The contrast between alienating work and fulfilling careers is an important one. One takes a job because they have to, another pursues career goals because they want to. While doing fieldwork may be necessary to advance knowledge (and get tenure), it is a privilege to have the option of doing so. Parenthood may be chosen, but childrearing is a necessity.

More than twenty years ago, Arlie Hochschild (1996) argued in *Second Shift* that the women's revolution stalled out. Women pursued careers in the labor market but came home to start a second shift. This disproportionate burden is even more pronounced among women without college degrees, representing an intersection of how burdens of class and gender may vary and interact. The response has been not just for men to help out more but for men to step up into the role of a lead parent. However, this has not been an easy proposition. Like women in the same position, men who take more than a few weeks off from work suffer from stigma and loss of prestige in a position. My own work slowed down substantially, stopping entirely during the first six months after the birth of our daughter. Rarely does the ability to stop or slow work with such flexibility exist outside of academia, except perhaps among the ruling classes. Clearly both men and women could benefit from reconsidering the expectations and relationship between gender, work, and parenting.

In a patriarchal and sexist society, it has traditionally been seen as "natural" that primary parenting is the domain of the mother. While feminism challenged a number of long-standing ideological assumptions about parenting, feminism does not provide for one clear, obvious framework to consider fatherhood. However, utilizing a theoretical model informed by feminism may help situate the role of fatherhood with regards to gender, equality, and intersectionality. For instance, see bell hooks's remarks on parenting in her landmark work *Feminist Theory: From Margin to Center*: "Seeing men who do effective parenting as 'maternal' reinforces the stereotypical sexist notion that women are inherently better suited to parent, that men who parent in the same way as women are imitating the real thing rather than acting as a parent should act. There should be a concept of effective parenting that makes no distinction between maternal and paternal care" (hooks, 1984, p. 139).

hooks reminds us that while patriarchy has been devastating to women, it has also been constraining men in how they experience parenthood. Stubborn stereotypes about masculinity remain entrenched in our collective conscience. For instance, the same year my daughter was born, New York Mets second baseman Daniel Murphy had to deflect criticism for missing the first two games of the season after his son was born. Prominent sports commentator Mike Francesa declared, "You have a job to do." I was heartened about the outrage expressed at the sentiment by many men (and women too), but the undertone demonstrated that sports are indeed a microcosm of society where there are clear cultural barriers against men staying home to take care of the family.

While paternity leave is increasingly common among the privileged, there are several barriers to new fathers taking on as much as they should or may want to. Even when fathers want to take extended absences to care for children, cultural norms and expectations prevent men from utilizing paternity leave. Men are often expected to return to work within a week or two after the birth of their child. Meanwhile, new parents in lower-wage occupations must return to work, not for fear of falling behind in their careers but because they have no other source of income. For example, a census bureau report demonstrates that men with a college degree are twice as likely to take paternity leave than those with a high school education (U.S. Bureau of Labor Statistics, 2016). Other studies have found that companies are more likely to offer paid leave benefits to college-educated workers and managers than the high school–educated rank and file (U.S. Department of Labor, 2013). For millions of new parents, there is no "choice" to stay home as a primary parent. Clearly there are class differences in how paternity, work, and childcare are negotiated.

Besides class differences in how maternity and paternity are experienced, there are clear and obvious gender differences as well. While role expectations have men boxed in as breadwinners, the near parity of women's participation (but not pay) in the labor force has put most women in a triple bind. Much has been written on the unequal division of labor in households where women bear a significant and disproportionate amount of unpaid labor. Nearly as much has been written on how to mitigate this disparity. Many thought that as more women would enter the workforce, household work would become more evenly distributed. Yet while men have picked up more of it, the problem persists, as household surveys invariably demonstrate that women do much more of the childcare and household work even when both spouses are employed full time. Learning to "talk" to your spouse about the share of unpaid work may be a good interpersonal skill, but it can hardly combat the structural inequities embedded in the societal structure of our work and family life.

Reflections

I would like to conclude by considering several key takeaways from my experience, with the benefit of four years of hindsight. Some of these conclusions are personal, others are political. There are some things that society—and more specifically, men—could do better.

My experience taking on the role of lead parent to an infant is not unique and certainly not heroic. Lots of fathers are stepping in to raise children—not usually because they "want to" but because circumstances beyond their control have mandated it. Men have been disproportionately impacted by recessions and economic restricting. Men with less than a college education have further seen their earnings and prospects for living-wage work plummet. As women have emerged as central breadwinners because they either have to or want to, the discourse of feminism has changed to reflect that reality. While feminism does much to illuminate social positions, power, and intersectionality, there is a lot that feminism can do for fathers that both men and women have not fully embraced. We should have a similar feminist reconsideration of the concept of fatherhood.

I do not have any sweeping revelations or epiphanies about supporting a partner in the field other than a few items that have no generalizability beyond my set of specific circumstances. For instance, if you decide to breastfeed, you need to acknowledge the built-in inequality in this. If you want to "share" in some work, your child may not always want to go along with it. My daughter mostly refuses to let me put her to bed when her mother is around, so I do the dishes instead. Sure, we are "sharing" work, but one is much more emotionally involved than the other.

I do not want to overstate my contribution to supporting my wife while she did fieldwork. I am extremely fortunate to have a job where I could take a few months off to follow my wife. I suffered no long-term career repercussions from a short gap in my vitae—certainly nothing along the lines of the "motherhood penalty" affecting women's wages and seniority. However, male lead parenting has only recently gained much acceptance.

Besides the incessant screaming, the hardest aspect of the six weeks acting as primary parent while my wife was in the field was the loneliness. There is not a lot of informal networking and socializing that goes on with full-time dads. Similarly, temporarily living abroad comes with a host of challenges and corresponding effects on the mood and psychology. Being a stay-at-home dad as well as a stranger in a strange land seems to have magnified this. I did not have any social support beyond online social networking. Such a dynamic creates a feeling of isolation. I tried binge-watching television shows, but this quickly exacerbated my bored househusband syndrome. Despite being a pretty committed introvert, I do need some interaction, which is a problem especially when faced with being so far from home and language barriers.

Earlier, I mentioned the isolation that I felt during the long, often boring days of parenting all day. Men can do a lot more for one another in terms of how they interact and talk about fatherhood. My experience was hardly out of the pages of Gillman's *Yellow Wallpaper*, but men have yet to carve out a common language for how we talk about parenting. When I try to engage my fellow fathers about the feelings and strategies of being a father, the conversation inevitably wanders into the much more comfortable (and safe) arenas of discussing sports, fishing, or home brewing. I think men can do better for one another to learn how to engage in emotional labor and then talk about the feelings that this produces. In contrast to pursuing a career, taking on a caring role is immensely fulfilling. However, men are reluctant to express the feelings that accompany this role.

I think one of the most profound lessons of my experience in six weeks as a primary parent is perhaps the most controversial: no matter how much you try, parenting is not equal, nor can it be. It is simply not possible to evenly split and balance parenting, housework, a career, and time for one's self. This is not a cop-out by any means but simply an acknowledgment of how the Millsian thesis impacts one's own daily life. Imperatives of biology along with cultural norms and social realities are always coalescing to interact with individual career and personal choices. Someone is always getting the short end of the stick, and that someone is almost always the mother. Just because it cannot be equal does not mean there cannot be approximations. Both men and women can and should do more to recognize the importance of fathers taking on a caring role.

Afterword

Nearly four years after my wife completed the fieldwork recounted here, the sudden shock of being new parents has given way to more routine matters: Our daughter is dropped off at day care. Now that she can talk, she lets us know when she is hungry or wants something specific. Our initial trials and tribulations as new parents caring for an infant have given way to the more mundane matters of daily living. Since then, I have learned how children can give you the highest of highs and drag you through the pits of Mordor.

I opened this piece with a discussion of primary and lead parenting, but neither my wife nor I are stay-at-home parents for any serious length of time; our situation, like so much in parenting and middle-class life, was temporary and enmeshed in relative privilege. Once I was done with my duties in support of my wife in the field, the three of us returned to the United States to begin a new schedule. Our daughter enrolled in nursery school; my wife started teaching again. I did get my sabbatical, which was blissful, but not for the reasons I imagined. I always imagined a sabbatical in a faraway land, working on a book or creative project unrelated to my immediate field, a chance to rest and reset. While the creative project did not unwind the way I thought it would, it did give me a chance to reflect and take a life inventory.

Being a father has helped me realize that I do not want my life just defined by my job. I'm not sure that's a very popular realization in a volume dedicated to negotiating fieldwork as a parent. It is an old male cliché, but nobody is on their deathbed wishing they spent more time in the office (maybe more people wish they spent more time in the field). I think my experience gives this tired phrase new meaning in the context of several propositions of feminist authors.

Regardless, the adage reminds us how important, but neglected, our family and friendships are. It was an extremely difficult time in my life to take on the role of a lead parent while my partner was in the field, but it was a period in my life that I will never regret.

Practical Tips

- Your newborn may prefer mom to you—this is hard when mom is gone most of the day. Do not take this personally; you may not know it, but you are sowing the seeds for an important bond that will manifest when the baby is older.
- In becoming a father, by default you are required to regularly step up and sacrifice. If you are married or in an otherwise committed relationship, you also agree to step back and let your partner shine at times. There is no need to be self-congratulatory about doing something that should automatically be expected of fathers anyway.
- Given the previous points, you should relish in your time away from work and the spotlight. Even if it is a financial burden, understand it as a positive dividend of changing expectations of fathers. Even if fathers of another generation were financially able to take time off to support a mother as she worked, it would have been regarded as absurd to do so.
- On a personal level, time together as a family is priceless. That said, if you need time for yourself, express that to your partner but prepare to negotiate, and do not be selfish.

References

Davis, A. (2009). *The meaning of freedom and other difficult dialogues*. San Francisco, CA: City Lights Books.

Hochschild, A. R. (1996). *The second shift*. New York, NY: Penguin Books.

hooks, b. (1984). *Feminist theory from margin to center*. Boston, MA: South End Press.

Mills, C. W. (1959). *The sociological imagination*. New York, NY: Oxford University Press.

Moravcsik, A. (2015, October). Why I put my wife's career first. *The Atlantic*. Retrieved from https://www.theatlantic.com/magazine/archive/2015/10/why-i-put-my-wifes-career-first/403240/

Slaughter, Anne-Marie (2012, July–August). Why women still can't have it all. *The Atlantic*.

U.S. Bureau of Labor Statistics (2016). Labor force statistics from the current population survey. Retrieved from http://www.bls.gov/CPS/

U.S. Department of Labor (2013). Paternity leave: Why parental leave for fathers is so important for working families. Retrieved from www.dol.gov/asp/policy-development/paternityBrief.pdf

Part IV

This Too Shall Pass

• •

Field Research before, during,
and after Motherhood

MÉLANIE-ANGELA NEUILLY

When my daughter was nursing, refusing to sleep for more than what seemed like five minutes at a time, I remember many dark and desperate moments in the middle of the night when the only two thoughts that would keep me sane were that morning would come again and that these difficult times would pass. When my daughter was between three and five months old, however, mornings did not bring their usual heart-lifting light, as I had to wake up bright and early to conduct ethnographic observations at a medical examiner's office. Aside from the vicarious trauma that this research itself inflicts on the mind, the physical toll of ethnographic observation was almost too much to bear for this sleep-deprived, lactating mama.

As we envisioned this anthology, both Bahiyyah and I were still very much in the early moments of motherhood. We traveled the world with infants and toddlers in tow, struggling with issues specific to these age groups. As we started receiving proposals for our nascent project, it became obvious that the solutions we had found to our new mom problems would not be relevant to parents with older children. It also became apparent to us that we needed to consider the issue over the life course as a succession of seasons. When in the throes of particularly challenging times in our lives, we can easily lose sight of the fact that all is transitory in this world. Fieldwork is no exception.

In this section, we offer a progressive view of what mothering from the field means at different stages and how the lessons we draw can differ depending on our standpoint in the life course. I share the specifics of my experience conducting ethnographic research while nursing an infant. Anne Hardgrove, finding herself in somewhat of a midway point of mothering, and Kimberly Garland Campbell, with grown children, offer perspectives looking back over the evolution of their own mothering in the field. To say that having read their contribution before I embarked on my own adventure would have been helpful is possibly the understatement of the century. But let's also be clear that just because the problems pertaining to mothering infants from the field come and go, it does not mean that other stages of life are without their own sets of issues. Like me, Anne Hardgrove contrasts pre- and postchild fieldwork but also provides a wide range of ways in which she has involved her family (or not) in fieldwork over the years. Kimberly Garland Campbell never knew fieldwork without children until now that they are grown, and through it all, she juggled with a field season that corresponded to her children's summer vacations. One unifying theme in this section focuses on presenting different facets of mothering from the field along with the importance of our support networks. This, of course, has been more delved into in section 3, including the voice of my husband, telling the counterpart story to my own, but it is worth reiterating that, no matter what stage in life you are in, support is what makes it all possible.

Section-Specific Takeaways

- First and foremost, let's remember to tell ourselves and each other, when faced with what may sometimes feel like insurmountable difficulties with regard to mothering in the field, that this too shall pass.
- As a corollary, let's also come to grasp with the saddening fact that whatever solution we found for one research trip may no longer work for the next one, as our children and situations will change.
- It may be really hard, but be sure to make memories too. Take advantage of your location and of the fact that you cannot be working 24-7 because of your children. Take pictures of the good times. The hard times may never truly fade away in your memory, but at least you will have pictures to remember the good times.
- Additionally, remember that if your child is big enough to remember these field trips, they will most likely not remember them as hard, and

instead, these trips will be the foundation for lifelong learning and incomparable experiences.

- Much like mothering from the field morphs and evolves with our life course and the age of our children, so does the impact that having children (or not having them) will have on our rapport in the field, negotiated entry, and our general approach to the methodology. This is what section 5 will expand upon.

9

Lactating in the Autopsy Room

• • • • • • • • • • • • • • • • • • •

Mothering from the
Field When the Field Is a
Morgue and Your Child Is
a Nursing Infant

MÉLANIE-ANGELA NEUILLY

In the summer of 2014, I led my husband and my three-month-old daughter on an adventure we (at least the two of us with fully developed memory functions at the time) are to remember for the rest of our lives. For six weeks, I tried to balance my responsibilities as a field researcher investigating institutional and cultural processes of death certification in Nice, France, with my responsibilities as a nursing mother and bearable wife. This was in stark contrast with my previous field experiences, which were very much inspired by my schooling in mainstream methodology, putting the work first and focusing on objectivity. Being a mother forced me to reflect not only on how motherhood had impacted my standpoint as a researcher but also on whether my supposedly much more "professional" previous experiences in the field may have benefitted from more reflexivity and some critical methods. It is my goal here to outline the trajectory that landed me at the Nice medical examiner's office, the strategy that sustained the three of us while there, and the methodological and policy-related lessons that emerged from analyzing the whole experience through a feminist framework.

What Was I Thinking?, or How One Should Never Embark on a Long-Term Research Project When Starting a Dissertation

I always enjoyed being in the field. From early on in my studies, I welcomed opportunities to witness the world with my own eyes, take it all in, and figure it out. As an undergraduate student in psychology, I was trained in ethnographic techniques, interview methods, and experimental design. Like many people, I strived when I got to get my hands dirty actually doing things, except those "practical" things I was being trained in were the building blocks of the craft of research. I knew then that I was interested in studying, researching, and doing it from scratch.

In graduate school, I discovered that one could explore the world through data collected by others. This did not inspire me. Why would I skip my favorite aspect of doing research, the "doing" part? I insinuated myself in a data collection project: extracting and coding information from police homicide files. We were doing something. Getting to the heart of each case was fascinating,; seeing how they all aggregated was like magic.

This was not my project, however, so for my dissertation, I developed my own ethnographic data collection project. I negotiated entry with contacts, designed my instruments, and went on to spend roughly six months collecting data in two sites. It was not all fun, however. My pet project happened to focus on medico-legal practices, so I spent my time at medical examiners' and coroners' offices, observing the daily operations of investigators and forensic pathologists, going to death scenes, and standing over dead bodies during autopsies with my little notepad. I let the work become my every moment, engulfed in the fascination of my investigation. I would become depressed, but I could not let it go. It was my life. I was single at the time, and my dissertation research was my number one priority—my baby.

Once I got a tenure-track job, I started thinking about my project again. I was itching to get back in the field, to continue my investigations, to further my understanding. And so I did. Once again, I was like a fish in water, glued to my topic. I had a serious boyfriend then, but we were mostly geographically apart for this time in our relationship, and it fostered my intense focus. I wrote a lot during that field season, feeling productive and purposeful.

After that, I simply could not wait to find funding for my next field adventure. It took a few years. I married my boyfriend, and by the time I was all set to go back to the field, I had a three-month-old baby, a real one, the year prior to my tenure year. I planned my research trip in a sleep-deprived haze, looking forward to it as my "going back to work" trip. Being a comparative researcher, the trip involved going abroad. No big deal for an international scholar like me. The baby was not sleeping through the night, but she would undoubtedly do by the time I would be starting the project. And I would figure out how to deal with my milk supply. It would be fine. My husband would be the main caregiver for six weeks. That would do wonders for my daughter's relationship with him, as he would figure out his own ways of soothing her, something he had been struggling with, as I mostly stayed home for the first three months of her life while he worked (albeit a reduced load, as he is also an academic; see chapter 8). So even though the perspective of a long transatlantic trip with an infant weighed on us, we embarked on it full of hope that everything would be OK, with me looking forward to discovering yet another research site.

How Did We Do It?, or How We Turned a Nightmare into Wonderful Memories

The Nightmare

Upon arrival, we discovered that our baby, who would indiscriminately nurse or take the bottle up until that point, had decided to reject the latter. Was it due to the craziness of the travel (we did some sightseeing and family visits on the way) or just a developmental phase? It didn't matter. I was going to be gone all day, five days a week; she would have to adapt.

The apartment I had painstakingly chosen to fit as many of our new little family's needs as possible turned out to be hot and overlooking a very noisy courtyard. The choice was then between overheating the infant or threatening the soundness of her sleep. We went for the latter.

After a couple of traumatic attempts to "break" our daughter from her bottle aversion, it became abundantly clear that we were the ones being "broken." I would simply have to meet my husband and baby for lunch every day and come home early every afternoon so that I could nurse. So much for the complete immersion that had sometimes led me to stay for two shifts in a row at my previous sites. So much for the flexibility needed when you never know what is going to happen next. Thankfully, this was France, the country of the two-hour lunches and the thirty-five-hour work week. And while I was reluctant to divulge my personal circumstances to the head of legal medicine at first, it turned out to be helpful in building rapport with some of the staff, gatekeepers of much of the information I needed.

The enthusiasm that lifted me through the exhaustion of my previous field-work, however, seemed gone. Sure, I was still learning new interesting things, and that was stimulating, especially to my mommy brain, but come 4 p.m., all I wanted was to meet my husband and child at the beach and enjoy some family time. Sundays brought dread, as I navigated the week sleep-deprived and always in transit between my research sites (there were three locations) and my infant. The times I was physically present at the sites were punctuated by regular cell phone checks, dreading my husband's frantic texts for help in the face of our infant's possible dehydration in the oppressive summer heat.

Part of me longed for the immersion of years past, while the rest of me pondered whether I had simply grown tired of my project. I worried about the scientific validity of my findings, fearing any focus under 150 percent would provide shaky results. Meanwhile, I obsessively took field notes and journaled about my every thought and feeling but mostly about my worries and insecurities about my performances both as a researcher and a mother.

Of course, my daughter came first, but the very fact that I had to assert it to myself revealed the deeply complex and entangled relationship I had with my research. Indeed, deep down, I wanted to be able to focus solely on my project. After all, the project was my first baby, and it was, and still is, very deeply tied to my identity as a criminologist, an academic, and even a person.

As a feminist and a staunch advocate of fully shared parenting, this situation was very hard for me to handle, let alone accept. I had only very reluctantly accepted to breastfeed our daughter, as I had serious concerns about becoming her sole provider of nutrition. Her willingness to take the bottle early on had eased my concerns, but it was nonetheless very difficult for me to embrace a behavior (breastfeeding) that I had so strongly opposed for so long. (It is not my purpose here to develop my argument against a practice so widely endorsed, particularly by the learned community, but lest it to say that some recent studies—Colen & Ramey, 2014; Hodinnott, Craig, Britten, & McInnes, 2012—along with a couple of well-written thought pieces [Kornelis, 2012; Rosin, 2009] summarize my position very well.) Now this very behavior was standing in the way between me and my methodology. It was an "I told you so" moment in which I really could not find any self-righteousness.

The Memory-Making Strategy

So how did we do it? We followed the advice given by one of my academic friends who had spent a year working in Denmark when her firstborn was a baby. She told us, "Take lots of pictures of the good times; it will help you through the challenging times." And so we did. But in order to take pictures, we had to create the good times first, which meant surmounting the inevitable moping that developed when we first realized the enormity of what we were facing.

My type of field research has always come with a serious side effect of depression. Spending extended periods of time observing death can do that (especially for someone as anxiety-ridden as me—some of us simply can't turn away from the flame). So each time I have ventured out in the field, I have had to develop a set of coping mechanisms. These have varied with time, from meeting my boyfriend at the bar to drink away the burden of death (not the healthiest coping mechanism) to a systematic run or yoga practice at the end of the day (I got healthier as I got older). Bringing my family along meant that my own potential depression was not the only thing I had to deal with; as the experience turned out to be a challenge for all, coping mechanisms involved a broader type of self-care. We thus implemented some rules to keep us going, mostly focused on bringing beauty and joy into our everyday lives so that we could turn our challenge into a set of opportunities. All those rules revolved around taking full advantage of our amazing geographic location.

Our first rule involved going to the beach every single day. Not everybody is given the opportunity to spend six weeks of their summer in Nice, a place that most foreigners and even French nationals regard as a tourism jewel. The pebble beaches there are world renowned, and as individuals living in a land-locked area, we set out to fully enjoy this feature of our summer residence. Every evening, I would meet up with my husband and infant at the light rail stop, and we would walk the short mile or so to the beach together. There, I would feed my daughter while my husband would get some much-deserved infant-free time in the water (his favorite element). We would then take turns watching over the child, taking her in the water, and swimming independently. I would even sometimes take my daughter in the jogging stroller on a short run on the Promenade des Anglais, the famous boardwalk. For about an hour, we would be like the tourists but also the local families, away from the stress of work or a screaming infant, together, doing fun things in an idyllic environment.

Our second rule came right after our first and involved good food. Again, spending time in Nice was an incredible opportunity to partake in some amazing culinary delights, and so we followed my French influence and used food as a way to bring joy and aesthetics to our everyday life. My husband made it a daily ritual for him and our daughter to go to the stores and get the daily allotment of fresh bread, refreshing rosé wine, fragrant tomatoes and basil, glistening fish, and amazingly varied charcuteries.

Our third rule involved making sure to eat that good food in great locations. As we had to meet up every day for lunch so that I could nurse our daughter, we were faced with the challenge of finding an adequate location: not too far for either my husband or I to get to and providing shaded and yet freely available space not only for us to eat but also for me to breastfeed. It quickly became apparent that these characteristics were not enough and that we also needed the space to be pleasant. After a few failed attempts, we found that the garden at the Chagall museum provided the perfect setting for our daily picnic, and eventually we even visited the museum, to our daughter's great fascination (as it turns out, Chagall's large, colorful paintings are very attractive to a four-month-old's little eyes).

Our fourth rule dictated that we get out of town every single weekend on some sort of sightseeing expedition. This allowed us to visit Monte Carlo,

Eze, Saint Paul de Vence, Fréjus, and more as we continually strived to take full advantage of our geographic location. As we had planned, and as I had budgeted the trip, my husband had questioned my decision to rent a car rather than rely on public transportation options, especially considering the fact that we had to keep the car in a paid garage during the week, as I took the light rail and bus to get to my field sites. Our weekend expeditions were the justification for the expense, as the car allowed us the necessary flexibility when traveling with a fussy infant. These weekend excursions truly transformed what was otherwise a work trip into a vacation.

Our final rule involved my leaving work behind when I would meet up with my husband and child. Considering how hard it can be to truly leave an emotionally draining job behind, this rule was often broken at first. However, I was soon able to meet my need for a daily debriefing after a day of observations by journaling extensively on my bus trip back from the medico-legal institute each afternoon.

Once those rules were in place, it was easy to apply my friend's principle and document all these wonderful memories we were making in between crisis episodes. Sure, my daughter was still screaming for extended periods of time every day, so much so that a concerned neighbor would come knock on our apartment door when my husband would be desperately trying to feed her using an eye dropper. Sure, I was still exhausted from having to wake up twice a night to nurse and then again early in the morning to get ready for a full day of observations, but we had things to look forward to every day, and it sustained us, and now we can look back on those things fondly and glance over the bad stuff.

Eventually, about a month in, my daughter's first two teeth broke through, and my husband decided to disregard my stance on solid foods. He bought a jar of organic mashed carrots in the baby food aisle of our local Monoprix and gave it a try. Our daughter loved it. I was upset at first when he confessed but quickly understood how much of a game changer this was for the two of them, and the last two weeks were a lot easier on him and thus me too.

Work-Life Balance, or How I Maintained Methodological Integrity through It All

Being a Mother as a Rapport-Building Asset

As all field researchers know, negotiating access to the field is a dynamic, ongoing process that goes much beyond the initial stages of site selection (Hennink, Hutter, & Bailey, 2011). Building rapport is central to ensuring access to the entire range of possible field experiences and sources of data. Rapport-building strategies vary based on a number of different variables,

FIGURE 9.1 Grace, then four months old, and I cuddling on one of Nice's world-famous pebble beaches after one of my days at the morgue, summer 2014. Those moments with my family after a long day of fieldwork made the weariness fade away, even if only for a short time.

including the type of individuals populating the field, the characteristics of the researcher herself, and the topic of the research.

At previous field research sites, I had focused on building rapport with forensic pathologists and medico-legal investigators, as they were the types of personnel I most interacted with and were those who could provide me access to the most information. This was mostly due to the structure of the medico-legal sites but also, in hindsight, related to my standpoint as a young, single, white, educated woman in the criminal justice field. Indeed, I would approach my medico-legal research sites in much the same way that I had approached the Robbery-Homicide Investigation Squad in which I conducted my first long-term field research experience in graduate school. As such, I saw medico-legal research sites as investigation-centered extensions of a certain law-enforcement culture of discovery of evidence mixed in with masculine scientific values. My role as the outsider was softened by my traditional gender expression, which complemented my position as an educated novice. This would lead me to view my approach as immersive and focus on following the action whenever and wherever it would take me (I will discuss this further later).

The specific characteristics of the Nice medico-legal institute combined with my new standpoint as a (slightly) older married mother led me to do much more rapport-building with the administrative assistant pool. Indeed, death scene investigations, which had been a large portion of my observation time, as well as occasions for rapport-building with investigators at previous research sites, were much rarer at the Nice site because of some institution-specific characteristics. Additionally, while a large part of my time was still spent observing autopsies, which had always been my main avenue for rapport-building with forensic pathologists, there were still fewer autopsies than at the American sites. Instead, the largest amount of my time was spent extracting archival data from autopsy report files, which were physically located in the administrative assistant pool offices. As my hours, constrained by my nursing obligations, mirrored the administrative assistant staff's more so than the forensic pathologists', rapport-building naturally shifted toward the administrative assistants, who were also the gatekeepers of the files.

While I was initially reluctant to disclose any information about my personal situation, particularly not the ways in which motherhood was "limiting" my ability to work, my status as a new mother, particularly in a country that very much glorifies mothers, became a tremendous asset. In an office with a majority of female workers, both administrative assistants and forensic pathologists, a large proportion of whom were mothers, my "otherness" as an observer was lessened by the commonalities of our motherhood experiences. This rapport-building strategy culminated on my last day at the office, a day for which all personnel had clamored for me to bring my daughter along so they could finally meet the dictator reigning supreme over my calendar. It was once each person present passed the baby along to bounce her on their knees that I fully realized the extent of my having been accepted.

Ethnographic Observation as a Continuum

As I stated repeatedly before, up until that summer, my experience of ethnography was very much all-absorbing, closer in many ways to complete participation than to the complete observation my research memoranda of understanding would state. While there was never any doubt that I was an observer, I would always strive to be accepted as one of the team (with varied levels of success), but most importantly, I would align my life to the life of the office where I was doing research. At a medico-legal site, that involves freeing one's schedule to accommodate trips to death scenes going over time or even, in the case of my American sites, observing not just the day shifts but also some night shifts as to ensure a more representative sample of observations.

In Nice, I was not able to do any of this. I had to report for nursing duty at specific times, which meant often being the first one to leave the autopsy room and never ever being able to stay behind to glean whatever last little nugget of information I could absorb. As I started reflecting on my inability to give my research "my all," it became apparent to me that my "limitations" were not solely my nursing child's "fault." The characteristics of the Nice medico-legal institute also meant a different type of observational experience there. First is the fact that French medico-legal institutes do not operate 24-7 but rather follow fairly bureaucratic office hours (after all, the dead can wait, can't they?). And second, the Nice medico-legal institute had a peculiar relationship with surrounding district attorneys' offices and police departments (who are the ones calling upon their services). Since a sweeping medico-legal reform had taken place, medical examiners only rarely went to scenes, making the likelihood of my going all the more diminished. So of course, I could have spent more time extracting archival data and observing those autopsies that went over time for slightly longer and maybe, maybe, gone to one scene (in the time I was there, forensic pathologists only ever went to a handful of scenes that I was made aware of). And yes, maybe that would have led to a different rapport being built. But it is unlikely that it would have drastically changed my conclusions on the site's inner workings.

When I felt anxious about the validity of my findings because I was not able to "give it my all," I was forgetting that complete immersion is not the only way to conduct qualitative observations. Indeed, just as we can be complete observers, participant-observers, complete participants, or anywhere on the continuum, we can dip in and out of our ethnographic work or, as some like to call it sometimes, sample. Using a positivist terminology, we tend to envision ethnographic work as a census of observations, but sampling is still on the menu, and we should not forget it (Hennink, Hutter, & Bailey, 2011).

Subverting the Patriarchal Ethnographic Framework

Considering the ethnographic observation continuum reminds us that those of us who go deep and turn their research into their lives embody a specific type of work ethic: one that is only possible when there are no other responsibilities in one's life (in my case, when I was younger) or in a patriarchal system when one (usually a man) can rely on a support system (wife, assistants, etc.) to take care of all other responsibilities. Field research in the social sciences has been shaped by this approach, going back to the origins of ethnographic work in modern anthropology, with Franz Boas and his study of Alaskan Natives (1888) or Bronislaw Malinowski in the Trobriand Islands (1922, 1929, 1935), or in contemporary sociology, particularly with the Chicago School, but also, of course, with Erving Goffman and his participant observation of psychiatric wards (1961), or Howard Becker's study of drug users (1973), to name a few. We see such approaches continue to dominate today's ethnographic scene, with high profile works—in chronological order—by Philippe Bourgois (*In Search of Respect: Selling Crack in El Barrio*, 1995), Sudhir Venkatesh (*Gang Leader for a Day: A Rogue Sociologist Takes to the Streets*, 2008), Alice Goffman (*On the Run: Fugitive Life in an American City*, 2014), and Matthew Desmond (*Evicted: Poverty and Profit in the American City*, 2016) despite some of them being questioned on grounds of ethical or methodological soundness.

So while qualitative research has typically been seen as a way for researchers to turn their backs on a reifying and oppressive positivist methodological paradigm (Law, 2004; Pascale, 2001; Sprague, 2016), a lot of the examples of ethnographic research we glorify rest on the very system at the basis of the rejected paradigm. As such, I want to propose that despite (or maybe because of) all the guilt I experienced as a result of not being able to shut the rest of the world off and dive deep into my research site, my careful observations conducted from nine to five, with a lunch break in the middle, and then put to rest until the next morning after being meticulously journaled on the bus ride home every day are no less valuable than those observations I conducted when I was twenty-seven, staying up for twenty-some hours in order to stay for back-to-back shifts and then going to the bar for my daily "debriefing."

How is it then that I and many other field researchers (and also academics who do not conduct field research, nonacademic professional women, and just basically everybody else) see motherhood as a limitation or a constraint? We hide it, deemphasize it, do everything in our power to minimize its "impact" on our work, and yet there is power in our motherhood. Indeed, what this has taught me is that far from a constraint or a limitation in research, motherhood is a standpoint. Understanding and accepting that has allowed me not only to better journal my experience in Nice but also to look at my previous field notes and memos through the lens of my standpoints at the time, something that I was not as apt at doing then because of the pregnancy of my positivist methodological training.

Doing research on death is taxing, whether one is a parent or not, but being a parent brought on new levels of distress to my reading of autopsy files. I could no longer feign objective detachment when extracting data about a child's death, sometimes even struggling to refrain from openly crying. This new sensitivity to my research topic brought into question my apparent callousness until then. What does it mean to be objective when your subject is death? If we are to reject the positivist ideal of objectivity, then why do I feel like a fraud when I fear that my methodological approach may not have been the exact same at all four sites? And what did it mean that I thought I could achieve that to begin with? Each site was very different from the next, and I conducted my observations at each one during different times of my life and in varied sets of conditions. This may have been a long-coming methodological as well as theoretical maturing, but I worry that this is not my mistake alone. If even one of the most critical methods of social science research can fall prey to the very structure it aims at analyzing, then we need to learn to unlock the true power of our respective standpoints and make our voices heard.

In Conclusion: When "Having It All" Means Going from Excess to Balance and Redefining What "All" Is

Before I endeavor in concluding, let me contextualize my standpoint: First, as I write (the first draft of) this, my toddler daughter is home sick from day care for the third day in a row, and I am on the phone with the nurse while texting with my husband to arrange the logistics of sharing the care work.

Second, I am a persistent leaner-in (in-leaner?), which has led me to be seriously overextended and feeling like work (whether professional or care) only ends when I close my eyes for a too short six-hour night before doing it all over again the next day: (1) wake up at 6 a.m.; (2) work out; (3) get ready while also tag-teaming the child with my husband to get her ready; (4) drop her off at day care; (5) commute to work; (6) juggle emotional labor and ideal worker labor between my too many service commitments to change university policy and increase gender equity while fulfilling an interim position as graduate director, research projects, and a full teaching load; (7) head back to pick the child up from day care; (8) play with her while alternating weeks of cooking dinners with my husband; (9) wrangle her through a bedtime routine while my husband cleans up or vice versa; (10) tidy up, clean up, and do chores throughout the week and on weekends; (11) fit in some social time as well as some dedicated husband-wife time, all of this through a nonstop barrage of emails on multiple devices at any given time; (12) collapse.

Do I have it all? Or am I just a very underpaid, more poorly coiffed version of Sarah Jessica Parker's character in the 2011 critical flop *I Don't Know How She Does It*? I have come to the conclusion that having it all means being the ideal worker (a very traditionally masculine and patriarchal concept) while also being the ideal embodiment of the private sphere (the perfect nurturer). It is this impossible imperative that Anne-Marie Slaughter discussed in her 2012 *Atlantic* piece, "Why Women Still Can't Have It All." But what if having it all did not actually mean being all things to all people all the time? What if it meant revolutionizing the ways in which we conceptualize the public and the private spheres, the ever-elusive work-life balance, or sneakier work-life integration? What if it meant equally valuing our respective standpoints and structurally supporting them? In terms of field research, what if it meant embracing policies that more strongly support scientists with families, all the while understanding that tenure requirements need to better reflect the rich diversity of scholarships, even when they all result from what can sometimes appear as a unified methodology (field research)?

In a follow-up book, Slaughter (2015) adjusted her commentary to reframe exactly what having it all meant and proposed that having it all meant to valorize care work. While her change of heart in the wake of her high profile 2012 article is indicative of a sea change in society at large (Sheryl Sandberg also had a change of heart on her *Lean In* doctrine after the passing of her husband in 2015, and *Daily Show* comedian Jessica Williams made a strong point of refusing to lean into what others saw as good for her career after Jon Stewart announced his retirement in 2016, to cite only two high profile examples), it is my argument here that there is still some work to be done, particularly when it comes to the academy.

The work-life balance literature often operates in a self-help fashion, putting the onus on the seeker of balance to find it, while the policy literature focuses on macrolevel solutions, mostly emphasizing ways to make workers better workers by alleviating some of the burdens placed on them by their private sphere responsibilities. While offering better and more affordable day care, paid family leave, and a host of other social policies is of course needed, my argument is that we also need to seriously rethink how we view work and life as almost opposites and instead consider viewing them as more inclusive of one another. This is of course where work-life integration comes in, and this is where academia operates as both the perfect test lab and a cautionary tale. Indeed, because we value the (traditionally male-dominated) public sphere and its ideal worker more than the (traditionally female-dominated) private sphere and its ideal nurturer, work-life integration has tended to mean the invasion of work in the nooks and crannies of every aspect of our lives. We tout flexible work schedules as advantages to working parents and millennials in search of a meaningful life (Anderson, 2016), but we end up responding to emails at 10:30 p.m. and eagerly waiting for nap time to catch up on grading during weekends. Sure, we are no longer desk-bound, but it only means that we can work in our pj's or from the beach. And soon enough, we are burnt out, no longer good at or fulfilled by our various occupations (Malesic, 2016).

But how can we avoid such destructive encroachment when our work is so intricately tied to our identities and often something we really care about? Is work-life balance something achievable when you see your work more as a vocation—like many academics do—than a job? And further, how do we establish balance in a socially meaningful way that is not based on individual responsibility or assumes the privilege of a solidly middle-class employment?

This idea that we can have more than a job, that we can have a career, and that it then can be embraced as integral to our lives is indeed an essentially counterrevolutionary middle-class concept. Many people do not struggle with when their work ends and the lives they work for begin (or fail to begin), nor do they feel the urge to work during nontraditional work hours. Maybe what needs to be changed are the values underpinning work/life delineation and their impact on the scientific method and academic policies.

The way I see it, Hochschild and Machung's work on *Second Shift* (1989) is still sadly too relevant. While men are sharing in more and more of the care and maintenance work (I am definitely married to one of the best) and the social conversation is shifting, "having it all" still very much implies "giving it all" (see earlier for what that means for me). It is easy to see how we have interpreted this aspirational goal through a typically American "100 percent, all in, all the time" lens. Our successes have to be high profile and individual, our care work has to be spotless and fulfilling, our marriages have to be fairytale-like.

Being French-born, I am often reminded of the large cultural gaps between my two seemingly similar countries. Reflecting on my 2014 fieldwork in France provides a wonderful contrasting lens of two work ethics at odds: in opposition to the "giving it all" American/protestant work ethic, the French work ethic, often exaggeratingly touted as inspirational in liberal circles across the Atlantic, offers a measured response of *un petit peu de tout*, or "a little bit of everything." In France, we mostly use this maxim with regard to our diet (never deprive yourself of anything, but also eat everything in moderation), but our social policies seem to attempt to make it an overall life motto. Aside from the very generous vacation package all working French people receive (five weeks of paid vacation), the reasonable accommodations for parents, subsidized day care, and free education starting at three years old, only to name a few of the policies emphasizing the importance of balance, the French government recently passed a law that forbids employers from emailing their employees after hours. Sometimes values have to be reinforced by policy.

Practical Tips

What does this mean in terms of our academic quandary? Here are my practical tips:

- A methodological revolution: First, we need to push for a methodological revolution that does not require the field researcher to operate in an unrealistic setting of circumstances limited to specific stations in life. This means accepting critical methodologies as valid and embracing more broadly the feminist notion of standpoint. Indeed, if all methods were to require questioning researchers' standpoints, the scientific endeavor would not only become more inclusive but also be strengthened overall, avoiding positivist blind spots.

- Institutional support for family-friendly policies: Second, and logically deriving from my first proposition, we need to ensure that all researchers are able to adopt the methodology that will most adequately answer their research question, regardless of their life circumstances. This may mean including funding for families to travel with researchers, childcare, and other types of financial support to the researcher. Policies such as Dependent Care Travel Funds are flourishing in Ivy League institutions and starting to spread beyond the small circle of private elite universities through ADVANCE grants at various top public universities. We need to continue pushing for more.

- Redefining our boundaries: But, and this is my third and larger point, it also means transforming the way we think and act about our careers. As I previously explained, work-life integration in academia has meant the dominance of work over every other aspect of one's life. Indeed, maybe we should not talk about work-life integration, as working is clearly part of our lives, but rather public life-private life integration. While the baby boomers have lured us into thinking that there was such a thing as pure leisure, which was achievable only if you made enough money, Gen Xers have struggled to achieve this elusive balance arguably only made possible in the first place by the combination of favorable economic cycles and a massive workforce due to demographic shifts. As millennials strive to find meaning in their professional and personal lives, we need to rethink what some have characterized as institutional anomie (Messner & Rosenfeld, 2004). Indeed, it is the unhealthy focus on financial success and its associated glorification of work that lead us to lose ourselves in what has become a race to tenure, a race for external funding, a race for indicators of success, and as a result, faculty burnout, women opting out either before or after tenure, and the increasing reliance on adjunct labor among other signs of academic malaise. Shifting the culture will require more than "family-friendly policies," even though these are necessary. It will also involve policies providing not only a baseline for faculty to meet expectations but also a ceiling curtailing the never-ending and ever-growing appetite for more, more, more (scholarship, external funding, teaching, advising, service)—something of an equivalent of the French law forbidding employers from emailing employees outside of regular office hours. We cannot be trusted to value our nonprofessional lives as much as we do our professional lives because our work is where our livelihood comes from but also because we, academics, do not see ourselves as workers. So we need to make it clear, and we need to enforce it. In other words, we need unions, not self-help (Fleming, 2016).

References

Anderson, J. (2016, October 16). This is what work-life balance looks like at a company with 100% retention of moms. *Quartz*. Retrieved from http://qz.com/806516/the-secret-to -patagonias-success-keeping-moms-and-onsite-child-care-and-paid-parental-leave/

Becker, H. (1973). *Outsiders: Studies in the sociology of deviance*. New York, NY: Free Press.

Boas, F. (1888). *The central Eskimo: Sixth annual report of the Bureau of Ethnology*. Washington, D.C.: Smithsonian Institute.

Bourgois, P. (1995). *In search of respect: Selling crack in El Barrio*. New York, NY: Cambridge University Press.

Colen, C. G., & Ramey, D. M. (2014). Is breast truly best? Estimating the effects of breastfeeding on long-term child health and wellbeing in the United States using sibling comparisons. *Social Science and Medicine, 109*, 55–65.

Desmond, M. (2016). *Evicted: Poverty and profit in the American city*. New York, NY: Penguin Random House.

Fleming, P. (2016, October 11). The way to a better work-life balance? Unions, not self-help. *The Guardian*. Retrieved from https://www.theguardian.com/careers/2016/oct/11/way -to-better-work-life-balance-unions-not-self-help

Goffman, A. (2014). *On the run: Fugitive life in an American city*. Chicago, IL: University of Chicago Press.

Goffman, E. (1961). *Asylums: Essays on the social situation of mental patients and other inmates*. New York, NY: Anchor Books.

Hennink, M., Hutter, I., & Bailey, A. (2011). *Qualitative research methods*. Thousand Oaks, CA: Sage.

Hodinnott, P., Craig, L. C. A., Britten, J., & McInnes, R. A. (2012). A serial qualitative study of infant feeding experiences: Idealism meets realism. *British Medicine Journal, 2*(2), 1–14.

Kornelis, C. (2012, October 31). A father's case against breastfeeding. *The Atlantic*. Retrieved from http://www.theatlantic.com/sexes/archive/2012/10/a-fathers-case-against-breast -feeding/264115/

Law, J. (2004). *After method: Mess in social science research*. London, UK: Routledge.

Malesic, J. (October 21, 2016). The 40-year-old burnout. *Chronicle Vitae*. Retrieved from https://chroniclevitae.com/news/1584-the-40-year-old-burnout?cid=VTEVPMSED1

Malinowski, B. (1922). *Argonauts of the Western Pacific: An account of native enterprise and adventure in the Archipelagoes of Melanesian New Guinea*. London, UK: Routledge.

Malinowski, B. (1929). *The sexual life of savages in north-western Melanesia: An ethnographic account of courtship, marriage and family life among the natives of the Trobriand Islands, British New Guinea*. New York, NY: Eugenics.

Malinowski, B. (1935). *Coral gardens and their magic: A study of tilling the soil and of agricultural rites in the Trobriand Islands*. London, UK: Routledge.

Messner, S.-F., Rosenfeld, R. (2004). *Crime and the American dream*. Belmont, CA: Wadsworth.

Pascale, C.-M. (2011). *Cartographies of knowledge: Exploring qualitative epistemologies*. Thousand Oaks, CA: Sage.

Rosin, H. (2009, April). The case against breastfeeding. *The Atlantic*. Retrieved from http:// www.theatlantic.com/magazine/archive/2009/04/the-case-against-breast-feeding/307311/

Russell Hochschild, A., & Machung, A. (1989). *The second shift: Working parents and the revolution at home.* New York, NY: Viking Penguin.

Sandberg, S. (2013). *Lean in: Women, work, and the will to lead.* New York, NY: Alfred A. Knopf.

Slaughter, A.-M. (2012, July/August). Why women still can't have it all. *The Atlantic.* Retrieved from http://www.theatlantic.com/magazine/archive/2012/07/why-women -still-cant-have-it-all/309020/

Slaughter, A.-M. (2015). *Unfinished business: Women men work family.* New York, NY: Random House.

Sprague, J. (2016). *Feminist methodologies for critical researchers: Bridging differences* (2nd ed.). New York, NY: Rowan & Littlefield.

Venkatesh, S. (2008). *Gang leader for a day: A rogue sociologist takes to the streets.* New York, NY: Penguin.

10

Fieldwork Adventures on the Mommy Track

•••••••••••••••••••••

ANNE HARDGROVE

> My Mommy lies over the ocean,
> My Mommy lies over the sea,
> My Mommy lies over the ocean,
> Oh, bring back my Mommy to me.

I love to sing with my son. Even before he was born, I sang to him. When he became a toddler, my son himself initiated a joyful singing session. But when I first heard—or noticed—him singing the "Bonny" song with "Mommy" as the subject, my heart sank. Certainly I would not expect him to understand the word *bonny* as "beauty." Yet "Mommy" more accurately fit his own situation. What had my beautiful young son internalized about the time I spend doing anthropological and historical fieldwork in India for my career as a university professor?

This chapter addresses the issues of conducting humanities and social science fieldwork in three different modes—as a single woman, as a mother doing fieldwork without my child, and as a mother doing fieldwork with my child in tow. Methodologically, each of these modes of research has been possible with the advent of feminism, and feminist anthropology, in particular, addresses these questions most directly. One's subject position—vis-à-vis the people being studied—is directly formed by sets of relationships. As a fieldworker building trust among communities, particularly those in India that understand and project social relationships in terms of kinship structures, there is no doubt that having a husband and offspring meteorically increases and deepens the rapport, the honesty, the friendships, and the relationships I create. And yet American norms of living and livelihoods pull too in an opposite direction—a husband whose corporate job has limited vacation time, a child who hates to miss a single day of middle school. As I finish this chapter a handful of days before returning to India for a two-week research trip, my American duties of motherhood go into overdrive—a last trip to the grocery store to stock up on necessities for my family, assembling a bag of "guilt gifts" for my son to open, one each day, during my absence.

Upper-middle-class American mothers in particular question the balance between time spent with children and time spent doing just about anything or everything else. Long debates over "having it all" capture the angst of the privileged middle-class mind-set to a tee. For the majority of academic mothers, no well-established model or path of academic motherhood exists. One side of my family was relatively affluent: women did not work. For the working-class side, women always worked in nonprofessional, hourly jobs while managing household and childcare. I find myself as a first-generation professional woman with no close familial role models. Colleagues, friends, and professional connections become my compass in the wilderness of being an academic mother. Other mothers have professional jobs defined by time spent in the office, or counting of hours working at home, and responsibilities cease at the end of the work day. But academics and professors have no hours on or off other than how they define it. It's a blessing and a curse. I know a handful of women academics who track their hours to improve time management and increase family time. Far too often, female academics find research and family mutually exclusive and irreconcilable. This is slowly changing. A former colleague wrote a book about her stillbirth as a way of reconciling her academic self with a lifelong absence of her son (Heineman, 2014). Weaving together academic and family identities is alien, but is necessary and can be therapeutic.

When the job of professor includes fieldwork, the hours, days, weeks, months, and even yearly demands of the profession become vaguer. Such jobs were done by men with wives running their home and managing children and family. When women joined academics in increasing numbers, including in fieldworking disciplines, women found themselves adjusting, probably more so than other professions. No academic mother or parent as primary caregiver—whether married, single, straight, gay, trans—is an island. We all rely heavily on a mixture of partners, parents, extended family, neighbors, paid childcare, and friendly colleagues.

Early on, as an unattached, child-free PhD student doing coursework, I observed mysterious graduate student / parent peers as tied to an unalterable schedule. A group project could only be done in the late evening, after children fell asleep. Family schedules were rigid, and other people needed to be flexible. It was a marked contrast to my all-the-time-in-the-world-put-it-off-until-tomorrow existence. And yet as my career advances, I now see that those family/work balance issues I first noticed in graduate school are the norm and not the exception. After two decades at a majority-minority institution, where the "typical" student is nontraditional and often a parent or caregiver, I have had many occasions to rethink relationships between academia and family life. This is as true for my students as it is for myself. Both students and professors navigate an academic system that was not organized for women with children. Evening classes—lasting until 9 or 10 p.m.—are a challenge. Add the necessity of traveling overseas in certain fields to research in foreign and acquired languages and it is no wonder that it is a battle to thrive, let alone survive, in this parenting-unfriendly system. I increasingly know more immigrant and second-generation academics in history and the social sciences who work on their home countries to mix research and grandparent time. I too use research libraries when I visit my parents. And for many reasons, many dual-academic couples in my field choose not to have children at all.

Policy issues related to academic mothers doing fieldwork research are complex, individual, and not one-size-fits-all. There is no one answer, but no answer either, for how to be both a participant-observer immersed in a foreign culture and a loving parent to a child who is wholly dependent on you for nourishment, shelter, and love. Anthropological fieldwork assumes a lone (male) researcher going 100 percent local in language, location, and culture—an "immersion." The original, nineteenth century idea was not to bring your own culture—much less a trailing family—with you. To best achieve this, the anthropologist was imagined to be male, single, wealthy, and unencumbered by extended or nuclear family issues, either sentimental or financial. The class and subculture privilege associated with this financially secure, autonomous individual is substantial. Frankly speaking, this model is virtually unattainable by most researchers—female or male, single or coupled, child-free or parent—in the field today. One of the most brilliant examples of mothering in the field—published as the book *Zenana*—is by a friend who married her Pakistani college sweetheart (Ring, 2006). Along with their oldest son, then four years old, they went to Karachi—the husband's home city where his parents still lived—and spent a year in an urban apartment complex. There, she brilliantly studied how women from varied ethnic backgrounds "make peace" with each other and with children, including her own, serving as proverbial ice-breakers among families.

Eventually, certain aspects of fieldwork caught up. Fieldwork grants and fellowships began to accommodate accompanying family members. "Fulbright Marriages" became an accepted category of social cohabitation, where granting agencies paid for legal spouses, an exclusionary category for same-sex partnerships until several years into the twenty-first century. This researcher model assumed a male head of household, with a "trailing" wife and children as an unbreakable unit accompanying the father in his work. This pattern of head researcher and flexible family was expected and presumed to continue throughout entire academic careers. As the "faculty brat" daughter of a small liberal arts college chemistry professor, this was my own experience of my parents' working lives.

Years spent in the South, in Florida and in Tennessee, were eye-opening experiences in an otherwise homogenous, 1970s midwestern milieu. Looking back, my experiences of difference within the United States certainly influenced my ability to adapt to new circumstances and my choice of professional training. From my mother's perspective, however—that of a working-class, first-generation college student—these sabbaticals interrupted her own world of nonprofessional work, and she left each job without assurance that she could go back to it once returning from sabbatical leave. But during the 1970s, middle-class mothers didn't just *leave* for extended periods, professionally or personally. This was unthinkable. My mother had initially started out—before marriage—as a high school teacher. According to state law, however, married women were expected to leave their teaching jobs at public schools. Her status as a mother trumped all other duties.

Once I finished a few years of adjunct teaching and earned my PhD, moving into full-time academic work as a visiting and then tenure-track professor gave me opportunities to see how other anthropologist-historians organized their research-teaching-life balance. Some colleagues began families as graduate students and were experienced in the research-teaching-children-life balancing act. One mother-colleague who does fieldwork in Central America coached me with the wisdom of her experiences. "Try to go away and do your research while your child is still very young," she advised. "That way, he or she won't remember it later and hate you for being gone." Her own children, especially the older one of two, had devised their own ways of coping with their own mother's fieldwork. "If you are naughty," the older girl told her sobbing younger sister, "Mommy will go away again to Guatemala for the summer."

Managing the discourse of parenting duties in academia is deeply inflected by gender stereotypes. Women are typically punished for childcare affecting their work, whereas male professors who parent are transformed into superheroes. Academic mamas are expected to meet a standard of "effortless perfection," seamlessly weaving together professional and family responsibilities, but academic fathers put forward "learned incompetence" as their performance of life-work balance. Male colleagues with grown-up children take for granted how much their wives supported them. You'll love being a mother, I was enthusiastically told while pregnant. Taking off the occasional weekend to just play with children is the best.

Some academic dads make a public game of ditching or belittling childcare responsibilities. At a university-wide teaching workshop I attended recently, I overheard a tall, burly younger male colleague apologize jovially for his late arrival to the conference hosts. "I got stuck with babysitting," he announced in a heavy European accent. The two female conference assistants beamed at him, handing over his nametag and folder of materials. In that moment, I bristled hearing this display of outdated, privileged thinking. "You are just overly sensitive," my husband commented later when hearing the story. I was reminded of Facebook story on the Dad's Network t-shirt that read "Dad's Don't Babysit (It's called 'Parenting')" (BBC, 2016). With so many wonderful, supportive parent-colleagues in my workplace, I couldn't imagine anyone I knew saying this. Perhaps it was a second-language thing. At best, perhaps it was an attempt to make an ironic joke. As much as such incidents scratch at our well-being, the languages of parenting remain locked in normative contexts. One day riding the work elevator with my son in a stroller, a stranger asked me how I liked working as a nanny. I mumbled my thanks for being told that I looked like a professional childcare provider when I was not.

I offer these last vignettes as evidence of the male-normative work environment of academia. Yes, academia is slowly increasing the number of women in its lower ranks, at least in some fields of study, but attaining the highest ranks remains challenging. Most importantly, fieldwork disciplines add experiences of women scholars of color, whose work-life balance is further complicated by assumptions stemming from racism and classism. Same-sex partnerships and single parents warrant other contributions to the discussion. Still, old habits of thinking die hard. Schools call mommy first when a sick kid needs to be picked up. I have the luxury of being part of a department where currently, every woman happens to be a mother. There is not, as there are in some places, a child-free women's control group establishing child-free norms, telling breeders that they should have made better choices. But there is a lingering sense that there is no obvious path to a consuming career and life with a family. Mothering fieldworkers do not imagine these life stresses, nor do they exist in a patriarchy-free vacuum. There is no companion volume, *Fathering from the Field*, to this book.

Are Parenting Academics versus Child-Free Academics as Polarized as Drivers and Pedestrians?

In about twenty years of working as a professor, I've been on both sides of the parenting fence. I spent my first thirty-seven years child-free until the last thirteen magical, life-changing years as I became a mother to my little boy (who is now taller than me). In fact, I was spouse-free too until the last wonderful fifteen. In my career, I've been lucky enough to become a tenured associate professor in a forward-thinking, vibrant city and a truly diverse, Hispanic-serving university with earnest and appreciative first-generation students whom I would not trade for anything.

The students bring to the table their own variety of backgrounds and experiences, from being the first generation to attend university, former and current military, "returning moms" who are finishing their education, and more. When I first started teaching, I was astonished by how many of my students were also parents. Since San Antonio is the United States capital of teenage pregnancy—and teenage mothers—it is not so surprising. Other cultural and social differences exist. I started lecturing one day about how people in India find the American ideal of leaving home for college incredibly sad and depressing. Then I realized that I was the only person in the room who might have aspired to that. My students find creative ways to integrate college and life, work and home, children and studying, into an integrated whole. Of those who succeed, the perseverance and drive to forge ahead in a sometimes unwelcoming academic context, and when higher education is not necessarily appreciated by family, is astonishing. I have become a much better teacher—and mother—in this environment. What is especially refreshing about the student body is their appreciation of educational opportunities—they don't display the entitlement sometimes seen at more affluent or higher-ranked institutions.

My work as a (child-free) historian and anthropologist of South Asia meant that for many years, I made regular trips to India (as well as Pakistan and Bangladesh) to conduct research in libraries and archives as well as anthropological fieldwork in the homes, shops, and offices of the Marwari business community, which is the subject of my dissertation and first book. In the 1990s, I traveled to India every summer and spent long stretches of time there. During this stage of my research, I mostly focused on the women in the community. These included several community leaders in business, the arts, literature, and philanthropy. My research with these professional women was largely formal, with timed appointments and conversations. I did "join" a Marwari social service organization, whose ladies' wing was organizing a mass marriage for less well-to-do couples. My participation with this group was more in the style of participant observation, where I served on a membership committee and helped facilitate the registrations of families who hoped to find an engagement and suitable match for their son or daughter. It was with young women of my own age or slightly younger with whom I had the most "down time" to get to know. These women typically lived with their parents and were often studying for advanced degrees in literature or philosophy, subjects deemed suitably feminine enough to not detract from their marriageability. I visited with these women mostly during the day, when their fathers and older brothers were away from the home, working in their offices and attending to the family business. The access I had to these young adult women came from introductions from mutual friends, my knowledge of Hindi (some of the women were more proficient than others), and also my own status as being in the same age range and having the same single marital status and student status.

Having my first book done and published before I got married, let alone had a child, was a completely different experience compared to what came next. After submitting my book to the publisher, I squeezed in some shorter fieldwork trips to begin work on my next project, which is a more literary-oriented study of marriage and sexuality in South Asia. I felt fortunate that I received some grants and fellowships to launch this work. The Social Science Research Council Sexuality Fellowship program gave me a year's leave to dive into the research literature, to travel to India and Britain for research, and to begin to write my results. Health concerns took up some of the time, and planning a wedding took work and time too, but I was able to publish a few papers as articles, feeling confident that I was making a mark on my new field of research.

Six months after getting married, my grant ended and I went back to my teaching, and I was thrilled when David and I found out that we were expecting a baby. Being an older mom comes with its health challenges, but it also came with confidence and economic stability, at least in our case. I experienced morning sickness fairly early on, in about week five or six. I'd gone to another state to give an invited lecture and spent the last day of my visit with a close friend and colleague. I threw up on her kitchen floor, and she guessed what was going on. From that day forward, throughout the rest of the pregnancy, I threw up every single day. Even, it turns out, on the day that I had the baby. I became a pro at timing my stomach problems to just before my teaching, with a trip to the bathroom to vomit before going off to lecture. I hadn't gained much weight, so my pregnancy wasn't obvious to those around me. Perhaps I would have been better off if I had been more open. One morning, I walked the dog around the block as was my usual pattern and ran into a neighbor who I was beginning to get to know. She waved at me, and I suddenly felt the lunge of my stomach as I heaved into some nearby bushes. When I looked up, she had turned and walked away down the block before I could say anything. I was puzzled by her reaction until I realized that she must have assumed that I was a raging alcoholic who couldn't hold my booze. I think that she knew that I worked as a professor—and assumed that I fulfilled the heavy-drinker public stereotype of researchers and writers. I never did get a chance to explain.

My last weeks of the pregnancy were spent on bed rest. I only got up to make very fast trips to the toilet. After only a few minutes of being upright, I would feel the baby's head pressing down, and I would leap back into bed so that gravity would be on my side. At thirty-five weeks, Jeremy entered the world through an emergency C-section. He stayed in the NICU for three long weeks, and I spent the time going back and forth to the hospital to be with him and learn to nurse in a large room filled with seventy-five-plus babies in cribs, nurses, other parents, and an army of computer screens that beeped at their own rhythms, providing biofeedback on each little life that was attached to them. Due to my bedrest order, I had the semester off. When I returned to teaching, I taught on nights and weekends so we could juggle childcare during my husband's more prescribed nine to five work routine.

During this sleep-deprived, happy time, I found out the good news that I had gotten a grant for four months in the field, for time to be back in India. It would start in about a year, giving me some time to plan and figure out how to manage. After my first semester back at teaching, the three of us made a research trip to Britain when Jeremy was nine months old. The plan was to stay at a bed-and-breakfast in Reading, where I would do archival work at the university archives, and David and Jeremy would explore local attractions. Since Jeremy was still nursing, along with eating cereal and other simple foods, we thought the research trip would be a breeze. Jeremy's new passport didn't arrive from the state department, so we had to hustle to get it reissued in time for our flights. The night before we left, Jeremy threw up a little bit, which is just what babies do, so we didn't worry. We boarded the plane in Houston and took off on our adventure. About forty-five minutes into the flight, as we were still squarely over Texas, I realized that I had come down with Jeremy's virus. The rest of the flight was a horrible blur of airsickness bags, severe stomach pains, and disgusted looks from nearby passengers. During the flight, Jeremy sat on his daddy's lap next to me, squealing with laughter each and every time I vomited. Another episode came once we landed and rode a series of trains to our B&B in Reading. After settling into our room, David went out in search of snacks. Upon his return, one look at his greenish face told me that he was the next victim of the stomach bug. Our recovery took several days, taking away time that I would have otherwise spent in the library. But eventually we got better, somehow managing to take care of a baby as we languished. The Caribbean-British owners graciously lent us toys to keep Jeremy amused. He particularly loved a ringing toy telephone that screeched "It's For You!" in a cockney accent. When we finally left for London, our host drove us to the train station but insisted we wait for a few minutes for something. He pushed a plastic bag into my hands, and when I peeked inside, I saw that they had purchased the same phone for us. I was so touched by this friendly, generous gesture. The phone still sits on my desk. No mother is an island.

My first trip back to India as a mother came when Jeremy was about twenty-one months old. He was still nursing at night. David insisted—wisely—that I wean him off before leaving. It would be bad enough having me *gone* for several weeks. But if Jeremy also expected to nurse while I was gone, it would have been torture. During my absence, my parents came to Texas to help with the household and taking care of the baby. We had partial, inexpensive childcare lined up through a local church to supplement an expensive childcare center. I spent several days in Bombay during my trip, conducting interviews and research in local institutions. Every day, David emailed a recounting of the day's adventures. All the little joys of being child-free—to have one's own schedule, to work late or early or both—were all possible again. I lay in bed reading newspapers and books without interruption until I fell into a deep, deep, sleep. I had not slept through the night since I couldn't remember when. The word for sleep in Hindi is *sona*, which also means "golden." Now, as a mother, this made perfect sense.

Why Bring a Car Seat When There Are No Seatbelts? Baby Does Fieldwork

Doing research in India requires a huge amount of foresight and planning. It takes about five years to acquire a research visa. The first step is to apply for grants and get one. Then the funding agency begins the two-year process of circulating your application to find a local institution affiliate, and the government ministries circulate and approve the proposal. They make sure that there is nothing offensive and nothing that could be construed as insulting to the country's national reputation and that your credentials are all in good and working order. Medical shots are next (hepatitis, typhoid, yellow fever, meningitis). Until the mid-2000s, India required a certificate saying that foreign researchers with long-term research visas were HIV-free. The logic was that HIV was a foreign scourge, spread in India from (1) long-haul truck drivers, (2) prostitutes, and (3) foreign nationals with long-term research visas. At first, India would accept results from any qualified American MD. The alternative, as one of my classmates chose, was to get tested at a stray-dog infested, severely substandard, underfunded government hospital in Kolkata. In the later 1990s, the rules got more stringent, limiting which MDs could provide such certification. In the final iteration, just before the program ultimately imploded, the Government of India announced that they would only accept certificates issued by the CDC, leaving me to wonder how I'd squeeze in a trip to Atlanta—much less an appointment—for such a routine matter. Thankfully, the requirement was finally dropped in time, and I didn't have to go to Atlanta—or to the Kolkata hospital, where the stray dogs often bit patients.

This is to say, in so many words, that obtaining permissions and a research visa is precious. Any sane person would spend as much time in the field as humanly possible. My four-month grant gave me the possibility of a two-year visa, which I mercifully secured. I initially thought about bringing both of my parents to help take care of the baby and staying the whole four months. But two additional round-trip plane tickets, not to mention housing and meals and local transportation in a rapidly liberalizing India, began to look exorbitantly expensive and well beyond our means. Instead, I used the grant in two separate intervals, paying for my extra plane tickets out of my own salary. The time I spent in the field added up to far less time than I had money for, about two months total.

The fact that my visa was still valid led me to realize that I should try to return to India. The "baby" was now almost four. A conference on translation, the topic of my new research, was an excellent opportunity to present my work and get feedback from scholars. With the miracle of frequent flyer tickets, the three of us decided to go to India together. I could do additional fieldwork in Delhi, staying a bit longer than my husband and son; we would travel south to a school where I hoped to establish an exchange program and finally to the conference, held in a former French colony I'd always wanted to visit. Bringing a husband, much less a child, to India was a completely new experience. Suddenly, in the eyes of my Indian friends and so-called anthropological "informants," I became a whole person, knowable by my own kinship network, and not some lone ship passing in the night. My son played with children his own age, visited a school where his curly blond hair was an instant attraction, and was thrilled to eat boxed Kraft macaroni and cheese at a friend's house. I relished showing my family around the fascinating country I'd spend thirty years studying. Of course, young children have their own agendas. When visiting Delhi's stunning Bahá'í temple, shaped like a lotus flower, Jeremy ignored our instructions (despite several signs labeled "Absolute Quiet") to be very quiet inside. Settling down in a chair in the front of the temple, with the vast dome overhead, he burst into song:

The stars at night are big and bright,
Deep in the heart of Texas. (clap clap clap clap)
Reminds me of the land I love,
Deep in the heart of Texas. (clap clap clap clap)

Our son didn't quite get to the final four claps when the temple security officers ran over to us, pointing in unison to the door marked "exit." No ifs, ands, or buts. We were loud, obnoxious Texans, fulfilling every last and horrible stereotype, and we had to leave. New Delhi's notorious pollution gave our son a bad respiratory infection. He coughed and was lethargic, content to sit on the bed under the mosquito net and watch *Dora the Explorer* in the South Indian language of Tamil. He learned Dora's Tamil expression for "Mommy! Daddy! No!," which he delighted in yelling whenever we were out. (Later, returning to San Antonio, he was pleased to report that Dora speaks Tamil *and* Spanish).

When we arrived in Chennai, our hosts at Madras Christian College sat us down for a delicious lunch. Our three-year-old took one disinterested look at the food in front of us and wandered off into the hosts' bedroom. We could not have been more than three or four luscious bites into lunch when the family maid rushed into the kitchen, yelling frantically in Tamil. Our hosts jumped up, running toward the bedroom.

Our son had managed to lock himself inside of the bedroom, closing the heavy, teak, colonial-era door. He must have stood on a chair to reach the lock because a chair was suspiciously on its side, having fallen over. Our host, a friend of my parents, explained that there was no way to open the door from the outside and that the windows were sealed with steel bars. He began to call the college carpenter to come and either saw through the bars or else to hack through the (beautiful, priceless, irreplaceable) teak door. I took a chair around to the outside, standing on it and looking through the metal bars. I peeled back the Velcro of the mosquito screen so that I could talk directly to my child. Having not eaten much during the last week, he must have been craving calcium because he was licking away at the newly limed walls. Lime wash itself isn't dangerous. Eventually, I talked him through the several steps to freedom: upright the chair, pull it to the right (he didn't know right/left at that point), stand on it, reach up for the lever, and pull the deadbolt back to its original position. Fifteen minutes later, to everyone's relief, he was freed. He loved the college, the students, the trees. It was the Hundred Acre Wood from his favorite book. Everyone who met him was very charmed. Of course, the shared experience and story of him locking himself in the room was a bonding moment and the starting point for interviews I managed to squeeze in.

Toward the end of our visit, we arranged for a car to drive us to Pondicherry. We would leave early, stop at a famous Hindu temple on the way, and reach the conference in plenty of time. I learned that I would be the first presenter, so we needed to be there on time. I had thought of bringing a car seat, but abandoned the plan when a friend pointed out that "there are no seat belts in the back seats, so a car seat would do absolutely no good." Details. Our host helped dress me in my sari, the expected attire for professional women in India. I am not good at managing the folds and pleats myself, and I was thrilled to have the help. By the time we left, I looked fantastic. What I did not count on during our journey was the fact that our son was thrilled to ride in a car without the confines of either a car seat or a seat belt. He rolled around on my lap, pulled on the beautiful folds of my sari, and played with my hair. We had some delays since our original car had a license for commercial passengers in Tamil Nadu but not Pondicherry government districts (equivalent to DC in the United States). By the time we arrived, I had to walk directly into the conference and up to the podium. Naturally, my sari and my hair were a complete wreck. As I presented my paper, which focused on histories of translations of

India's famous sex manual, the *Kama Sutra*, I became aware that my sari was coming undone and slowly unwrapping itself, sliding to the floor. I hid behind the podium. When I finished, a very kind woman escorted me directly to her conference center guest room and helped me pull my clothes back on. When I reported the story later to my husband, telling him how embarrassed I was and that my attempts to look professional were completely undone by our squirrelly child, he threw his head back and laughed uproariously. "Are you kidding?" He said. "An American woman doing a strip tease while talking about the Kama Sutra? It must have been a huge hit!"

The rest of the trip had nowhere to go but up. We got our son to a doctor, and antibiotics hit his sinus infection and fever head-on. Dora continued to speak Tamil. I reverted back to the much-easier-to-wear long tunic and pants—a *salwar kameez*—for the rest of my time at the conference. The talk eventually became a journal publication.

My subsequent research and fieldwork trips—because of logistics and expense—have seen me go solo to Beijing, Hong Kong, and Japan. I showed off pictures of my family to Asian colleagues and received shocked expressions from those wondering how I could travel without them. Yes, I get more done.

FIGURE 10.1 My family visits the Taj Mahal in Agra, India, during a research-related trip in 2010. Mom and Dad, who both have PhDs, are awestruck by the beauty of the tomb. But toddlers have their own agendas and sometimes just need to run off their unending levels of energy.

No question. But to most people, particularly in Asia, a mother-on-the-go without children is a strange sight, and they are right. There is no easy path—with or without.

Motherhood has transformed my fieldwork experiences. Certainly my early career extended fieldwork would have been impossible—or at least very different—with a child in tow. My fieldwork opportunities are more limited by familial obligations. Yet motherhood enriches my fieldwork experiences immensely. The same kinship that I shared with the Marwari girls seeking husbands in their twenties has evolved in to a parental kinship with professional contacts in the field. As a mother—and specifically as a mother to a son—I am in India's patriarchal, family oriented society a complete person, opening the door to understandings and discussions that may otherwise not occur. Bringing my family into the field is seen as a sign of commitment and trust, an acceptance of the gracious hospitality that Indian families extend to their guests.

Going to the field—in my particular case, to India and South Asia and previously to Pakistan and Bangladesh too—is a major undertaking, organizing passports, visas, permissions, immunizations, plane tickets, and itineraries, making contacts, and conducting interviews. Even renting a cell phone takes several days of applications, permissions, and patience. There are considerations of safety and travel advisories. Staying well digestively takes planning—for example, locating accommodations that offer evening meals so that unaccompanied women are not out at night, a time at which they draw inquisitive stares. The deadly problem of serious air pollution poses dangerous risks to anyone living in India's cities or visiting them. These factors vary according to the season, the place, and the people.

Generally, if fieldwork is a regular part of a professional career, it is important to try to find some way for family to make at least one short visit. It has helped my parents, my husband, and my son understand what life is like in the field and its challenges, rewards, and demands. In families with two academic parents who are studying India, or if one parent is from India, full-family visits and longer stays are easier. But in cases like mine, it is more productive when my family is not there every time. Just like the time at my American university, I get far more done—and do it far faster—when I can throw myself into my work with fewer distractions and demands on my time and energy.

As I left the dinner table to put the final touches on this chapter, my thirteen-year-old took a break from singing a Justin Timberlake song to comment, "Mommy! You should be writing this in five years! Not today!" I asked him to explain. "Well, you still have five years to go," he said. "If you wait five years, you will be finished. And then you can tell the whole story. You're not done yet!"

I listened to his wise words as I pushed my chair back and prepared to hide in my study, ignoring the mess in the sink and the general chaos of the kitchen. I lovingly smiled at him, saying nothing. I will always define myself as his mother. In my heart, I hope and know that for a parent, and a mother, there is no "end" to the adventure of parenting and fieldwork.

Practical Tips

Fieldwork in anthropology and history is a transformative life experience. Here are suggestions for parents engaging in fieldwork in these disciplines and funding agencies and universities that help support their research.

- Fieldwork is expensive. Most researchers rely on fellowships, grants, and their home institution to cover transportation, living expenses, local transportation, supplies, entrance to libraries and archives, photocopying or camera fees, and so on. Granting agencies often cover the expenses of an accompanying spouse and children. Agencies and universities should evaluate their own policies positing the model of researcher and trailing spouse as the normative unit of childcare in fieldwork settings. There are several scenarios, including my own, where it would be impossible for a spouse to leave a job for an extended period. Were I to bring my child, I could only manage my professional and parenting duties by bringing another adult with me, such as a grandparent or other relative or a paid nanny. Agencies should be willing to fund an accompanying adult who provides childcare. This imaginative, flexible, open-mindedness about definitions of family would serve researchers who are single parents or parents like me who are singly doing fieldwork. When the Obamas moved into the White House, Michele's mother moved in too. Relying on extended family is increasingly the norm. There are many models of and models for families. Agencies should consider real-world demographics in funding guidelines, especially when considering who counts as a "fundable" person accompanying the researcher.
- Historical and anthropological fieldwork has been defined as long, uninterrupted stays in the field site and is the mainstay of academic research and the publication of ethnographies. Yet this "norm" of fieldwork is out of sync with modern family demands. No researcher is an island. Each of us has demands and responsibilities placed on us by our loved ones. By leaving family members behind, more frequent, shorter visits to field sites spread out over a longer time period helps create family-friendly possibilities for fieldwork research. Often agencies impose arbitrary deadlines to exhaust funding, but they could explore how funding could be used over longer periods of time. A three-month fellowship aimed at summer research might be more efficiently used in

smaller units of time over a longer period, perhaps two or three summers, anticipating multiple departures and arrivals. Agencies offering dependent support might pay instead for multiple plane tickets for researchers whose family stays home. Fieldwork during the school year might be advantageous for families remaining at home.

- The changing world of childhood is an important backdrop to this collection. Today, children live with far different expectations and circumstances and a more varied cast of family members. Bigger cities and neighborhoods affordable on academic salaries are not as sheltered and idyllic as once imagined. Walkable neighborhood schools are mostly illusory. Children are driven to and from school, playdates, sports, libraries, music, robotics, gyms, swimming pools, and birthday parties. Easy, organic neighborhood play is no longer commonplace. Twenty-four-seven news cycles remind us of terrible things that can happen, no matter how rare. Fieldworking mothers report that it takes a huge number of people to replace them—as drivers, organizers, and back-up planners. Perpetuating the nuclear family myth has outlived any imagined usefulness. Dual working parents, single parents, and families with a stay-at-home adult all face individual and collective challenges as we pass through various life stages, doing our fieldwork and striving to make our professional and personal lives mesh together.

- Fieldworking mothers share challenges of other professional mothers who balance parenting with careers. While this point may seem obvious to some (and perhaps debatable to others), we must consider this when navigating our personal and professional lives. Fieldwork researchers find themselves in work circumstances that nonresearchers may not comprehend. But we can also relate, as professionally employed mothers, to the doctor, the teacher, the custodian, or the artist whose child is friends with ours. Crafting parental networks outside of academic bubbles helps develop effective support systems that ground us in local communities. Networks and friendships provide space away from our work so we become more fully defined as individuals—not only in roles as researchers and mothers but also as friends, neighbors, and participants in our own communities.

- We confront frustrations in our academic or family lives with acts of love. Our love for our families differs from our love for our discipline, but we sacrifice for both because they provide fulfillment beyond material rewards. When our priorities come into conflict, we should expect the discipline to be as forgiving as our families have been. Fieldwork pulls us from our families, but birthday parties, household duties, holidays, and visits to childhood homes pull us from research. This is as it should be and gives balance to our lives.

References

BBC (2016). The fathers saying "dads don't babysit." Retrieved from http://www.bbc.com/news/blogs-trending-36144487

Heineman, E. (2014). *Ghostbelly: A memoir*. New York, NY: Feminist Press at CUNY.

Ring, L. (2006). *Zenana*. Bloomington, IN: University of Indiana Press.

Wood, L. M., & Townsend, R. B. (n.d.). The many careers of historians: A study of job outcomes 2013. *A Report to the American Historical Association*. Retrieved from https://www.historians.org/jobs-and-professional-development/career-diversity-for-historians/career-diversity-resources/the-many-careers-of-history-phds

11

Mommy in the Field

• •

Raising Children and
Breeding Plants

KIMBERLY GARLAND CAMPBELL

I was in the back of a van driving from Hermosillo to Ciudad Obregón,
Mexico, to attend a wheat breeding conference at the International Maize
and Wheat Improvement Center. Suddenly, my cell phone rang, and my colleagues heard me say, "You put the hot dog in first and set it to twenty sec-
onds and then put the bun in for ten." It was my eight-year-old son. He was
asking for instructions on making an after-school snack. "Expensive hot dog,"
my colleague commented. My cell phone became my most effective parenting
tool because my kids could reach me, although they often didn't know where I
was in the world. I currently work for the United States Department of Agriculture Agricultural Research Service (USDA-ARS) as a wheat breeder and
geneticist. I've been a wheat breeder for twenty-five years, first in Wooster,
Ohio, as faculty at Ohio State University (OSU) and, for the past nineteen
years, with the USDA-ARS in Pullman, Washington. We live across the state
line in Moscow, Idaho.

My husband and I met as U.S. Peace Corps volunteers. We were based
in the Antigua West Indies working with sugar cane agronomy and pasture
development (me) and building-trade instruction (him). We came back to
the states, married, and then moved to North Carolina so I could go to graduate

school and he could continue his work as a subcontractor for interior trim carpentry. Our first daughter was born as I finished my master of science degree in soybean breeding at North Carolina State University (NCSU). My graduate advisor allowed me the needed time off, although much of it was without pay. We had little money and no health insurance. The general contractor that my husband worked for had declared bankruptcy, owing him thousands of dollars. Meanwhile, our dog had seven puppies, and we would sell puppies to afford diapers. We said we couldn't have another child until we paid off the first one, which took us three years.

Then we had insurance and another daughter. It was 1991, and I was midway through my PhD program in tobacco breeding, also at NCSU. Among the graduate students, my PhD advisor had a reputation as a curmudgeon. It was not easy to discern his mood. He had an unnerving habit of bowing his head and covering his face with his hand while listening. He would get carried away ruminating over new ideas and not speak to us. We students thought we had done something wrong, but he was actually just deep in thought. He had not advised many women because there weren't many female PhD students in traditional agriculture departments in the 1980s. He was quite the opposite of his reputation and was actually quite supportive and kind to those who met his expectations for excellence and creativity. He made a place for my daughter's bed in my office and for her baby swing in our greenhouse and taught me to love the plants that I worked with, to stay curious, and to always care deeply for research. I never doubted his support through graduate school and later in my career.

Our third daughter arrived three years later, when I was an assistant professor in wheat breeding in the Agronomy Department at OSU. It was easier to have children in graduate school than when dealing with the intense stress of a tenure-track faculty position. The expectations for success at OSU were unclear, and the department didn't have formal mentoring for untenured professors at that time. We were based at the Ohio Agricultural Research and Development Center in Wooster, Ohio. My husband operated a home remodeling and trim carpentry business. Wooster is a small Midwestern town with pretty parks and lots of kid-friendly activities, located midway between our friends in North Carolina and our extended families in Chicago and Philadelphia. Fortunately, many of our friends in Wooster were our age and had young children, so we could get together for fun and trade childcare in emergencies.

The emergencies happened. I suffered a cerebral aneurysm when my youngest daughter was two. Luckily, my husband recognized that I didn't just "have the flu," as I was insisting. Our family doctor was a skilled diagnostician, and we were close to the Cleveland Clinic. They patched me up, mostly intact. The small town where we lived took care of us. While I was in the hospital, the crossing guard stopped my daughters to re-braid their hair because their dad

FIGURE 11.1 Katie Rose Campbell, six months old, on her swing in the greenhouse at NCSU in Raleigh, North Carolina, 1991. The tobacco in the background is Kim Garland Campbell's PhD research project.

was untrained in that art and too worried about me. I recovered slowly; my second daughter wouldn't leave my side, so she had to repeat kindergarten. I started working again from home and then in the lab after three months. Two years later, our son was born, unplanned. (Actually, all of the children after the first one were unplanned). My son was premature because I had toxemia, and we weren't released from the hospital for several days. Again, two weeks after release, I went back to work, my son in his baby carrier, because the wheat seeds had to be packaged for planting.

Unfortunately, during recovery from the aneurysm, and for many years afterward, I would forget common words while speaking to people. Due to these lapses, teaching became quite difficult, and we realized that I needed a more research-focused position without a large teaching responsibility. Fortunately, I was asked to apply for my current job with the USDA-ARS based in Pullman, Washington, affiliated with Washington State University. As a federal research scientist, my primary mission is to conduct research to provide new knowledge, and since our research unit is colocated at a university, we are easily able to work with undergraduate and graduate students.

Plant breeding is largely a field-based endeavor. I work with winter wheat, so we plant in the fall, take notes in the spring and early summer, and harvest in July and August. During harvest, I typically work sixty-hour weeks, including several hours in the field and more at home analyzing data. My summers are spent walking along single-row "head rows," taking data in small yield plots, and traveling throughout Ohio and, now, the Pacific Northwest to view wheat in the field. When the kids were young, I would coordinate fieldwork with their father's schedule or hire babysitters for after-school hours. When there was not another option, I brought them to work as honorary assistants. My son rode in the child backpack when I walked head rows. Many of our fields had tall crops like rye planted around the wheat to isolate the pathogens we were working with. The kids would play hide-and-seek in the rye.

Although I worked long hours, I was often able to arrange time to attend soccer games, cross-country meets, track meets, and band concerts. When possible, I would combine these events with visits to wheat fields. But too often, I would reply, "I have to be out of town" or "I have a grant deadline" when asked to come to teacher conferences or attend a school event. Several major decisions, including whether to get a new cat and which college my daughter would attend were made after long phone conversations because I was out of town. My kids also confessed, via e-mail, to crashing the car, getting stiches, taking their dad in for emergency surgery, and setting the kitchen on fire while I was in another country. With my long hours, travel, and the need to focus on grant and paper deadlines, my husband made an early decision to be the "readily available" parent for our children. He carried diapers and LEGOs in his briefcase when the kids were young. He visited their schools, picked them up from events after school, and taught them how to behave at a nice restaurant for a steak dinner when I was out of town. Our children's elementary schools weren't accustomed to calling dad first when there was a problem. They often called me to pick up a sick child, and I would then call him from five hundred miles away to ask him to drop by the school. Old assumptions about working dads and available moms were, and still are, pervasive.

My office is anywhere that I am with my laptop and wireless internet. When the kids were young and on summer vacation in Moscow, I would take them to the pool on August afternoons. While they swam, I sat under an umbrella in my bathing suit with a large shaved ice and my laptop to analyze data and make selections in the plant-breeding program. Ice cream was a useful parenting tool. I would take the kids to the main campus in Columbus, Ohio, when I taught a class or to rural Ohio, Idaho, and Washington when I went to look at plots. They enjoyed the journey if not the actual event. My children have walked with me across so many wheat fields at all stages of the crop cycle. We've stirred up nesting birds, walked our dogs, and gotten soaked from the dew on the wheat leaves. I would take notes for a couple of hours, and then we would go to get ice cream. We know every ice cream shop around.

My other secret parenting tool was spray paint. Early in the breeding cycle, many of our selections are made visually using different colors of spray paint to designate "keeps" or discards. I'd hand my young daughters a can of spray paint and tell them to mark the "yellow wheat." At less than forty-five inches, they were the right height to see the spotted and yellow leaves and tell me, "Bad one." They did a great job because, face it, kids love spraying paint. I brought my eight-year-old son to work in the summer of 2008 and asked him to paint the handles of our sickles orange so we wouldn't lose them in the field. I should have realized that a whole can of spray paint is like Nirvana to an eight-year-old. He emptied the entire can onto twelve sickle handles. We had to open up all the windows in the seed house to avoid passing out. Even considering the potential health risk, those sickles have never been worn down to their original wood color.

After twenty-five years, I still love my job, at least most days. I'm out in the field all summer and in the greenhouse, laboratory, or computer lab in the winter. Plants are fascinating, with their ability to create large, green, self-sustaining structures and seeds out of light, water, nutrients, and air. Genetic diversity, viewed in a field full of wheat varieties, is beautiful, especially at the end of the day when the western sun is shining gold through the green leaves. I also get to be a bit of a badass and drive tractors, four-wheelers, and large trucks all around the Pacific Northwest. Like most scientists, publications are my main product; unlike most of my counterparts, I get to witness the tangible results of my work. Farmers grow the wheat varieties that are developed in my breeding program. They produce grain that becomes bread, noodles, cakes, and cookies. Recently, I was driving with my mother through eastern Washington and realized that I had developed the wheat in the fields on both sides of the road and across to the horizon.

I know of few other female scientists with four children, but family life is just as complicated regardless of the size of the family. The greatest challenge has been the unpredictability of children. They just don't adhere consistently to schedules. The stress of managing day care was tremendous, especially when the kids were sick. When I was in graduate school, we were only able to afford day care for part of the day, so I would go into the lab from 5 a.m. until 1 p.m. and then pick up my daughter and take her home. My husband worked as a finish carpenter from 9 a.m. until 6 p.m. I would return to the lab from 7 p.m. until 10 p.m. This worked well, I thought, even though I was sleep deprived. Suddenly, in January, our day care provider, who was the wife of an Egyptian engineering graduate student, said she could no longer provide day care. I took my daughter over to my office and placed her on her blanket on the floor. Then I laid down on the floor next to her, hugged her, and cried. We both slept for a while, and then I got back up, and we found another day care. I hoped that the stress of managing day care would be solved when I had a better paycheck, but that was not the case.

I was still trying to find a workable solution ten years later, when I moved with the kids to start my current job while my husband tied things up in Ohio. At that time, the older girls went to after-school care; my youngest daughter was in all-day preschool; and my son, who was a year old, was cared for in a neighbor's home. Our monthly childcare bill was greater than our rent. I would leave work promptly every day at 4:50 p.m. to make the mad dash to pick them up at four different locations before the 6 p.m. closing time. My son suffered from complications from asthma. In March, when he was one, he had a severe attack and had to spend a week in the hospital on oxygen. I called up the parents of my daughters' friends, whom I barely knew, and begged them each to take a girl for a week. When my son recovered, and I drove around town to reunite with my daughters, my youngest daughter asked to take up permanent residence at her friend's house.

My children have brought challenges and wonder into my life and career. I am a better scientist, mentor, and supervisor because of my children. They have taught me to have patience, to listen well, and to be flexible but have clear expectations. My current research group includes three technicians, six graduate students, and six part-time undergraduate students. My grown children give me advice. Two years ago, they all opined that I was too nice to my graduate students and that I needed to treat them as I had treated my children. I assume this means that I was meaner (or at least more strict) with my children. So I took my kid's advice and implemented new expectations in the lab group.

My group tends to have more women than men, and I have experienced most of what they are encountering in science and in work. My students who are mothers and fathers often bring their children to seminars, lab meetings, and work in the greenhouse. My third daughter was able to work for a colleague for three summers while she was in college. In our family, she has the best understanding of my daily activities, and we were able to work together frequently. When she quit to go back to school, she told me that she admired what I do but that she definitely didn't want to do it. She helped me understand that even though I consider my main occupation to be a wheat breeder, my vocation is to mentor all these young people. I'm not sure if they will become research scientists, but I do want them to use their talents and skills so that their career is a journey that they love. Over the years, I have received three awards from various organizations for mentoring, and each time, my students nominated me. I always thought of myself as somewhat scattered, driven, and antisocial, preferring wheat plants to humans, so these awards were a surprise. I have learned any skills that I have in mentoring from my children.

The kids are now grown—my oldest daughter owns her own business, my second is a jeweler, and my third daughter and son are in college. Time went by too fast, and I wish I had spent more time with them when they were children, but they tell me they are grateful because they were raised to think for themselves. My husband and I were the opposite of "helicopter parents." We were learning parenting in real time and not as fast as we needed to. Consequently, we encouraged our children to seek advice from other adults in their lives as well as from us. The kids are all self-confident, fiercely independent, and determined to work at what they love. We tried to convey to them my father's advice to find a vocation rather than just a job. He would say, "If you love what you do, you never work a day in your life." He was a salesman, not a scientist. My daughters are all in sales, and not one of the kids wants to go into science. My son, who is studying civil engineering, has a fondness for soil, and I like to think that he learned that from me. I know that they understand some of my total absorption in my work because they are doing the same thing with their endeavors. In addition, they are all creative and active and love working outdoors.

My husband and I have been married for thirty-four years. My oldest child was born when I was thirty and the last when I was forty-one. The friends of our children had parents who were much younger than my husband and I. He was often mistaken for my son's grandfather and is now retired from carpentry and is working in the elementary schools. He has a second career where he gets to support young people who need another adult in their lives. We made the early decision to support my career at the expense of his. While I know other women scientists who have made these same decisions, I also know many talented women who are working in job categories that are beneath their talents because the decisions were to emphasize the career of the other spouse. In field-based research, we are often based at remote locations without good opportunities for both spouses. My husband's work in carpentry allowed us to be more flexible, but we as a society haven't yet figured out how to integrate satisfying careers for both parents with child rearing. The traditional television-family structure where one spouse worked outside the home and the other was a full-time caregiver is no longer the norm, if it ever was. Too many workplace policies still support that structure to the exclusion of others. We who are biologists need to use our creativity to devise healthy environments that support the organisms working within.

I don't really have a separate work and home life. They are intertwined or, rather, a tangled mess. My work and my family bring me great joy. Currently, the whole family is living in Moscow, Idaho, and we are able to get together frequently for dinner and to watch sports, and we ski and hike together frequently. The challenges of trying to find some sense of harmony continue, however, as I spend more time with my mother since my father passed away two years ago. I'm trying to learn from the past and make the time to just be with her without distractions, but I have a long way to go to be successful. This past year has been difficult, as I have said yes to too many committees, meetings, and writing assignments. Last year, my youngest daughter called and said, "My sister wants to talk with you but I told her she has the wrong person." Later, my older daughter came in asking, "Mom, I need your advice on how to get a better 'work-life' balance." I laughed, "That balance doesn't exist." However, we do have to try to find equilibrium. Field-based science is a demanding occupation requiring lots of travel and activities that are time and seasonally driven. Raising children is the same; children become sick, they need to talk, they need care, and our parents and friends need care. The balancing act operates like a seesaw, swinging high in one direction with a sudden bump in the other when the ground intervenes. The bumps can be jarring, but the swings are thrilling. Our goal has to be to maintain the center with enough weight on both sides so that the ups and downs are fun and we can rejoice and see the view from the top with wonder.

Practical Tips

Some of my thoughts to support women and men with children:

- Institutions need to develop clear rubrics for performance expectations. Too many young scientists are working without clear expectations for their performance, and they are stressed out trying to meet unrealistic expectations that they have set for themselves. This is especially true for those on the tenure track. These rubrics should describe the level of accomplishment needed to meet expectations and to exceed expectations. There are many trade-offs involved when pursuing a career and raising a family. When the rubrics for success are explicit, people have the ability to decide that "meets expectations" is sufficient. For example, I was heavily involved in foreign development projects that required a great deal of international travel, but this travel wasn't necessary to my advancement as a research scientist. My son was having difficulties at school and was in counseling. I decided to cut back on the international work so I could be home for him. Now, ten years later, I am starting again to participate in foreign development projects.

- Incoming employees need mentoring. Supervisors and graduate advisors should be trained in mentoring skills, and peer mentoring should be encouraged. These mentoring groups should include both sexes and meet a least quarterly.
- Flexible scheduling should be implemented and encouraged. In the medical field, it is common to work four ten-hour days with three days off. In the oil industry, it is common to work two weeks on and two weeks off. Conferences, writing, and e-mail can all be performed via remote access. Even data collection can be more automated using sensors and drones. Although face-to-face meetings and observations of plant material are critical, alternatives enable more people to be involved.
- All parents should be supported as caregivers in the workplace, regardless of gender. Many of the changes that were implemented in workplaces for the benefit of mothers need to be recommended and supported for all parents. One of these is leave after the birth of a child.
- Sick leave should also apply to child illness. My medical leave covers family illness, but this is not universal.
- Extension on tenure and promotion clocks should be automatic when family medical leave is requested. Up to two additional years on the tenure or promotion clock should be encouraged for parents who welcome new children into their home or experience major illnesses. Many institutions have this policy in place, but the process to request it can be complicated. It should be automatic. Over a thirty-year career, another year or two to support family life is not too much to ask.
- The natural world is a curious place with much to study. We need to have fun. Scientists should take some time from meetings and grant writing to talk to K–12 teachers and offer to do a unit or host a field trip about their work. My lab group extracted DNA from fruit with local fifth graders. Seeing their enthusiasm when the DNA precipitated energized me for weeks. "Wow, it's like snot!" was a common remark.

We've hosted field trips at the greenhouse and mentored several high school students who are exploring genetics and plant science. One of them continued to work with us as an undergraduate and graduate student. She just successfully defended her PhD and is off to a prestigious postdoctoral position. She tells me that she wants to keep in touch because when the day finally comes and I retire, she will apply for my job. (So at least I've convinced one person to follow in my footsteps).

- The overemphasis on the value of professional life should be reduced. Too often I hear students and young scientists say they are concerned about having children because they may be perceived as being "not serious" about their science. This way of thinking is a false dichotomy between a scientific career and family that is largely based on an outdated model of family structure. Those of us in mentor positions have the power to make these changes, as did my own graduate advisors when they supported me. My predecessors rarely brought their children with them in their field endeavors. Due to my husband's and my schedules, my children were with me often in the field. We started to establish a new norm because we did not have a choice. Institutional change is needed, and it only happens when a critical mass of people creates the acceptance. We must broaden the idea of vocation to include our whole environment. The two current "hot" areas of plant science, soil health and sustainable crop production, emphasize that soils and crops are not distinct, but each contributes to the health of the other. Similarly, family and work are not distinct entities— rather, they are necessary components to an entire worthwhile and gratifying life.

Part V

What *Is* the Field, Anyway?

• •

Mothers Redefining
Field Methodologies

MÉLANIE-ANGELA NEUILLY

As the previous sections make clear, mothering in general—and from the field in particular—is not for the faint of heart. The deep, basic universality of the experience goes perhaps most strongly against neoliberal ideals of individualism and uniqueness, of agency and choice. As such, mothering blurs the lines of otherness and scrambles the pieces of long-established fieldwork traditions. Following a neoliberal ideology of agency and choice making and a positivist epistemology of objectivity, we have often tried to contain mothering, cap it, segment it, as to ensure it would not encroach on our methods. In a similar way, we have told stories of our fieldwork that attempted to portray these experiences as pure, perfect, and rigorous. But neither is possible nor desirable.

Instead, we argue here that it is not the researchers who need to fit their motherhood into the ideal fieldworker's mold, but rather it is the mold that needs updating. We need to reconceptualize fieldwork methodology. When we use feminist theory, we can question the validity of an unquestioning and unquestionable ideal field researcher archetype. Mother-researchers' perspectives are important on several levels: first, because researchers should be understood as complete humans with full lives, whether these lives include motherhood or not; second, because motherhood, like many other statuses, can be value added when it comes to negotiating entrée and building rapport in the field; and finally, because motherhood as an inescapable status and standpoint highlights the impossible mandate of the separation of public versus private spheres. This final point might be the most important, as it offers a starting point in questioning what the field actually is. As we offer to redefine not just who the fieldworkers are but also what the *field* in field research is, we truly open possibilities for change that go beyond academe. We propose that mothering from the field can be just the radical resistance tool we need to fight oppression and be the change.

Whether it is Sarah Kelman, Marylynn Steckley, or Deirdre Guthrie, our conversations in this chapter emphasize the pregnancy of the labor of mothering on the processes and outcomes of fieldwork. Kelman and Steckley offer a study in contrast between the presence and absence of children in the field and evidence that one's motherhood is an identifier that transcends the physical presence of offspring. Deirdre Guthrie's contribution proposes motherhood as an intricate canvass through which we can better understand our development as researchers. In conclusion, our conversations with Aprille Ericsson, her sister Dawn Ericsson Provine, and their children and nephew open an important debate only briefly touched upon in other chapters throughout this volume: that of the field as a place of learning not just for us researchers but also for our children. By flipping the gaze onto the field as an educational tool, they emphasize what many of us know but are either too busy to notice or too timid to state: when we bring our children to the field, we not only empower ourselves, embracing the complexity of our multiple roles; more importantly, we empower our children by providing them embodied and aspirational role models but also exposing them to realities they would otherwise not benefit from.

Additionally, when we look at the field from our children's perspective, we also widen the range of possibilities for what the field can actually encompass. Having operated under patriarchal definitions of field research, it is time we question not just who field researchers are but also what qualifies as the field. This is central as we push for methodologies that are more inclusive of self-reflective perspectives. Indeed, the lab can only be considered separate from the field if we agree with the epistemological premise that the positivist ceteris paribus is actually achievable. From our feminist perspective, we argue that all research environments should be given the same self-reflective treatment traditionally prescribed within the context of qualitative social scientific research. If we argue that motherhood, like any other standpoint, impacts research to the same extent that research impacts the researcher, then the context within which research is conducted should not be the sole focal point. Rather, the field becomes relative to one's discipline and/or area of expertise. In other words, it all becomes the field.

Section-Specific Takeaways

- The reality of mothering from the field is a complex and diverse one. In no way does one experience embody mothering from the field better than another. And motherhood impacts our field research whether or not our children are physically with us when we conduct it.
- Motherhood should be viewed as a lens through which we can better understand our research. It is not only a standpoint we should always reflect on; it is also a way of being in the world that should inspire our research.
- As we consider our research from our motherhood standpoint, we must keep in mind its fluidity, its culturally and context-specific meaning, and its deeply intersectional implications.
- Finally, we ought to remember that as we question the impact of motherhood on our research, we should never forget that our research also has an impact on children. When we bring children to the field, they too get to learn, grow, and become empowered.

12

Entangled Knowledge

• •

On the Labor of Mothering
and Anthropological Fieldwork

SARAH KELMAN

All PhD students in anthropology are told that they will need to conduct field-work in order to write their dissertations and earn their degrees. If their advisors are kind and attentive, as mine were, then students will be warned of the crushing homesickness, loneliness, and feelings of dislocation that will ensue. What they will likely not be told is that bringing a baby to the field will not mitigate these sensations—if anything, they will become heightened and even more debilitating. I learned these lessons for myself in 2014, when my husband and I, along with our six-month-old son and the family cat, packed up the contents of our small apartment into six suitcases and made the long plane journey from California to Malaysia. For a period of eighteen months, I conducted ethnographic field research in and around Kuala Lumpur, carrying out interviews, engaging in participant observation, and undertaking the immersive cultural experiences that accompany living and working in a place other than one's familiar environment. This approach comprises the anthropologist's toolkit of fieldwork—a constellation of practices, cultivated habits, and "deep hanging out" that can be thrilling, monotonous, and awkward all at once.

Part of the task of anthropological fieldwork is to forge meaningful connections with collaborators in our field sites (Holmes & Marcus, 2008) so that through these relationships there will emerge deep, experiential learning (Ingold, 2011) borne of the "thick description" (Geertz, 1973) of our observations—in short, brilliant, original, ethnographic knowledge. But cultivating these relationships and producing this ethnographic knowledge require an exhausting, never-quite-achievable vigilance to be finely attuned to the activities, words, emotions, and affects of others, all while trying to minimize the disorientation and loneliness of living in an unfamiliar place. For a new mother like me, with a nursing infant and no support network to speak of in my new city, this work seemed impossible. With an enormous amount of parenting help from my husband, and due to the privilege of being able to afford childcare in Malaysia, I gradually found myself with larger pockets of available time to begin to undertake the fieldwork activities that I had proposed to do—attending events, holding interviews, and otherwise hanging out with entrepreneurs and financiers in Malaysia's emergent start-up scene. Although I managed to perform some version of the work that anthropologists do during fieldwork, I worried constantly that it was incomplete and insufficient. I worried then (and still do now, to some extent) that my dissertation and any subsequent publications that emerged from my research should have an asterisk that says, "Sorry, I brought my baby with me. This was the best that I could do."

From the vantage point of a few years later, I can say that my experience of mothering an infant while doing fieldwork was not only difficult and full of second-guesses; it also affected the kinds of knowledge that I produced. This chapter explores ways in which the politics of that production are always situated in relationships and obligations and the labor of care for others and self. The fact that I mothered while doing fieldwork should be no shameful secret or an asterisk on my research project and dissertation. Mothering while doing fieldwork is one of the political stakes of what anthropology asks us to do—to make meaningful relationships and be reciprocally obliged and entangled with those around us as a means of generating knowledge about the world (Clifford, 1980). We anthropologists like to think of ourselves as more longitudinal in our studies and therefore highly committed in a set of ethical obligations that link us forever with the subjects and interlocutors of our research. We are not information extractors—we are meant to develop lifelong friendships and even kin relationships with the people that we study and from whom we generate anthropological knowledge. Yet if we are to remain tied to others in such a way for the sake of our professional work, what kind of space does that leave for the equally reciprocal and entangled work of mothering? How do these forms of production—of anthropological knowledge and human life—reflect the politics of the labor that made such products possible?

Through my own experiences of fieldwork and mothering, I learned several valuable lessons about what it takes to actually perform the work of knowledge production and why this work is so central for anthropologists and others whose job it is to generate insights about cultural landscapes outside of their familiar milieus. I offer these lessons learned not only as pieces of practical advice for others who intend to take the same path of fieldwork and mothering that I took but also as a reminder that knowledge is not made in a solitary endeavor. The products of our research are not simply the result of an interface between researcher and research subject—such insights are not "discovered"; they are produced, often within the context of relationships of power that situate researcher and subject unequally. Although mothering while doing fieldwork did much to alter those relationships between me and my interlocutors, in many ways drawing us together on more intimate terms, it also underscored the power dynamics that create a sense of distance between us. I find that I am best able to understand these relationships of intimacy and distance, which are critical to the process of producing anthropological knowledge, through similar sensibilities that I experienced through the work of mothering. While my scholarly aim is to tell a divergent story to the mythology of the singular fieldworker and mother, my personal goal is also simply to normalize some of the intense sensations and experiences of this labor of mothering from the field, with the ultimate purpose of examining what *other* forms of knowledge emerge from these stories, labors, and modalities. To explore these issues, I offer a closer look at my experience of trying to perform the concomitant labor of fieldwork as an anthropologist while also performing the work of mothering, highlighting the key lessons that I learned in the process.

The Politics of Production

Although my experiences of fieldwork and mothering coincided, anthropology often treats fieldwork—the research and data-gathering phase of our discipline's efforts at knowledge creation—as a separate enterprise from all other forms of labor. Anthropologists can certainly be mothers, although it is less common than one would think (Redden, 2008), and anthropologists must do fieldwork—but it is rare to consider anthropologists as field researchers and mothers concurrently. However, there is some overlap. Both motherhood and fieldwork never really end. Even though there are prescriptive "expiration dates," so to speak, for what kind of roles we play as field researchers and as mothers and how long those are supposed to last, the experiences end up haunting us for much longer. Consider the fact that gestation changes a mother's cellular structure—she exchanges DNA with her child, and the child in utero also exchanges DNA back with the mother in a process that makes them both chimeras (the scientific term is "fetal-maternal microchimerism"; see Chan et al., 2012; Martone, 2012; Sanders, 2015). Mother and child are recombinant. I cannot pretend that fieldwork is exactly like this, for I know that while *I* was much changed after returning from my eighteen months of research in Malaysia, life for my interlocutors back in Kuala Lumpur has continued, much the same, as if I had never been there. Still, part of me wonders if there is some sort of recombinant reverberation that continues, between fieldwork site and researcher, between mother and child, long past these eighteen months and forty weeks. It is this reverberation that interests me, for it foregrounds a set of relationships and reciprocal exchanges at the heart of what it means to be an anthropologist and a mother—utterly entangled with others, both in our ways of knowing and in how we teach others what we know.

Anthropology's knowledge projects, or its ways of producing information about "Other" people, are intimately tied up with projects of colonialism, imperialism, and domination. In these contexts, fieldwork is as much a way to gather the data necessary to produce knowledge as it is an exercise of power. Such exercises include census-taking, surveying land and water, counting crops and domestic animals, recording stories and myths, and observing performances and forms of production and exchange—all of which generate anthropological knowledge through the creation of "knowable" subjects. In the discipline's old days, from roughly the late nineteenth century to the mid-twentieth century, the gatherers and producers of this knowledge were almost always white, Euro–North American men, often in the employ of colonial or imperial governments that sought to know more about (and therefore exert power over) their subjects. This is not to say that women never accompanied men into the field, but their roles usually remained limited to "research assistants" or simply the wives who cooked, mended, and sometimes took photographs and film recordings. Notable exceptions include women who became anthropologists in their own right—Zora Neale Hurston, Hortense Powdermaker, Ruth Benedict, and Margaret Mead, for example—and some brilliant ethnographic accounts have been written by other women anthropologists who carried out their own research projects while accompanying their husbands to the field.[1] But by and large, women were afterthoughts when it came to doing research for their own benefit. Moreover, the idea that a woman could bring her child or children to the field, raise and look after them, *and also* do her own ethnographic research was mostly unthinkable.

In today's landscape, fieldwork looks quite different from its early and mid-century precedents. There has been nothing short of a revolution in anthropological thought and writing in the late twentieth century, which ushered in a sense of postmodern reflexivity to our work. These philosophical changes reconfigured how we write about the subjects and objects of our study and how we conduct the research to support this writing and knowledge production (Clifford & Marcus, 1986). Yet other conceits have remained unchanged. Fieldwork still involves, for instance, researchers "going away" to another location, preferably not one in which they currently reside or were raised, and "immersing" themselves in an unfamiliar cultural world. Fieldwork is also rarely carried out by anyone other than an individual anthropologist—unlike other social science disciplines, such as political science, economics, or even anthropological subfields such as archaeology, cultural anthropologists prefer to work alone. We rarely share data or field sites, and you will not easily come across anthropologists researching or writing in teams or pairs—except for the occasional pairing of domestic and intellectual labor found in a team of spouses or partners.[2] In addition to being a solitary venture, fieldwork is also thought of by anthropologists as a rather fetishized rite of passage. According to the unspoken conventions of our discipline, field research marks a distinction between the vetted researcher and the "armchair anthropologist" (Sera-Shriar, 2014)—a demarcation that matters a great deal for gaining the authority necessary for scholarship and knowledge production. But like many rites of passage, the "real" stories behind fieldwork—its difficulties, disappointments, and dead-ends—are often left out of the journal articles and books that result from this fieldwork. Why we hide these hard stories away is somewhat counterintuitive to me—it is not as if our readership is much larger than a circle of fellow anthropologists who have experienced the hardships of fieldwork for themselves. Nevertheless, fieldwork remains embedded with myths and silences and with an unwillingness to acknowledge just how difficult it is to undergo this rite of passage that marks us as anthropologists who have done "real" work in our discipline.

What I find significant about these myths and silences about the nature of fieldwork is that, in an uncanny way, they mirror the stories (and the parts left out of the stories) about mothering. The origins of these stories seem divergent at first—the first emerges from an image of the Cartesian, Enlightenment-era rational thinker (scientist, researcher, knowledge-producer), while the second is a more recent product of neoliberal ideology met with body politics, the woman who found herself with a baby because she "chose" her fate.[3] But if you dig back far enough, these narratives form a conjoined stream of thought—one that puts people in charge of their own destinies and leaves them on the hook for what are seen as their own shortcomings. Individualism entreats us to pull ourselves up by our own bootstraps because, as discrete units of one, we can and must do it alone. I would like to write against individualism.[4] This approach is a deeply self-centered way of thinking about how life is generated and sustained and about to whom we are indebted in our ability to be alive. But how do we tell a different story about what it takes to produce knowledge and grow children? If this is not a story of makers, inventors, and cloistered geniuses, then what kind of story is this? For me, it starts with a reframing of both knowledge production and mothering as forms of labor that are deeply political, personal, affective, and enmeshed in the lives of those who sustain me and my work as a mother and as a researcher.

The Labor of Fieldwork and Mothering

In addition to the myths, silences, and inherited assumptions about field-work that we learn throughout the course of graduate school, what we rarely get to see about fieldwork is that it is also *work*. My own research activities in Malaysia required me to show up to places, every day, ready to talk and engage with people—to take notes, snap pictures and videos, and process informa-tion and think. The labor of fieldwork is endless, and to gain even a few brief conversations required an enormous amount of supporting work—none of which I could really do with my child around. It is difficult for me to explain why, except when I am able to frame this work *as* work. We do not ask sur-geons, or welders, or garment finishers to work with their young children and babies in tow. Sometimes it is a necessary if temporary measure, especially in cases of emergency or illness, but most workers know how distracting it can be to try to carry out the duties of their labor while also minding their own children—it is essentially like trying to do two very different jobs at once. As a field researcher, I often found myself unable to perform this simultaneous labor of fieldwork and mothering, especially because my advisors had warned me that fieldwork alone would be an immersive, all-encompassing experience that was critical for producing anthropological scholarship and left little room for distraction.

Fieldwork therefore required me to arrange for sufficient childcare to allow me to leave home for several hours a day to carry out research activities. I inter-viewed babysitters, who were mostly Filipina immigrants looking for higher-wage work in nearby Malaysia, and was lucky enough to find a warm, brilliant woman in her late forties who had worked in Jordan for decades as a nanny, sending remittances back home to her large family in the Philippines. She came to our house every morning at eight, filling my son's day with cheerful singing and leisurely walks around our apartment building's compound. As he got older, he accompanied her on daily calls to visit other Filipina nannies and babysitters in the apartment complex who would share gossip and sweets as the children played or napped. Eventually, she started taking him to a nearby nursery school in the mornings, and between her efforts and those of the "aun-ties" at school, my son was walking, talking, and learning to play and get along with other children. They did much more for him than I ever could have done caring for him alone.

Yet on the first day that I left my son at home with his new babysitter, I cried for the entire walk from my apartment to the nearby commuter rail sta-tion. These emotions were a confusing mixture of relief and guilt, sorrow and happiness. However, after a few short hours of being away from home, these feelings gave way to an unabashed sense of buoyancy that I had not felt since giving birth to my son. To be alone—*completely* alone, without my child in arms or in his nearby stroller—was a rarity for me during the first year of his life. I finally found myself able to do the work of fieldwork, if only for a few hours a day, and as my advisors had warned me, this work was indeed difficult. But I was thrilled to be doing it, for it was the only time in my day when I was not fully immersed in my "other" work of mothering. Fieldwork was why we had moved our family to Malaysia in the first place. It was part of my identity as an anthropologist, and it was work that I loved. I was invigorated by meeting new people, traveling through unknown routes around a fascinating city, and sharing experiences with interlocutors who taught me about their aspirations and desires.

I have not often come across stories, at least in public circulation in the United States, from mothers who look forward to going to work. The dominant discourse on motherhood is a narrative about how regretful new mothers are that they cannot stay home longer with their children or that they are unable to bring their children to work with them. While I acknowledge that these narratives have arisen partly because of the United States' dismal parental leave policy and the stigma attached to actually using that leave for infant care,[5] I remain dubious of this discourse because it forecloses the possibility of mothers desiring and identifying with other kinds of work that they do. It assumes that all work outside of the home and away from children is alienating, and it also assumes that work done *in* the home and *with* our children—that is, the work of mothering—is *not* alienating. Nothing could be further from the truth, at least for me, although it is a difficult thing to admit. I find great comfort in the words of anthropologist Sarah Bakker Kellogg, who wrote about her experience of motherhood and ripped open the black box to announce that, after childbirth, "everyone falls silently apart" (2016, p. 8). Few are brave enough to argue, like Kellogg does, that a new mother's mental health, sense of self-worth, and sheer quality of life often improve when she is able to hand over some of the childcare duties to partners, day care, and babysitters.[6] However challenging the work of fieldwork was, it was also a place of solace for me—a place where I could, just for a few hours, be apart from my child because it was what I desired.

If we accept the premise that fieldwork is actual work, which necessitates a break from parenting in order to remain receptive to the many forms of social engagement that fieldwork requires, then we must also recognize that mothering is also work. This work is a distinctive form of labor that social analysts call "emotional labor" (Hochschild, 2003) or more recently, "affective labor" (Hardt, 1999; Muehlebach, 2011; Negri, 1999), which is often performed by people who are gendered as women or femme and involves the care of others' well-being and their emotional and physical health. One of affective labor's most distinguishing features is that it is ubiquitous and necessary for the survival of others, yet it rarely gets remarked on, let alone paid for. Affective labor is in the air that we breathe—it makes all other forms of labor possible, for it regenerates households and keeps children alive while adults earn wages, and it includes the unseen work of worrying, thinking, and planning. The challenges of affective labor become even more magnified when put in the context of anthropological fieldwork, which exerts its own sort of affective demands, such as managing the intimacies and distances that fieldwork engenders. In effect, neither the work of mothering nor the work of fieldwork can be deferred, and yet each proves to be nearly impossible to perform simultaneously with the other. This is not simply a matter of the researcher-mother's skill or dedication. Instead, the impossibilities are deeply rooted at the heart of what these all-encompassing forms of labor require of those who perform them.

Mothering practices rub up against the other relationships in our lives, but these frictions also produce deeply politicized and hierarchized understandings of what counts as work and what should be prioritized as such, considering that the demands of these multiple obligations are endless. Furthermore, mothering's constant necessities to perform affective labor means that, even when we anthropologists are expected by all norms and conceits to be fully immersed and attuned in our fieldwork, mothering while doing fieldwork means that you are *never really fully doing fieldwork without also doing mothering.* You cannot separate the two.

As Amber E. Kinser puts it in *Feminist Mothering*, mothering is a form of "relational consciousness" in which the multiplicity of selves, obligations,

FIGURE 12.1 Me and my child in Kuala Lumpur, Malaysia, 2014

and relationships results in blurred boundaries between mothering and other forms of work (2008). As a mother, the work of field research was thus always somehow diluted—if not derailed—by the work of mothering. For an anthropologist, this is bad news because the work of field research is supposed to be all-encompassing and immersive. So how did I do two jobs that require constant vigilance, neither of which could be abandoned over the other? The answer is that I did both rather sloppily, which is to say that I did them both how they normally get done. Just as knowledge is always partial—incomplete and biased[7]—so is the work of fieldwork and mothering.

Of Distance and Radical Difference

Although I have now come to terms with the fact that I eschewed the work of mothering during the hours that I chose to do fieldwork, meaning that I did not bring my son with me to the vast majority of the interviews, observations, and events that I attended for research, other problems arose from this arrangement. Many of my interlocutors were pious Muslim women who saw themselves as good Muslims *because* of their roles as primary caretakers for children and other family members, and some chided me for not bringing him along to our meetings. When I would reveal that I too was a mother, they looked confused. "Where is your child?" they would ask, peering around to see if he had followed me into their homes, where I often conducted interviews. "He's home with his babysitter," I would say. More often than not, this was met with frowns. As a friend explained to me, leaving very young children with paid childcare workers was not something that other women from her community of Malay Muslims[8] often did, even if they could afford it. Outsourcing childcare seemed counter to an unspoken ethos, a mixture of religious and cultural norms that naturalized the wage-earning roles of men while also celebrating the strength of women who ran the domestic domain.[9] Even though they may not have intended it as such, my Malay interlocutors' explanations of why they did not employ childcare workers often felt like implicit critiques of my decision to do so.

Although I often felt embarrassed that the women I spent time with were disappointed by my child's absence in our meetings, their feelings were understandable. Seeing my child helped them see me as less of a complete stranger and more of a person with a child and family, just like them, despite the differences of nationality, ethnicity, religion, class, and generation that remained between us. As time went on, I began to understand that their ability to see me this way was an issue of safety for my interlocutors. Fieldwork requires an enormous amount of trust on the part of the people with whom we work, for we ask them to let us in on the intimate details and contours of their lives. Every request for an interview or meeting with an interlocutor was also a request for them to open up their homes, workplaces, and places of worship, community, and learning to me. Even if I only just hovered awkwardly around the edges of people's lives while doing fieldwork,[10] I was always asking others to make themselves vulnerable. Declining to bring my child to these interactions often felt like I was declining to reciprocate this vulnerability. Thus the absence of my child, and the presence of differences of opinion on the matter, remained a wedge between me and my interlocutors, smoothed over with much effort and often left unacknowledged.

This wedge between researcher and interlocutors is no surprise. After all, many forms of unequal privilege and power—economic, social, and political, among others—had to be in operation in order to even bring me to Malaysia[11] and put me in a position to be able to afford childcare. Nevertheless, it is a hard thing to feel. As an anthropologist doing fieldwork far from home, among a community comprising people that I did not know very well, at least at first, I wanted desperately to find some sense of like-mindedness with my interlocutors. Coming across moments of disagreement, particularly when I realized how much I did not identify with my interlocutors, felt discouraging and demoralizing. This sense of disappointment that I felt was, in large part, due to another strong anthropological pretext in which researchers doing fieldwork are supposed to avoid being at odds with them, lest we view them as "repugnant cultural others" (Harding, 1991). In fact, affinity and connection, not distance and disconnect, is really what fieldwork is about for many of us (Abu-Lughod, 1995). Yet I sometimes found myself in outright disagreement with my friends and interlocutors in the field. We were opposed on a range of issues, from child-rearing and medical philosophies to foreign policy, racism, and feminism. Distressingly, we disagreed about *me* and my decisions to forego the primary responsibilities of childcare in favor of doing fieldwork. Their critiques and comments about my child's absence in our meetings—which, to be fair, they may not have seen as real work—stuck to me like tiny needles, wilting my already thin confidence that doing fieldwork in Malaysia with my family was the right thing to do.

Today, I can come to terms with these distances because I understand more about what they mean for fieldwork and anthropology at large. This meaning is rooted in some of the significant changes that the discipline of anthropology and its related fields have undergone in recent years, starting with the emergence of "radical difference" as an analytical and methodological approach to our knowledge projects. In the "ontological turn,"[12] for instance, where primarily Western-educated anthropologists strive to exist alongside with—but not overtake or speak on behalf of—the non-Western, often indigenous peoples who are our interlocutors, the recognition of a difference between "their" and "our" way of thinking is crucial. Anthropologists who embrace this ontological turn are supposed to respect the views and ways of our interlocutors, recognizing that this respect requires stifling the urge to rationalize, justify, or speak for the "Others" that we study—a move that often results in the reinforcement of separations between "us"/ self and "them"/Other. Some anthropologists have critiqued this ontological approach, though, and argue that radical difference in the guise of respectful engagement only reifies the "normal self" and exoticizes the "different Other," who is ultimately the bearer of difference. If anthropology has taught me anything, it is that there is no ethics in an attempt to merge my experiences with those of my interlocutors. Recognizing difference is necessary to producing anthropological knowledge, and while it still allows for room to commonality and affinity, it does not hinge on a complete dissolution of the membranes between anthropologist-self and interlocutor-Other.

Producing Dividual Knowledge

Through (but also despite) the work of mothering, I was fortunate enough to forge close relationships with a number of interlocutors during fieldwork, and while these relationships remained entangled in both distance and intimacy, they allowed me to generate a culturally situated social analysis of life within Muslim communities of entrepreneurs in Malaysia. This analysis, and the insights on which it is based, are at the heart of what anthropologists consider to be the products of our labor doing research in the field—scholarly objects such as articles, books, and chapters that are collectively gathered under the umbrella of "knowledge." But if we accept the premise that the work required to produce such knowledge is the deeply politicized labor of fieldwork and mother-work, and the conditions of this production are underscored by social dynamics such as intimacy and distance, then what kind of knowledge is being produced? What does this knowledge production say about us, the producers?

It is critical to explore this issue of knowledge production in conjunction with acknowledging the concomitant work of mothering and fieldwork because the knowledge-making process, and the role that these forms of work play in it, comprise a particular narrative that I think is imperative to dispel. This narrative is that the only producers of knowledge are the free-floating "individual selves" of our fieldwork mythologies—the solitary, monastic researchers who write and think alone. But the counternarrative that I would like to propose is that those doing fieldwork, like those doing mothering, are always selves entangled in relations with others. If not through the very definition of the anthropologist's ethnographic labor, which nearly *requires* that we have relationships and entanglements with the people and places that we study, then this entanglement emerges at least through the acknowledgment that relationality is exactly what it means to be alive. If I take Sarah Bakker Kellogg's essay seriously, which I do, then the conclusion that I must draw from her work is that entanglement is the human condition. We are made up of our relationships, and there is no individual self—only, as Kellogg reminds us, the "dividual" self (Strathern, 1988). But what kind of knowledge does this dividual, entangled self produce? In my case, it is a knowledge *that is also dividual and entangled*. Entanglement, even when it fosters distance and underscores difference, is the basis for webs of connection to be forged. These connections are not outside of the "producer of knowledge"—they make up the producer as a person.

The knowledge resulting from these forms of labor—affective, endless, and unyielding—is not made up of what we know but *who we are in relations with*: our partners, our children, our caregivers, and kinfolk. In other words, this knowledge is a piece of collective labor produced, in part, by those who we depend on and who depend on us, on our "ordinary devotion" (Kellogg, 2016, p. 22). Our selves, these dividual repositories of relations and connections, are always beholden to others. The knowledge that we produce is therefore bound to those who have made it possible. To write against the individual is therefore to acknowledge and honor the notion that the labor of fieldwork and of mothering is collective, relational, and affective. This does not mean that the knowledge that results from such labor is insufficiently scientific or empirical—if anything, my hope is that this acknowledgment helps normalize the entangled, situated ways of knowing the world and our experiences in it. I am sometimes tempted to think of my own efforts at mothering and fieldwork as somehow incomplete or insufficient, when guilt, doubt, and my attachment to the mythologies of individualism cast a thick cloud over my sense of self-worth. But then there are moments of flashing clarity, when the care and generosity of others who have made my own mother-work and fieldwork possible comes into view, and the collective force of that human connection becomes a powerful energy, crackling with vivacity. This power—dividual, entangled, formidable—becomes the true product of our labor as mothers, field researchers, and anthropologists. It is with this power that the work of fieldwork and mothering are done.

Conclusions: The Things We Take Away

What does the conclusion of fieldwork bring for those who engage in this entangled labor of mothering in the field? For many of us, the end products of fieldwork take the form of everything from key "takeaways" and insights to copious amounts of field notes. Through the process of writing, editing, and rewriting, these products eventually transform into conference papers, job talks, and peer-reviewed publications—the stock-in-trade of scholars and professors. The outcomes, products, and end results of our fieldwork are incredibly valuable and have the potential to make or break a career. But when we leave the field, we also take with us precious knowledge, other people's stories, objects of art and beauty, images and photographs, and shared experiences with our interlocutors.[13] Moreover, we also engage in considerable production. We generate wisdom, and hopefully it is not "taken" but deposited with care and respect. Thus instead of something to be taken away, I offer these pieces of lovingly and collectively produced wisdom from my time in the field specifically to other graduate students embarking on fieldwork while mothering:

- Do not be afraid to turn down opportunities if they prove to be too logistically difficult to take up. Try not to regret the opportunities that you did not (or were not able to) take. You cannot do all of the things all of the time.
- On the other hand, do not be afraid to ask for help in order to take opportunities that seem to be logistically difficult. All things are difficult with a baby, so just because something is not easy to do does not mean that you are automatically discounted from doing it.
- If you can, try to share the emotional labor of parenting and fieldwork with others who can listen and pitch in to help. Whether this person is a partner who is there with you, or a therapist who can listen to your worries, or an interlocutor, or a family member, just try not to shoulder this work alone.
- Representatives of your institution, including your dissertation committee members and advisor, may not understand how best to support you. Universities are often structurally biased against student parents, and you may need to assert your needs and rights in order to get the resources you need to carry out fieldwork. Whenever possible, try to recruit allies among professors and administrators who can help with these efforts.
- Try not to compare yourself to anyone else—this includes people in your cohort who do not have children, or those who did fieldwork in different places than you did, or others who produced different knowledge than you did. Each scholar has his or her own journey, and each will finish producing the fruits of his or her academic labor in their own time. Also, try not to compare yourself to mothers back home. They are not going through what you are going through.
- Finally, know that you are enough—enough of a mother and scholar—and the products of your labor are enough too.

Notes

1 Rosemary Firth's monograph *Housekeeping among Malay Peasants* (1966/1943) is one such example, and her focus on the domestic (read: feminine) economy of rural

Malay households mirrors a similar division of labor between her and her anthropologist husband, Raymond Firth, whose published work from that time period focuses on male fishermen.

2   Of course, there are always exceptions, such as Hardt and Negri (2000; 2004; 2009), J. K. Gibson-Graham (2006), Roelvink, St. Martin, and Gibson-Graham (2015), and Anna Tsing (2015), among others, who count themselves part of a team of researchers exploring anthropological and social questions.

3   I am indebted here—and throughout this chapter—to the insights of anthropologist and friend Sarah Bakker Kellogg, who made me think about this dualism between the mind of the researcher and the body of the mother in her essay "Anthropology and the Argonauts" (2016).

4   I am not the first to do so, and the inspiration and intellectual lineage for this argument stretch back through feminist anthropological literature on gender, kinship, and labor whose authors write that there is no such thing as a truly discrete, individual person who needs no one else to survive (see Ortner, 1984; Strathern, 1987; Yanagisako & Collier, 1987).

5   This stigma is particularly associated with paternal leave—see examples from journalists Miller (2014) and Weber (2013), among others.

6   Let us not forget that this is an incredible privilege to exercise—many women and families cannot afford safe, comprehensive childcare.

7   My thanks are to Don Brenneis for emphasizing this concept in my first year of graduate school.

8   Malays comprise the 60 percent ethno-religious majority in Malaysia. They constitute a growing middle class—although historically as a community, Malays have undergone economic struggle.

9   It is much less common for Malaysian women to put their children in childcare to return to work. Many women simply do not work until their children are of an age to be in primary school, and the idea of placing infants and toddlers in childcare (either for the sake of returning to work or for other reasons) is not one that is fully embraced by many, although the Malaysian workforce suffers from a noticeable absence of childbearing-age women (Boo, 2014; Yeoh, 2014).

10 I am beholden to this image rendered in a most lovely way by Kirin Narayan (1995).

11 Consider, for example, the visa situation. United States passport holders can stay in Malaysia for up to ninety days on a tourist visa that is easy to obtain and renew on arrival, while Malaysians who wish to visit the United States must go through extensive in-person interview processes at the U.S. embassy in Malaysia, applying for their tourist visas well in advance and facing the likely prospect of rejection.

12 Again, I am indebted to Sarah Bakker Kellogg's essay and her clear explanations of the shift toward ontology as an analytic approach in the field of anthropology.

13 Hopefully this is done with the permission and consent of participants, according to convention and the ethical mores of fieldwork concretized in the American Anthropological Association's "Principles of Professional Responsibility" (2012).

References

AAA Web Admin. (2012, November 1). Principles of professional responsibility. Retrieved from http://ethics.americananthro.org/category/statement

Abu-Lughod, L. (1995). A tale of two pregnancies. In R. Behar & D. A. Gordon (Eds.), *Women writing culture* (pp. 339–350). Berkeley, CA: University of California Press.

Boo, S. (2014, July 1). Malaysia's missing women workers. *Malay Mail Online*. Retrieved from http://www.themalaymailonline.com/malaysia/article/malaysias-missing-women-workers

Chan, W. F. N., Gurnot, C., Montine, T. J., Sonnen, J. A., Guthrie, K. A., & Nelson, J. L. (2012). Male microchimerism in the female human brain. *PLoS One, 7*(9), e45592. https://doi.org/10.1371/journal.pone.0045592

Clifford, J. (1980). Fieldwork, reciprocity, and the making of ethnographic texts: The example of Maurice Leenhardt. *Man (new series), 15*(3), 518–532.

Firth, R. (1966). *Housekeeping among Malay peasants*. London, UK: Athlone Press. (Original work published 1943)

Geertz, C. (1973). *The interpretation of cultures: Selected essays*. New York, NY: Basic Books.

Gibson-Graham, J. K. (2006). *The end of capitalism (as we knew it): A feminist critique of political economy*. Minneapolis, MN: University of Minnesota Press. (Original work published 1996)

Harding, S. (1991). Representing fundamentalism: The problem of the repugnant cultural other. *Social Research, 58*(2), 373–393.

Hardt, M. (1999). Affective labor. *Boundary 2, 26*(2), 89–100.

Hardt, M., & Negri, A. (2000). *Empire*. Cambridge, MA: Harvard University Press.

Hardt, M., & Negri, A. (2004). *Multitude: War and democracy in the age of empire*. New York, NY: Penguin Press.

Hardt, M., & Negri, A. (2009). *Commonwealth*. Cambridge, MA: Belknap Press of Harvard University Press.

Hochschild, Arlie. (2003). *The managed heart*. Berkeley, CA: University of California Press. (Original work published 1983)

Holmes, D. R., & Marcus, G. E. (2008). Collaboration today and the re-imagination of the classic scene of fieldwork encounter. *Collaborative Anthropologies, 1*, 81–101.

Ingold, T. (2011). *Being alive: Essays on movement, knowledge, and description*. Hoboken, NJ: Taylor & Francis.

Kellogg, S. B. (2016, April 22). Anthropology and the Argonauts. *Medium.com*. Retrieved from https://medium.com/@sbakkerkellogg/anthropology-and-the-argonauts-d6b02c199795#.lgdn33ijo

Kinser, A. E. (2008). Relational consciousness. In A. O'Reilly (Ed.), *Feminist mothering* (pp. 123–143). Albany, NY: State University of New York Press.

Martone, R. (2012, December 4). Scientists discover children's cells living in mother's brains. *Scientific American*. Retrieved from http://www.scientificamerican.com/article/scientists-discover-childrens-cells-living-in-mothers-brain

Muehlebach, A. (2011). On affective labor in post-Fordist Italy. *Cultural Anthropology, 26*(1), 59–82.

Miller, C. C. (2014, November 7). Paternity leave: The rewards and the remaining stigma. *The New York Times*. Retrieved from http://www.nytimes.com/2014/11/09/upshot/paternity-leave-the-rewards-and-the-remaining-stigma.html?_r=0

Narayan, K. (1995). Participant observation. In R. Behar & D. A. Gordon (Eds.), *Women writing culture* (pp. 33–49). Berkeley, CA: University of California Press.

Negri, A. (1999). Value and affect. *boundary 2, 26*(2), 77–88.

Ortner, S. B. (1984). Theory in anthropology since the sixties. *Comparative Studies in Society and History, 26*(1), 126–166.

Redden, E. (2008, November 25). Fieldwork with three children. *Inside Higher Ed*. Retrieved from https://www.insidehighered.com/news/2008/11/25/anthro

Roelvink, G., St. Martin, K., & Gibson-Graham, J. K. (2015). *Making other worlds possible: Performing diverse economies*. Minneapolis, MN: University of Minnesota Press.

Sanders, L. (2015, May 10). Children's cells live on in mothers. *Science News*. Retrieved from https://www.sciencenews.org/blog/growth-curve/children%E2%80%99s-cells-live -mothers

Sera-Shriar, E. (2014). What is armchair anthropology? Observational practices in 19th-century British human sciences. *History of the Human Sciences, 27*(2), 26–40.

Strathern, M. (Ed.). (1987). *Dealing with inequality: Analysing gender relations in Melanesia and beyond*. Cambridge, UK: Cambridge University Press.

Strathern, M. (1988). *The gender of the gift: Problems with women and problems with society in Melanesia*. Berkeley, CA: University of California Press.

Tsing, A. (2015). *Mushroom at the end of the world: On the possibility of life in capitalist ruins*. Princeton, NJ: Princeton University Press.

Weber, L. (2013, June 12). Why dads don't take paternity leave. *The Wall Street Journal*. Retrieved from http://www.wsj.com/articles/SB10001424127887324049504578541633708283670

Yanagisako, S., & Collier, J. (1987). Toward a unified analysis of gender and kinship. In J. Collier & S. Yanagisako (Eds.), *Gender and kinship* (pp. 14–52). Stanford, CA: Stanford University Press.

Yeoh, T. (2014, January 15). Women in the workforce. *The Sun Daily*. Retrieved from http://www.thesundaily.my/node/237830

13

"Manman, Poukisa Y'ap Rele M Blan?" (Mama, Why Are They Calling Me a White?)

•••••••••••••••••••••

Research and Mothering in Haiti

MARYLYNN STECKLEY

Introduction

On a spring day in 2013, I was pregnant, sweating, and biking my son, Jwa, home from school on a rocky dirt path in the town of Desarmes in rural Haiti. We were a sight in any context, but there were a few particulars that made us odd here. It was unusual to be *gwo vant* (big bellied / pregnant) and biking in Desarmes (admittedly more so to own a bike with a child seat), but mostly we were hypervisible because we were *blan* (white people / foreigners). My son, perched in the child seat, was chatting away about his morning at school as I struggled around the potholes and trenches in the road. When middle schoolers let out in front of us, our pace slowed to a crawl. The fuss began straight away. Gathering around, the group gaped at my son's curly blonde hair, reached out to feel the smoothness of his small, bare arms, and yelled out excitedly to get our attention—"Blan!"

By now, we were accustomed to this kind of attention. We had been living as the only *blan* in Desarmes for more than a year. But there was something about the intensity of this commotion that started to feel a bit threatening. Maybe it was the tone and persistence of the shouts or the sheer number of students surrounding my son that day. Maybe it was the heat. The attention set Jwa off. He was crying and angry. "Alé! [Go away!]," he yelled. "Pa touché m! [Don't touch me!]." I sensed his panic.

As an ethnographic researcher in rural Haiti, my goal was to explore how persistent race-based social hierarchies and ideas of inferiority among the peasantry—legacies of colonial slavery—influenced food choices and, in particular, the tendency to valorize imported foods over locally produced ones. My chief objective as a researcher was to establish relationships of trust that would permit me to explore how racialized ideologies manifest in local cultural patterns and practices in ways that undermine healthy food systems and sustainable peasant livelihoods. But on a personal level, I also wanted to convince people that I was more than *blan*. I wanted friendship. This was a tall order in a country where race-based social hierarchies have persisted for more than two hundred years. My skin color carried enormous historical baggage, but I wanted to figure out ways to minimize the significance of my skin. I had a personal ambition to bridge racial divides in whatever small ways I could, and one of Marx's greatest axioms resonated deeply with me: "Why should we be content to understand the world instead of trying to change it?" In practice, this meant that I did my best to chat in the marketplace and in the fields, to engage in conversation when people called me *blan*, to adopt the local style of dress and diet. My goals and identity as a researcher meant that I wanted to uphold a certain code of conduct: openness, friendliness, patience.

But on that hot afternoon on our bike, when my son was crying, when I saw his vulnerability, my researcher identity took a back seat and my mother-self ruled. Sweating and (admittedly) frantic, my solidarity turned toward my son. I yelled for people to back off, I ignored people who were asking innocent questions, and I pushed my way through the crowd in an effort to gain momentum on my bike. Though some of the teens were running behind us, I got a lead down the dusty road and took a breath, turning around to check on my crying toddler. He looked up at me with big, blue, teary eyes and a head full of curly blond ringlets. "Manman," he said, "Poukisa y'ap rele m blan? [Mama, why are they calling me a white?]"

In this chapter, I investigate the challenges and possibilities for mother-researchers in cross-cultural field research contexts, focusing on three interrelated research questions:

- How do mothering and research impact one another?
- What happens when mothering and research objectives conflict?

- How can mother-researchers negotiate identity to enhance research *and* mothering?

To explore these questions, I draw from more than five years of work, research, and mothering experience in Haiti, including more than two years in Port-au-Prince, where I worked as a food policy analyst from February 2007 to July 2009, and nearly three years of ethnographic experience in Desarmes, from November 2010 to July 2013, where I lived with my family while I conducted my doctoral field research. My children were born during these periods: my son, Jwasiys, at a birthing clinic in Port-au-Prince, and my daughter, Solette, at a rural hospital near Desarmes. I rely on both my personal notebooks, which detail daily activities of our family, personal reflections, and lines and comments from my children and their friends, as well as my research field notes, which comprise observations of and comments from community members related to gender roles and race relations in Desarmes.

As a first step, I explore the fluidity of the mother-researcher identity and argue that the mother and researcher positions are flexible social locations, constantly shifting and always complicated by a host of other unstable signifiers including "race," class, and place. This discussion takes the "mother" as the analytical focal point to contribute to a growing body of literature that challenges the conceptualization of field researchers as either "insiders" or "outsiders" (Merriam, Johnson-Bailey, Lee, Ntseane, & Muhamad, 2010; Corbin & Buckle, 2009). Next, I draw from my own experience, to explore the impact of mothering on research, paying specific attention to how the belonging or exclusion of the mother-researcher in the field is bound up both in how research community members imagine the researcher and also in how researcher self-identity impacts integration, highlighting that children can be an important part of integration and relationship building in field research. In the third section, I offer my family's challenges related to childcare, health, and identity in the field as a way to encourage discussion about the impact of research decisions on mothering and children. One of my core objectives of this section is to name some challenges for mother-researchers who are committed to field research in sites of scarcity and to encourage more openness about the realities of academic mothers in development studies in particular. Finally, I explore possibilities for negotiating the mother-researcher position in the field in order to enhance both research and mothering goals. It is my hope that by articulating both the tough *and* rewarding aspects of mothering "in the field" and sharing some of my own strategies for negotiating my identity, I might contribute to efforts to creatively imagine possibilities for mother- and child-friendly research opportunities in cross-cultural research contexts.

The Flexible Identity of the Mother-Researcher: Race, Class, Place, and Self-Perception

Around the world, the position of "mother" carries incredible power, responsibility, and meaning (Moore, 1996). In fact, the self-definition as "mother" is stronger and more gripping than many other aspects of identity, including marital status and occupation (Macdonald, 2009). And yet the construction of the mother identity—including the values, expectations, and ideals associated with motherhood—is fluid and changing. What it means to be a mother is influenced by place, cultural context, work status, sexuality, and nationality, among many other things. The "mother" identity is a signifier that shifts. Even within one's self-perception, it is flexible (Johnston & Swanson, 2007). Likewise, the researcher identity is fluid and interpreted differently depending on context and place (Thomson & Gunter, 2010). Cross-cultural field researchers in particular deal with conflicting and varying perceptions of his or her researcher identity, which are inevitably tied up in uneven power relations. In particular, the perceived race, gender, sexuality, nationality, and guest or intruder status of the researcher may amplify or limit access to information or resources. The position of mother-researcher, then, is in many ways akin to other identity positions: it is fluid.

Shifting Identities in the Field

I first went to Haiti in 2007, and from my first steps on the streets of Port-au-Prince, I knew experientially that skin color mattered. Over time, I came to learn that my own social location as a *blan* was constituted by the country's colonial history and that the significance of my skin was tied up in the persistent color-coded class hierarchies that tend to organize contemporary Haitian society. My skin shade marked me as *blan*, my partner was *blan*, and two years after we arrived, and I birthed my son, he was designated *ti blan* (little *blan*).

I was privileged to have a dear friend and mentor who helped me navigate my "outsider" position. In fact, my husband and I spent so much time with Ari while I was pregnant that he named himself the *paren* (godfather) of our unborn son and gave him the *Kreyòl* name Jwasiys. When the nurse at the birthing clinic came to record the birth certificate, she was troubled by the name. "No," she said. "You can't name a white baby that. That's a Black peasant name." This incident was one among many that highlighted to me the fortitude of race-based social hierarchies in Haiti. To name a *ti blan* "Jwasiys" was unorthodox: it disrupted social expectations. More acceptable may have been Pierre or Jean or Michel. As parents, we were also chided for using the *Kreyòl* spelling—Jwasiys—rather than the French—Joicius. Using *Kreyòl*, Ari told us, was provocative because it signified that we were naming our baby "down," like a peasant. Time and time again, we were met with giggles when we shared our son's name. Jwasiys was unconventional, but it did not shift my son's status as *blan*. That shift was still to come.

Alongside skin, place bore heavily on my family's perceived status in Haiti—particularly on our belonging or exclusion—and, as such, on my research and mothering experiences. In Haiti, the color- and class-based social hierarchy has a geographical imprint, with the lighter-skinned Haitian elite and expat community concentrated in the wealthy hillside suburbs of Port-au-Prince and with people of "darker" phenotypes tending to live in the country-side. In this context, I quickly came to understand that there were places where my *blan* pregnant body belonged and places where it did not.

The social tendency to "imagine communities" has long been theorized (Anderson, 1991). Not only is there a strong relationship between iden-tity, place, and belonging; the social significance of identity markers (i.e., race, gender, and age) can change quite dramatically across spaces (Ching & Creed, 1997; Gupta & Ferguson, 1997). In Haiti, my experiences as a *blan* mother-researcher seemed to differ quite substantially depending on place and context. Perhaps obviously, in places where it was uncommon to see *blan*, or the lighter-skinned urban elite—in the *maché* or *tap-taps* (public pick-up trucks)—I was especially unusual as a pregnant *blan*. For this, I received lots of attention. More than once, my appearance was met with playful or teas-ing comments like "Gade gwo vant la k'ap vini! [Look at the pregnant *blan* that's coming!]" and "M pa't konnen blan yo konn fé bagay tou! [I didn't know *blan* have sex too!]" In contrast, my presence was rather unexceptional at the air-conditioned supermarket or at upscale restaurants. In these spaces, com-ments about my belly came in the form of questions: Who would my prenatal doctor be? Would I fly to Montreal or Miami for delivery?

After my children were born, I noticed that place also impacted my expe-riences of mothering, the advice I was given, and how I was received. For example, when I lived in Port-au-Prince, I taught exercise classes at a gym patroned mostly by upper-class Haitians and expats. Gym members wore brand-name athletic gear, sipped coffee in tiny cups in the adjoining café, and chatted in French or English. When I brought my infant son to class, women approached me freely to offer advice that centered around some key themes: finding an appropriate and trustworthy nanny; accessing the latest equipment for bottle cleaning and diaper disposal; and directions to the baby boutique where I would be able to find all the imported toys, clothes, and baby gear that I would need. Some women warned me not to breastfeed for fear that my breasts would droop.

After my daughter was born, I led exercise classes for women in Desarmes. In this context, I taught on a small patch of dirt outside of a school, most of us went bare-foot, and we chatted in *Kreyòl*. Sometimes I would bring Solette to class, and the advice was much different than what I had received in Port-au-Prince. I was encouraged to "mare vant mwen [tie up my tummy tightly]"; I was offered advice on leaves to use when bathing and teas to drink to help heal and increase my energy; and women who knew me better asked if I had an animal in the "lakou [yard]" to make sure that if bad spirits were sent our way, they would land on the animal and not my baby.

I want to emphasize that both in Port-au-Prince and Desarmes, the care and advice that women gave me was incredibly heartening. In both cases, offers of counsel were gestures of goodwill. They signified friendship and a generosity of spirit and made me feel accepted. I valued these efforts to connect immensely. It is also important to emphasize that my mothering experience, the advice I was given, and how I was received shifted quite dramatically by place and context. I highlight the dynamic relationship between place and the mother identity here because I think it's important to challenge the myth of "the field" as unitary and homogenous. Even though cross-cultural ethnographic researchers are "always everywhere in the field" (Katz, 1994), the "field" is diverse and differentiated, and my social location as a mother-researcher varied *within* the field.

The Tangly Relationship between Race, Class, Place, and Belonging

Place is obviously only part of the picture in making sense of the divergent reactions to my position as a *blan* mother-researcher in Haiti. The enormous class and resource disparities between urban and rural Haiti also bore heavily both on the mothering advice I received and on the significance of my position as *blan*. In other words, my perceived class status impacted whether my skin color was met with surprise or nonchalance. My son, for example, was born in a small maternity ward in the hills of Pétion-Ville, a wealthy suburb of Port-au-Prince. My ob-gyn was a lighter-skinned doctor who spoke to me in English, vacationed in France, and enjoyed a clean, air-conditioned, modern office, where I was received as "Marylynn"—rather than *blan*—by the professional secretary. My birth experience here cost upward of US$5,000. When I shared with Haitian friends or colleagues the birthplace of my son, no one was ever surprised to hear that I was being cared for in Pétion-Ville. On the other hand, my daughter was born at a rural hospital—the only hospital in the province. Lineups were chronically tedious, the paltry administrative staff were separated from the masses of patients by way of large plexiglass windows, the pitifully insufficient hospital beds meant that most patients were on the floor, and the hospital was so underresourced that patients were required to bring their own linens, soap, toilet paper, and even water (after my daughter was born, for example, the nurse looked to my husband to provide the nasal aspirator). Solette's birth cost US$250.

The disparities between my birthing sites reflect the trenchant economic inequality that plays out spatially in Haiti, and overlaying this is the strong relationship between class and color, "with lighter Haitians being richer and darker ones poorer" (Rogozinski, 2000, p. 216). This tendency was compatible with my prenatal experiences in Port-au-Prince and Desarmes. At the Port-au-Prince ob-gyn office, for example, I noted that the large majority of patients were light-skinned. In contrast, I never saw a *blan* patient at the rural hospital (though I did see *blan* volunteer doctors). There were even a few occasions when patients mistook *me* for a doctor, and since I was not in hospital gear of any sort, I can only presume that my skin color played a role in conjuring this impression. While my *blan* status seemed par for the course in Port-au-Prince, I was a spectacle in the rural hospital. I was treated differently from those around me by patients and administration alike. On the whole, I was prioritized, and while I waited for prenatal appointments—which was usually a wait in the ballpark of three to six hours—I overheard scores of racial remarks and had many experiences that illustrated both the uncommon nature of a person with my skin shade in the hospital and also broader race relations. For example, people frequently encouraged me to move to the front of the line and asked me why I was there. The race-based comments even came with me into the surgical ward, when my daughter was born through an emergency C-section. When I began shivering during the procedure, the doctor commented, "I didn't think *blan* would ever get cold." But my position as *blan* spurred more than rhetoric: it meant that regular hospital rules did not apply to me. For example, while other patients were made to leave their bags and backpacks outside of the hospital entrance,[1] I was permitted to bring all my personal items into the hospital. While other patients were made to wait without attention for hours in line, I was often encouraged to cut the line and was checked on more frequently by nurses and staff. In addition, I could access doctors and hospital management with relative ease, other *blan* doctors would often stop to chat with me, and my family was permitted to use the hospital swimming pool whenever they liked. Following Solette's birth, I was wheeled to the only private room in the hospital, while other mothers and their babies were packed into crowded rooms, some with beds, some without. I have no reason to believe that my special treatment was a result of anything other than my skin color.

My contrasting maternal health experiences in Port-au-Prince and Desarmes not only reflect the enormous economic disparities between rural and urban Haiti but also help illustrate how race, class, maternal health care, and field research can be intertwined. Although I'm not sure how popular it is to be pregnant and give birth in the field, it is important to appreciate that academic women may opt not to put families on hold for field research. In my case, I was a doctoral student in development geography with an interest in rural Haiti, and I found it stifling to imagine that my academic path could not continue alongside a family. Later in the chapter, I will return to issues of maternal and child health care in the field once again, paying specific attention to my struggles related to the ethics of mothering in research sites where resources are scarce. Here though, my intention is to draw from my own experience to illustrate how cross-cultural field research and pregnancy in tandem can reveal much about social relations and can contribute to research in this way and to illustrate the shifting nature of the mother-researcher identity *within* the field.

The Impact of Mothering on Research

When we arrived in Desarmes in 2010, Jwasiys was nearly two years old. One of the first kids we met was a three-year-old boy named Bélando. Jwasiys and Bélando were fast friends. I gallivanted with those two all over the place: to bathe in the river, to play in the *dal* (a concrete canal that the kids used as a water slide), and to pick *kanép* (canapés) and chew on sugar cane. Bélando was a daily visitor at our house. We read books, did crafts, and shared snacks. Bélando called me *blan* for nearly a year. But Jwasiys was Jwasiys.

FIGURE 13.1 Jwasiys and friends eating popcorn. Desarmes, Haiti, 2012.

Race-relations in Desarmes were akin to those in Port-au-Prince, although our family was more chronically hypervisible. This was a concern for me because I knew that if I was perceived as an outsider, it would be more challenging to develop the relationships of trust that are so important for ethnographic research. Bélando's lengthy time to eschew my *blan* label was analogous to the broader reception of me in town. I liked Desarmes and the people, and I wanted them to like me. I did my best to speak *Kreyòl*, to learn the banter and gestures of the market women, and to dress like the women in my neighborhood. But I walked in the town as a *blan*. I knew it as well as everyone else. Once, I was buying carrots in the local *maché* (open marketplace). "How much are these?" I asked the *machann* (market woman). "Sixty gourdes," she replied. With a bit of time and know-how under my belt, I was wise to the local pricing and knew that I was being swindled. "What!?" I said, smiling and trying to joke. "I know that other people get them for 40 gourdes." Straight-faced, she looked at me and said, "Yes, they *are* 40 goods for other people, but you are not a person. You are blan." Touché. But for Jwasiys, it was different. To him, the market would lovingly hand over bits of bread or sweets. Everyone knew him, and it was rare that anyone called him *blan*. He was just Jwasiys.

Both in my research and in my personal friendships, my children turned out to be an invaluable source of connection—both in utero and postpartum. Before Jwasiys was born, for example, I found it difficult to build relationships with Haitian women,[2] and I felt uneasy in male-dominated spaces. For example, government officials and leaders of community development, human rights, and advocacy organizations tended to be male, and sites of agricultural production—the fields—tended to be male-dominated as well. These spaces were ones where I witnessed and experienced sexual jokes and advances. They were spaces where I felt vulnerable and sometimes threatened. In addition, the domestic and market spaces that tended to be dominated by women were difficult to penetrate: women often seemed shy or standoffish, and I was regularly asked why I didn't have any children. Consequently, both the institutional and agricultural contexts that were dominated by men and the domestic and market spaces that were dominated by women were challenging sites for me to navigate.

When I was visibly pregnant, however, many of these dynamics changed. I noticed that I experienced fewer sexual remarks in office spaces, and my pregnant belly felt like a ticket to friendships with Haitian women. Additionally, it seemed that my identity as a mother dimmed my outsider status. For example, instead of being called *blan*, I was often called *Gwo Vant* (big belly)—a good-humored nickname used for pregnant women, *blan* and Haitian alike. Women at the *maché* also seemed more willing to engage in conversation and offer mothering advice when I was pregnant. In large measure, I attribute many new female friendships to my pregnancy. My pregnancy bonded me with other women through a common experience and enabled more intimate friendships. From the outset, my kids seemed to help bridge the social divide.

When he was older, Jwasiys's integration and identity as a *ti blan* in Desarmes was also immensely helpful at the level of research. At the *maché*, for example, Jwasiys's nationality, citizenship, and status was a frequent source of interest and discussion, and these conversations were fascinating windows to social perceptions of race, identity, and belonging. For example, one conversation topic that popped up with regularity was Jwasiys's identity status: was he Haitian or *blan*? In general, the most common questions raised were, Does being born in Haiti make you Haitian? Do you need to be *nwa* (Black) to be Haitian? Could a *blan* really be Haitian? Being privy to these conversations was not only insightful for my research on race relations; the attention Jwasiys received facilitated my own integration in Desarmes. For example, over time, I shed the name *blan*, and became widely recognized as *Manman Jwasiys*. It seemed that people in Desarmes became more familiar and trusting of me *because* of my son.

Everyone in our neighborhood knew Jwasiys and Solette, and their acceptance and integration helped me establish both friendships and research connections. For example, when we were out for walks in the fields, there were times when a farmer would stop to give the kids a piece of sugar cane, and this would enable me to ask questions and make contacts. I learned valuable insights on social life and behaviors, agricultural seasons and work patterns, community and social relations, and belief and meaning systems through my walks with my children and their friends. Additionally, the friends that Jwasiys and Solette made paved the way for friendships with their mothers, which led to lots of story swapping. Sharing mothering experiences with other women in Desarmes—the horrors and the delights—was a joy and immensely personally fulfilling, but it also deepened my field research, broadened my research network, and helped me develop relationships of trust in Desarmes.

The Impact of Research on Mothering and Children: Education, Health, and Identity

As I argued in the previous section, children can be valuable resources in helping facilitate cross-cultural field research, but what effect does field research have on mothering and on children themselves? Of course, one of my core objectives as a mother, regardless of place, is to create a loving, healthy, and nurturing environment for my children. Desarmes was in many ways a child's paradise, full of friends and enchanting places to explore. My children loved splashing in the river, washing their clothes in the canal, driving on the motorcycle to school with their dad, collecting *grenn legliz* (love peas, or *Abrus precatorius*) on our walks, and the independence of trotting off with five gourdes to the Jano's corner to buy a pack of *bonbon sél* (crackers). There were abounding joyous moments when I felt very grateful to be mothering in Haiti. But there were also sorrows and sicknesses, and I would be remiss if I did not also say that there were times when I felt that my research decisions—in particular, my research site—jeopardized my mothering and my children's lives. There are three arenas of parenting that were particularly challenging, and I will deal with each in sequence: education, health, and identity.

Childcare and Education in the Field

One of the foremost challenges of mothering in the field in rural Haiti was balancing childcare and work. Our family struggled fairly persistently with the childcare dilemma. Initially, it was our intention to enroll Jwasiys in a local preschool. We had been told that schools in Desarmes no longer use corporal punishment, but when we visited the school and I saw a teacher smack one of the students, it was a deal breaker. Our second option was a part-time nanny for Jwasiys, and there were times this worked marginally well, but we also had some major pitfalls. In the care of our first nanny—who lasted a week—Jwasiys poured Clorox down the front of himself, got ahold of a machete, and got into and perhaps swallowed a number of pills (that luckily turned out to be vitamins). We tried again, and this time, Jwasiys passed a few happy months spending his mornings with a delightful young woman who read to him in *Kreyòl* and French, sang songs, took him for long walks to the river, and taught him about the plants and trees in the neighborhood. Over time, we had a few minor issues—things missing, odd behavior—but nothing set off alarm bells until we learned that the nanny had not really been taking Jwasiys on long walks but had been taking him instead to the homes of her friends and (we suspect) boyfriends. I was horrified not because I thought there was any harm done but because I felt a deep loss of trust. Unfortunately, this soured the nanny option for us, and for months, my partner and I juggled childcare on our own. Later, we opted to try another school, one connected with the organization my partner worked with. I adored Jwasiys's teacher and although, like any rural school in Haiti, it was enormously underresourced, the two teachers were positive and encouraging and had an excellent rapport with students and parents alike. Jwasiys seemed to thoroughly enjoy his time there. Unfortunately for us, the teacher went on maternity leave and was replaced by another who reintroduced corporal punishment. We made the difficult decision of leaving the school and spent our final year in Haiti juggling childcare once again.

I share these stories to emphasize that the logistical challenges of bringing children to the field can be compounded in research sites where social services are scarce. I also hope that these stories highlight that even when childcare plans don't work out as planned, there may be benefits to the struggle. Specifically, Jwasiys had the opportunity to learn *Kreyòl* and some French both with his nanny and in school, and this has allowed him to continue French education in Canada and the United States. He also enjoyed the unique opportunity to learn about Haiti from Haitians themselves, and I am confident that his schooling helped with his integration with other children. In addition, I learned that it wasn't so bad having children in tow for interviews—it was fun, helped break the ice, and made it easier to make connections with women. In the end, the childcare challenges and worries—which, admittedly, sometimes caused havoc on our nerves and emotions—were bore by my husband and myself. Jwasiys is none the wiser.

Child Health in the Field

Bringing children to research sites that are underresourced can carry a unique set of challenges. While my family lived in Desarmes, there was no running water and no electricity in the town, and few people had latrines. We bathed in the river or collected rainwater from our roof and were careful to use Clorox to treat it. Still, sometimes it felt like the decision to live in rural Haiti was akin to *deciding* to sicken our kids. Jwasiys and Solette suffered innumerable gastrointestinal infections, parasites, and boils. They both had malaria and dengue fever. Solette was hospitalized for more than a week with a threatening case of infant pneumonia, and Jwasiys was once evacuated out of Haiti because of an illness that has never been diagnosed but gave him recurrent seizures and left him unable to walk or talk for three very terrifying days.

On one hand, the memory of these illnesses still haunts me—did my research put my children in harm's way? On the other hand, I felt elitist, inhumane, and hypocritical when I prioritized my kids' development, education, and health care amid such scarcity and deprivation. When I compared my family's position with our neighbors' in Desarmes, our disproportionate privilege mirrored global maternal and child health inequalities, and I felt the weight of this. Haiti's maternal, infant, and under-five death rates are the highest in the hemisphere: a Haitian woman has a 1 in 275 chance of dying during childbirth[3] compared to a risk of 1 in more than 14,000 in Canada; the infant mortality rate in Haiti is more than 50 per 1,000, compared to 4 per 1,000 in Canada (CIA, 2015; WHO, UNICEF, UNFPA, the World Bank, & the United Nations Population Division, 2013; UNICEF, 2010). Faced with this reality, my children's illnesses seemed minor, yet faced with a three-year-old having seizures, I felt like a terrible mother.

It felt impossible for me to balance my ethics of equity with my love for my children. While in Desarmes, I was reading authors like Gandhi, George

Beckford, and Wendell Berry: the goals of voluntary simplicity, accompaniment, and radical equality moved me. I frequently reflected on how much more difficult but effective it would be if the well-known verse was instead "Love your neighbor as your children." I could see no greater purpose than to aim for this kind of equity, and I wanted my research and my life to reflect that purpose. And yet when my children were sick, I easily threw these goals to the wind. Once, when my son and I were in the thralls of another bout of giardia, I was annoyed and complaining that I had to drag my feverish self down to the clinic with our stool samples in matchboxes to get checked for parasites. That day, I also learned that a dear friend—my daughter's namesake and mother of three—had been suffering from malaria for more than a month. I felt liked a whiner and was embarrassed by my lack of humility and sense of entitlement.

So often I struggled with the ethics of raising my kids in rural Haiti. I was simultaneously worried that my research site decisions were putting my kids through unnecessary pain and illness and guilt-ridden that our family could access the enormous privilege of health care when our neighbors could not. My mothering responsibilities and my ethics felt in conflict, and I couldn't make sense of what was right. I felt both compelled and allergic to benefiting from my class and race position by way of health care. As I put food on my children's plates, I knew my neighbors didn't have enough. It sickened me, and I couldn't escape it. Many times I felt like a failure for seeking medical help, for whisking my daughter away to Port-au-Prince when she had pneumonia, for evacuating my son for care in Toronto when he had recurrent seizures.

Long-term field research in rural Haiti entailed both sickness for my children and mental health struggles for me. I am still trying to come to terms with how my research decisions and site impacted my kids' health, and this remains a concern as I continue to think about the future of my research, career, and family. I share the impact of my research site on my children's health here for two reasons. First, I suspect that many mother-academics who conduct research in the Global South are confronted with the decision to either conduct research accompanied by family and avoid research in underresourced sites or to spend long stints away from family in order to conduct field research. My hope is that by sharing my own experience, other mother-researchers in development studies might be moved to share their own. Second, as a mother-researcher in Haiti, I left the field in a state of ill mental health, and my hope is that my experience will help contribute to calls for greater institutional support of mother-researchers who conduct field research in challenging field sites. There is a growing body of research in the field of humanitarian mental health that investigates the relationship between aid work and psychological stress (Eriksson et al., 2009; Beristain, 2006; Shah, Garland, & Katz, 2007). This is an area that requires more attention in university departments of global and development studies. Specifically, I hope that we might begin to strategize possibilities for supporting mother-researchers who are committed to research in sites of scarcity.

Child and Maternal Identity during Cross-Cultural Research

Mothering in rural Haiti, where my children's skin was a visible marker of their difference, was both perpetually entertaining and rife with challenges. One consistent puzzle that I stewed over was how to best help my children navigate their difference and self-perception in Desarmes. Although it might be obvious that I fielded a myriad of race-based comments from people in the community, another important barrier to our integration was related to my *own* self-perception and mothering goals. In particular, I confess that my self-concept—my ideas about my own identity, my comforts, and my goals for mothering—were quite stubborn. I felt a visceral connection to my Canadian-ness—however ambiguous—and longed to incorporate that into my mothering and family life. Our CBC radio connection, for example, was one of my most cherished comforts; privacy never ceased to feel luxurious; and I made conscious efforts to ensure that the infamously Canadian Robert Munsch stories and Raffi songs were prominent on our family's reading and playlists. I loved Haitian food, but I couldn't seem to quell my belief that porridge was the way to start my kids' day off right, nor could I squash my hankering for crisp apples and creamy yogurt. I loved the life of the Haitian countryside—splashing in the river, chewing sugar cane, and chasing rabbits around the neighborhood—but I also felt pangs of guilt for not exposing my kids to libraries and swimming lessons.

On this front, my children were an invaluable source of self-reflection and learning. Their fondness for rural Haiti and deep intimacy with our neighbors was moving and helped me grow to be more open-minded about my goals for them. One important milestone for me was when I realized that although my self-perception was still very much bound up in Canada, Jwasiys's internal magnet had a strong pull to Haiti. He longed for *diri ak sòs pwa* (rice and bean sauce) and fresh coconut and delighted in playing chase and football with his friends. As noted, Jwasiys experienced a much deeper integration into community life in Desarmes than I did. He had the tastes, the talk, and the swagger of the other kids in the neighborhood. People said he "spoke Kreyòl like a rat," which is to say fluently. Some even called him a *ti blan Ayisyen* (little white Haitian). Jwasiys also loved to bike around the neighborhood wearing a red *mouchwa* (bandana/scarf)—a powerful symbol in Haitian folklore and the voodoo religion—so folks would call him *Bawon*,[4] an undeniable Haitian moniker. Jwasiys's comforts and joys were different from my own and those that I grew up with, but it was a pleasure and an honor to learn from him and his friends and to find ways to support their interests.

While there were many advantages of Jwasiys's integration, I would be remiss if I did not share that Jwasiys never shed his skin completely, and his difference as a *ti blan* in Desarmes was sometimes a challenge to parent. Because his skin color marked his difference, Jwasiys received near constant attention in Desarmes, ranging from *machann* (market women) doting on him, to individual greetings, to troubling comments. On numerous occasions, people passing by would ignore his friends but offer him a special shout-out—"Bonjou Jwasiys." I also heard many comments like "Jwasiys looks just like a doll, what beautiful eyes and hair" and "Jwasiys has better hair than us. God loves him more." On one hand, Jwasiys was often the recipient of special treats—sweets, breads, and rides on donkeys—and small affections, but he was also a target for snide comments. One recurrent scenario involved adults saying to him, "Ba m yon bagay [give me something]." For example, one day, Jwasiys and his friends were strolling down a path sipping from a *saché dlo* (small bag of water) and snacking on *bon bon sél* (crackers), and he was singled out by a passerby: "Jwasiys, ba m sa [Jwasiys, give me some of that]." When Jwasiys didn't share, he was met with comments like "li chiche kòm yon blan [he's cheap just like a *blan*]." On other occasions when Jwasiys was too busy or distracted to return someone's "Bonjou [Hello]," I would hear comments like "li pa byen ave m paske m nwa [he doesn't like me because I'm Black]." At the level of research, these comments were insightful and helped me conceptualize the relationships between skin color, status, and social differentiation in Desarmes. Yet at the level of mothering, these comments were cause for concern—how was Jwasiys internalizing his difference? How would I address this?

It was important to me to keep in touch with and value Jwasiys's self-perception. In Desarmes, some people conceptualized Jwasiys as *blan* and others accepted him as Haitian, but for his part, Jwasiys seemed to have a strong self-perception as Haitian and a profound sense of belonging in Desarmes. It really struck me that—having been born in Haiti and spending the better part of his early childhood in Desarmes—this was not "the field" for him. It was home. For most of his years in Haiti, Jwasiys seemed to cope well with his difference. He was accustomed to people calling him out and seemed to either engage with or ignore people depending on his mood. Sometimes I did my best to shield him from comments, and sometimes I let him handle them on his own. But the incident on our bike ride home from school that I mention at the outset of this chapter was a watershed moment in his childhood. I realized that day that this incident had pricked his consciousness about race relations in Desarmes and his position as a *blan*. Although he had heard it countless times before, this day when confronted with people yelling "blan," he was troubled. "Manman, poukisa y'ap rele m blan? [Why are they calling me a white?]." *How do I mother this?* I thought. "Because you are *blan*," I tried to explain, "but you're Haitian too."

In Haiti, my identity as a *blan* mother-researcher was flexible, and so was that of my children's. There are certainly meaningful challenges related to identity and integration for mother academics who engage in international field research. However, it is important to recognize that mother-researchers can play active roles in shaping their identity construction, and there is reason to believe that mother-researchers can negotiate their positionalities both to overcome challenges and to enhance research and mothering goals. As Macdonald (2009) emphasizes, "Mothers choose which aspects of existing norms to embrace and which to resist," and researchers too enact and negotiate their positions in various ways through language, dress, and body language (Ergun & Erdemir, 2010). In this way, mother-researchers might consider "playing up" or "playing down" their position depending on context. In the next section, I explore situations in which I negotiated my identities successfully (to amplify either my research or mothering experience) and situations I wish I had handled differently.

Negotiating the Mother-Researcher Position

Researcher identity—including race, ethnicity, gender, age, and language— impacts research topics, methods, decisions, and outcomes (Muhammad et al., 2015). The mother identity is akin to these, and it is important to recognize that just as gender or language or ethnicity impact a researcher's "insider" or "outsider" status in community-based research, there are ways that mother-researchers can utilize and negotiate their positions to the advantage of their research. In my case, my "race" position and mother status were the identity markers that most strongly influenced my research methods and decisions in the field. For example, as a mother with children, I sometimes felt limited by whom I could interview and how far I could travel from Desarmes. But conversely, my realization that my children could help facilitate relationships with women enabled me to push my research in new directions—to research market women about household reproduction, for example. In many ways, my particular position as a *blan* mother-researcher enriched my understanding of race relations and community life. In other ways, my position was limiting. But this is par for the course—identity impacts research! The question for mother-researchers is this: To what extent are our mother-researcher positions flexible in the field, and how can we negotiate our positions to the advantage of our research and mothering practices?

In Haiti, I learned that I could lean on (or play up) my *blan*, mother, and researcher positions in different contexts to enhance my research, develop friendships, and liberate me from social rules that I disagreed with. For example, my position as a *blan* researcher paved the way for meetings with government officials and representatives of international organizations. In contrast, as noted earlier, I could amplify my mother identity by bringing my kids along to interviews with women. With a basic understanding of social relations and behaviors in Haiti, I could negotiate my identity positions to advantage my research in other ways as well. For example, in preparation for meetings with authorities, I never wore a traditional peasant dress, I never carried a *jakout* (basket associated with the peasantry), and I never brought my children. And when I arrived—pressed and shiny-shoed—at the gates of office meetings, I offered a greeting in English or French, and security guards always permitted my entrance. No question. In contrast, when I arrived for interviews with rural dwellers, I wore flip-flops and a peasant sun hat and dress and often had a *jakout* and a child in tow. When I introduced myself in *Kreyòl*—and especially when my children spoke *Kreyòl*—I was received warmly.

There were undeniable research and personal advantages of my *blan* mother-researcher identity. Yet being a *blan* mother in Haiti also carried with it a stifling set of expectations and suppositions that I had to learn how to navigate. For example, when I was pregnant with my daughter, a friend told me I would not be able to "push out" my baby because "blan women do not have strength to push" and instead I should schedule a caesarian section. Because I was *blan*, many women expected me to use disposable diapers, not to breastfeed, and to buy Gerber baby food, which carried social prestige. Other expectations were related to culturally appropriate mothering codes: don't leave your *lakou* (family courtyard) until three months after the baby is born, always make sure babies have socks on, never bathe babies after sunset. Sometimes I adhered to these norms, sometimes not, and my perception is that it was my position as a *blan* that granted me more freedom to take these recommendations with a grain of salt.

Alongside social expectations of how I would mother, my *blan* position also meant that my children and I were I often treated with an overblown courtesy that was sometimes embarrassing and often made me cringe: we were often seated at the front of the congregation in church services, we were prioritized in hospitals, and we were even (by some) perceived as closer to God. Once, when I was walking in the mountains with Jwasiys, a young girl approached us. She was carrying a toddler who was visibly paralyzed on one side. "Reach out and touch her," instructed the young child. I turned around. "Why do you want her to touch me?" I asked. "Because you're closer to God, and you might help heal her," the girl replied. Comments like this were alarming, and I increasingly felt compelled not only to *understand* race relations in Haiti but also to *resist* and *subvert* race-based ideologies. I strategized ways to downplay my *blan*-ness. I bought traditional peasant dresses, I used a *jakout* when I went shopping, and I ate local and traditional foods—even ones that were disdained and associated with the peasantry, like *pitimi* (millet or sorghum) and *mayi moulen* (cornmeal; Steckley, 2015). Some of these strategies worked. When I was wearing a voodoo dress, I noticed that I was often called a *Voudouizan* or *peyizan* (peasant) rather than *blan*. When I asked for *pitimi*, some people commented, "Madamn sa se Ayisyen nét [That someone is completely Haitian]."

Certainly, I found ways to enact my mother, *blan*, or researcher status in ways that helped maximize advantages in different contexts. However, alongside the benefits of a malleable identity, there were instances where I bent my perceived identity in ways that I regret. When I was pregnant with my daughter, the lineups at the hospital near Desarmes were tedious, and it often took four to six hours to meet with the doctor (if you had an appointment). Inevitably a nurse would notice me and encourage me to cut the line. I resisted these offers for months, but at one appointment, the weight of my belly and the sweltering day at the hospital weakened my resolve. I went with the nurse. On that day, I managed my identity—my position as a *blan* mother—to gain a health-care advantage over the other women around me. The shame that has stemmed from that decision has haunted me. Looking back, I am disgusted with myself not only for my blatant impertinence but even more for what little it took—heat, frustration, mild discomfort—for me to succumb to the temptation of privilege that came with being *blan* in Haiti. Most rattling though was that there was no protest. No one questioned why I was being taken to see the doctor or why I was cutting the line. The worst part of that day was the ease with which I could benefit merely from my skin color, and everyone else accepted it as natural.

Of course, it is humiliating to share this story, but I offer it to emphasize that negotiating one's identity in the field, especially when done to the advantage of the researcher, has dangerous potential to reproduce social inequalities and prejudice. In Haiti, my skin color meant that I had an enormous power advantage, and it is inexcusable that I used this to my benefit. So I am not advocating for "negotiating" identities at all costs. And yet, as noted in the introduction, mother-researchers in the field face particular challenges and risks—and there is a need to find creative ways to overcome these in practice. I think that negotiating our identities in the field, when done ethically and responsibly, can be a valuable tool that can enhance not only research but also mothering goals.

Conclusion

As noted in the introduction of this book, academic women often feel compelled to choose between babies and careers. This choice is perhaps more complicated for those of us whose careers are tied to international field research. Mothering in the field can certainly entail unique sets of challenges, and balancing research and mothering can become more tangly when research sites are remote and where resources are scarce. In my mind, empowering mother academics to do their best work means liberating women to conduct field research with children. For this to happen with more frequency, it is important for mother-academics to be able to imagine and create field opportunities that will both enhance research *and* contribute positively to their children's lives. In light of this, there is the need to identify strategies for mother-academics to successfully carry out fieldwork and mothering in tandem. While I certainly think that there is room for more institutional support of mother academics (i.e., mental health resources and funding opportunities), in this chapter, I offer my own experience of negotiating my identity as a practical tool that helped me cope with the challenges of balancing research and mothering in Haiti. My hope is that my experience might help spark more ideas about how the "mother" identity can be negotiated to enhance research and alternately, how research opportunities can enhance mothering and children's lives.

Kawalilak and Groen (2014) point to the disproportionate challenges that young female academics face and suggest that sharing experiences can be "therapeutic, healing, and affirming." In this chapter, I have shared some of my own experiences as a mother-researcher in Haiti with goals to convey both the delights and rewards of mothering in the field and to be honest about some of the challenges. One of my motivations is to help normalize the presence of children during fieldwork and to encourage confidence among academic mothers who are considering the adventure of mothering in the field.

Practical Tips

- Make strategies early on to help you embrace your mother-researcher identity, and draw from those identities to amplify your research and writing.
- Advocate for mother-researchers within your university.
- Alongside networking with the giants at academic conferences, your children are a great resource with connecting in the field—let them help you!

Dedication

The opportunity for mother-researchers to contribute to this book is encouraging, and I am sincerely grateful for this opportunity. I am also confronted by the fact that my contribution here is a glaring symbol of my class and color privilege. As I give voice to my own experience in this chapter, the silencing of many friends in Haiti weighs heavily. On my part, I am especially grateful to Solette and Gerda for graciously overlooking my many faults and mistakes, for their patient and persistent teaching, and for loving my children. As a way forward, it is my hope that as mothers and academics, we can utilize our privilege to the benefit of mothers in the communities that have served us and our research so well. There is much more possibility both for research and for relationships. *Ann Alé*!—Let's go!

Notes

1   One hospital staff member explained to me that patients and visitors are restricted from bringing in bags because the hospital has had issues with theft. I presume that I was not considered a threat because I was *blan*.
2   This is a challenge that Smith (2001) also describes.
3   The Latin American and Caribbean regional average is one in more than five hundred.
4   Short for *Bawon Samedi* (Baron Saturday), which is one of the *Lwa* (gods/spirits) of Haitian voodoo.

References

Anderson, B. (1991). *Imagined communities: Reflections on the origin and spread of nationalism*. London, UK: Verso.

Beristain, M. (2006). *Humanitarian aid work: A critical approach*. Philadelphia, PA: University of Pennsylvania Press.

Ching, B., & Creed, G. W. (1997). *Knowing your place: Rural identity and cultural hierarchies*. New York, NY: Routledge.

CIA World Factbook. (n.d.) Country profile Haiti. Retrieved from https://www.cia.gov/library/publications/the-world-factbook/

Dwyer, S. C., & Buckle, J. L. (2009). The space between: On being an insider-outsider in qualitative research. *IJQM*, *8*(1), 54–63.

Ergun, A., & Erdemir, A. (2010). Negotiating Insider and outsider identities in the field: "Insider" in a foreign land; "outsider" in one's own land. *Field Method*, *22*(1), 16–38.

Eriksson, C. B., Bjorck, J. P., Larson, L. C., Walling, S. M., Trice, G. A., Fawcett, J., Abernethy, A. D., & Foy, D. W. (2009). Social support, organisational support, and religious support in relation to burnout in expatriate humanitarian aid workers. *Ment Health Relig Cult*, *12*(7), 671–686.

Groen, J., & Kawalilak, C. (2014). *Pathways of adult learning: Professional and education narratives*. Toronto, ON: Canadian Scholars' Press.

Gupta, A., and Ferguson, J. (Eds.). (1997). *Culture, power, place: Explorations in critical anthropology*. London, UK: Duke University Press.

Johnston, D. D., & Swanson, D. H. (2007). Cognitive acrobatics in the construction of worker-mother identity. *Sex Roles*, *57*(5), 447–459.

Katz, C. (1994). Playing the field: Questions of fieldwork in geography. *Professional Geographer*, *46*(1), 67–72.

Macdonald, C. (2009). What's culture got to do with it? Mothering ideologies as barriers to gender equity. In J. C. Gornick, M. K. Meyers, & E. O. Wright (Eds.), *Gender equality: Transforming family divisions of labor* (pp. 411–434). New York, NY: Verso.

Merriam, S. B., Johnson-Bailey, J., Lee, M.-Y., Ntseane, G., & Muhamad, M. (2010). *Power and positionality: Negotiating insider/outsider status within and across cultures*. New York, NY: Routledge.

Moore, H. L. (1996). Mothering and social responsibilities in a cross-cultural perspective. In E. B. Silva (Ed.), *Good enough mothering? Feminist perspectives on lone mothering* (58–75). London, UK: Routledge.

Muhammad, M., Wallerstein, N., Sussman, A. L., Avila, M., Belone, L., & Duran, B. (2015). Reflections on research identity and power: The impact of positionality on community based participatory research (CBPR) processes and outcomes. *Critical Sociology, 41*(7–8), 1045–1063.

Rogozinski, J. (2000). *A brief history of the Caribbean: From the Arawak and Carib to the present*. New York, NY: Penguin Group.

Shah, S. A., Garland, E., & Katz, C. (2007). Secondary traumatic stress: Prevalence in humanitarian aid workers in India. *Traumatology, 13*(1), 59–70.

Smith, J. M. (2001). *When the hands are many: Community organization and social change in rural Haiti*. Ithaca, NY: Cornell University Press.

Steckley, M. (2016). Eating up the social ladder: The problem of dietary aspirations for food sovereignty. *Agriculture and Human Values, 33*(3), 549–562.

Thomson, P., & Gunter, H. (2011). Inside, outside, upside down: The fluidity of academic researcher "identity" in working with/in school. *International Journal of Research & Method in Education, 34*(1), 17–30.

UNICEF (2010, January 23). At a glance: Haiti. Retrieved from http://www.unicef.org/infobycountry/haiti_2014.html

WHO, UNICEF, UNFPA, the World Bank, and the United Nations Population Division (2014). Trends in maternal mortality: 1990 to 2013. Retrieved from http://www.unfpa.org/publications/trends-maternal-mortality-1990-2013

14

Birthing the Social Scientist as Mother

● ●

DEIRDRE GUTHRIE

Introduction

This work describes how my own definition, process, and experience of caring and fieldwork have evolved over the past twenty years, from the time my mother passed away and I entered the professional world to when I became a mother, quite unexpectedly, at age forty. It positions fieldwork as providing the context and opportunity for a developmental journey, not unlike those accompanying motherhood, with its stages of initiation, incoherence, and integration.

Becoming a mother was the catalyst I needed to let go of previous conceptions of what practicing social science should look like. This meant releasing the notion that I had to remain a detached observer, accepting the impossibility of work-life balance, and disconnecting my sense of self-esteem from the validation of the academy. This level of newfound acceptance arose following what Brown (in Cunningham, 2012) describes as a "willingness to let go of exhaustion as a status symbol and productivity as self-worth" and from an increasing concern with how to make my call to social justice work sustainable alongside my call to be a good mother. Occupying dual work-life roles meant redefining my value not so much in terms of the standard audit culture—meeting economistic goals of efficiency and performance outcomes—but in terms of

FIGURE 14.1 *Hacia un Nuevo Amanecer* (*Toward a New Dawn*), acrylic by Beatriz Aurora. The artist describes how the image represents her and her daughter Camila traveling in a Mexican moon-boat to meet with the Zapatistas. I purchased this image as a postcard in Chiapas during a work trip in 2017. I taped it next to my own daughter's bed and promised her that when I was far away, we could still visit each other in our dreams. (Reproduced with permission from the artist.)

valuing the practical wisdom my lived experience as a mother-scientist brings to the fields of relationships I encounter every day.

Yet this orientation toward work is often met with institutional pushback even from within humanitarian organizations I currently study and work with that have caregiving as central to their mission. While they have formally moved from a model of "aid to accompaniment" with affected populations, a philosophy that argues that responses to social problems must be collective, many still celebrate the ideal social justice worker as a heroic change agent: able-bodied, privileged, and free from personal caretaking responsibilities. As one new humanitarian mother explained, "I used to be a top performer, and I know [becoming a mother] is going to affect my job, and this [realization] has been a gut punch. I'm going to be tired, and there is always someone younger and peppier ready to take my role. My organization purports to be about family, but informally there is a lot of discussion around mothers not pulling their weight. The superstars are workaholics who peak at roughly thirty or maybe thirty-six and set the gold standard. After that, once they are parents and seen as having diminished capacities, they are marginalized."

I also used to fear that owning a new set of limitations while honoring any form of self-care would be seen by my colleagues—mostly male with wife-centered support systems at home—as a lack of the stoicism needed to do the job or a weakening of my commitment to change systems of structural violence. But once I became pregnant and took ownership of my work in the context of my caretaking responsibilities, I became less concerned with these "others" and more confident in my own internal compass.

It is true that becoming a mother *changed my entire way of being in the world.* To start, the neat compartmentalization of my professional and personal life became impossible because my body, which was now the source of food and life for a dependent human, was carried into both worlds. It sometimes leaked, and my circadian rhythms and their corresponding levels of alertness and sleepiness were intimately intertwined with my child's feeding cycle and attachment needs. The time for writing and research now takes place in those precious predawn hours before my child awakens. I have ceased to be self-conscious when colleagues peel stickers off my back or politely look away when glittery balls bounce out of my briefcase. As my stoic professional persona has begun to erode, I am challenged to live the feminist philosophy I espouse, one that privileges questions of ontology over epistemology and embraces an anti-Cartesian resistance to the binary oppositions that I know were always blurred in fieldwork (mind/body, nature/culture, sacred/profane, emotional/rational, home/field).

In terms of working definitions for this paper, then, I conceive of *the field* as this blurred site of shifting locations of encounter on which we come to know who we are in relationship with others. Given the politics of daily life for the mother–social scientist, the field is an unstable, dynamic realm of possibility and struggle, a living laboratory that she enters as an outsider with purported investigator expertise that remains impotent until it meaningfully engages with local knowledges. In such settings, occupying a highly translatable role such as mother may help transcend daily politics and affirm bonds with others across cultural boundaries, especially with mothers who are often pivotal actors in their own local communities.

As I now conceive of it, *to mother* is to embody the virtue of care and to strive to bring compassion into daily practice with others in a way that affirms our mutual humanity and enacts presence. In the language of humanistic nursing, enacting presence involves a "mode of being available or open in a situation with the wholeness of one's unique individual being; a gift of self which can only be given freely, invoked, or evoked" (Paterson & Zderad, 1976, p. 122). It emphasizes being over doing, and in my current work supporting the well-being of humanitarian and global health-care workers, *presence* may include active listening, offering emotional support, and practicing moral solidarity and responsibility in a way that feels energizing and not depleting. It is an inherent trait in those who are called—as I and my mother and grandmother, all social workers, were—from a private to a public space of practicing care work, where work becomes an extension of service, and service becomes an extension of life.

Ethicists distinguish *care* (meeting the needs of those who cannot meet their needs themselves) from *service* (meeting the needs of those capable of self-care). Care and service can be considered existential acts and ethical commitments that arise amid and in spite of the uncertainty and danger that define the human condition. Service, aligned with the lived principles of accompaniment and restorative justice, can be distinguished from the colonial mind-set of helping or fixing, where "helping, fixing and serving represent three different ways of seeing life. When you help you see life as weak. When you fix you see life as broken. When you serve, you see life as whole" (Remen, 2017).

Mothering in the field as scientist thus means that one is committed to both care and service—both daily nurturing practices as banal and intimate as wiping noses and bottoms, breastfeeding, and carrying children and, more expansively, extending compassion and social responsibility into one's professional life in relationship with strangers and vulnerable others. We learn to enact care or service well to the degree that we were well cared for. Therefore, at its most basic level, mothering draws from the universal field of love and attention from which every human being begins as a beneficiary.

Mothering is among the most challenging and rewarding calls because one must expand to become better than she is. The gift is in the stretching. For those of us who conduct social science work in the field, in settings where we engage and seek meaning in particular human problems, processes, or practices, such stretching beyond the self means acknowledging that *the way we occupy these lived spaces matters*. We may cultivate the quality of being reflexive to inform our daily experience in the field, awake and aware as compassionate *accompagnateurs*. We may be willing to identify and question our assumptions and blind spots as they arise as growth opportunities, committing to the deep listening of others, seeing interpersonal conflict as the expression of unmet needs, patiently resting in the *bardo* of what is uncomfortable and unknown before rushing to action. Or we may avoid all of this complexity and potential distress because we lack the capacity or willingness to identify and regulate the difficult emotional fallout such a collision of worldviews may entail, "coping" instead through disconnection, avoidance, or compulsive behavior.

After years of honing the ability to dispassionately witness and record reality with my highly attuned yet fallible sensory body instrument, becoming a mother has deepened my desire to cultivate the qualities of *active* witnessing suffused with compassion, presence, and awareness of process. Developing these qualities as well as validating them in others (both men and women) feels more authentic in recognition of the human condition, such that we are always acting in ways that are mutating, emerging, and vulnerable. Too often we deny this vulnerability and pretend that embodied emotions do not under-pin our daily work practices and relationships. And yet when that emotional content is missing, we experience its absence viscerally as anomie.

This chapter documents my developmental process as a field researcher and mother-in-training in terms of how I continue to learn to accompany others through embodying a mothering mind-set at work. This process involves learning to recognize the interrelationship of my more slippery, subterranean processes to my external fieldwork "performances," which in turn has led to an uneasy but sustainable integration of the "back" and "front" stages of my life. In this paper, I focus on the stages of development I went through to achieve this mothering mind-set as I navigated different field contexts as activ-ist, reporter, and advocacy researcher committed to addressing structures of violence through participatory methods.

Reimagining Mother Narratives: Lessons from the Field

Joseph Campbell (1990) conceptualized the hero as part of a universal pat-tern of human development and expression found in myths and stories across the world. Borrowing from James Joyce, Campbell called this one story "The Monomyth" or "Hero's Journey," composed of the elements separation, initia-tion, and return. Early anthropologists constructed their own heroic rite of passage in which the civilized hero left home to bravely venture into the world of "otherness" in the (uncivilized) field. What if, instead of reenacting the hero's monomyth—which often prescribes a hyperresilient figure who crosses from the mundane into the supernatural, conquering fantastic obstacles along the way before returning home victorious—we could see ourselves more fully in a journey modeled after the experience of mothering? In such a journey, which traverses not foreign lands but our own shadow, we might experience a catalyst to our identity in some field of encounter—without foreclosing the other—linger in that space of ambiguity, and eventually reintegrate our new narrative toward acknowledging our profound interdependence.

What if we learned to live in that liminal space or field of struggle that is the permanent human condition, in which there is no solution but an endur-ing awareness of our conscious behaviors and unconscious longings, our sun-lit frontstage consensus reality, and the shadowy backstage domain of private dream and intuition? What if we were to let go of the need to reduce each dimension of being/becoming to the other and increase our tolerance for ambiguity and dichotomy? We might learn to plant seeds of patience, accom-pany others in a way that is as receptive as it is giving, and eventually return "home" to share our practical wisdom.

Each of the field settings described in the sections that follow offered lived experience that informed my views on relationship, intimacy, witnessing, accompaniment, and mothering/caring. Each setting provided identity catalysts that challenged my worldview, forcing me to reconcile and reform meaning and purpose. The formal training I received to navigate this journey did not take into account the bodily, emotional, and spiritual/ethical fallout that coincides with rupture to one's worldview. I had to resource these capacities from elsewhere—from the memories of my own childhood, values my mother instilled in me, wise guides I met along the way, and spiritual teachings. I break this personal journey into the following ritual stages, which I conceive of as circling throughout one's life rather than unfolding neatly in a linear progression.

- Leaving home / initiation: where we question the known and the familiar. Following my mother's death and the accompanying loss of home as both material and emotional refuge, I formally entered the field.
- Rupture/incoherence: where narratives and norms lose meaning. As social scientists, we are at least partially prepared for how the friction of destabilizing encounters across difference results in a collision of social norms and routines. But we are less prepared to navigate the psychosocial effects of the journey, especially witnessing suffering and trauma, not to mention reconciling our identities as mothers with our identities at work.
- Integration/coherence: where, in the wake of rupture, existential crisis may occur. In my case, this crisis pivoted to a turning point where I sought the techniques and tools necessary to cope with moral distress.
- Coming home: where the field/home dichotomy is transcended and the new narrative is shared. Through adopting the mothering mind-set as a social scientist, I rediscovered meaning and purpose.
- Repeat: where this journey repeats with each new major life transition. Specifically, the journey toward subjective coherence, meaning, and purpose never ends and is situated in a broader human "field of struggle that remains elusive, transitory, and unevenly distributed" (Jackson, 2011), highly dependent upon our social contexts, locations, and access to opportunity structures.

Stage One: Leaving Home / Initiation, or Planting Seeds

My experience of field research, preceded and triggered by the death of my own mother to nonsmoking-related lung cancer, was complicated from the outset. In 1994, I wrote to a group called Red Thunder on the Fort Belknap Indian Reservation, located four miles southeast of Harlem, Montana, whose members were protesting the actions of Pegasus Gold, a cyanide heap-leach gold mine. They accused the mine of poisoning the groundwater and destroying sacred cave paintings in the mountains. Red Thunder invited me to join their protest movement against the mine and paired me with a respected elder named Dora.

That year was my first immersion into the messiness of fieldwork research as I became enmeshed in the web of fraught relationships nested in reservation politics, alcoholism and poverty, and gender-based violence, as well as the spirit of revival derived from sweat lodge, vision quest, spirit lodge, and sun dance rituals. Research as studious inquiry changes when you live among people, particularly when you are invited into their ritual spaces, smudging your body with braided sweetgrass, eating from the communal bowl of berries, and greeting each smoldering "grandfather rock" placed in the pit of the sweat lodge. Objectivity becomes complicated when you ride on horseback with drunk native cowboys howling at the moon and pouring cups of sticky Thunderbird over the graves of their friends lost to suicide. Impartiality is difficult when your neighbor shows up with bruises all over one side of her face, inflicted by the man you work beside, who, in turn, shares his heartbreaking poems about fighting in Vietnam. You are implicated in these stories as elders show you their grade-school photos and recall how the nuns made them cut their long hair, a sign of grieving in their native tradition. Over time, you, the ethnographer, are exposed as well, overcome, tired, awkward, and vulnerable.

My job was to share with outside reporters and environmentalists the data we had collected on the mine's illegal and unsafe practices by testing our own samples to prove that the water was contaminated despite its "self-monitored" claims. Ultimately, we were successful. The mine was ordered to pay a landmark $36.7 million pollution settlement to come into compliance with state and federal water-quality laws. I was elated to have played a small part in such an important victory against all odds (Guthrie, 1997).

But the victory was short-lived. As described later by Diamond (2005) in his book *Collapse: How Societies Choose to Fail or Succeed*, the mine declared bankruptcy and avoided all cleanup costs by transferring its assets to other corporations owned by the same individuals. Today, I tell the story of my initiation at Fort Belknap into the field of social justice work as a cautionary tale to underscore the importance of cultivating the quality of perseverance and to value process over outcome, especially when the results appear mixed or even as failures.

Often, the willingness to acknowledge one's limitations in present circumstances enables one to sustain the work in the long run. In a similar vein, an activist mentor taught me to regard social justice work as "planting seeds," undeterred by whether they might bear fruit in one's lifetime. To me, this idea of remaining present in social justice work—tending to and watering the seeds of our efforts so that they have a strong start and then, in time, stepping away so that the stems might grapple with the elements to strengthen their roots, bend with the wind, and so on—sounds like tried and true parenting advice. Perhaps one of the most difficult aspects of growing into the role of mother is learning to trust that we will instill enough valuable nutrients into our children to release the need to control their process as they become who they are in and through the world.

Writer Rebecca Solnit (2016) speaks of the faith in this kind of invisible ripening that lies underground, beyond our watchful eye, in terms of social justice, where "the fruiting body of the larger, less visible fungus" may even suddenly sprout into the mushroom of ideas and revolution. But more than a decade would pass before I regained my faith and showed up with confidence in my convictions and humility in my limitations, what Joan Halifax (2009), in her book on hospice work, calls a "soft front and strong back." In the meantime, something in me had hardened. I took my investigative skills in witnessing, reporting, and writing with me to the lower east side of Manhattan and attempted to compartmentalize the rest.

Stage Two: Rupture and the Fallout of Vicarious Trauma

After a demanding year in New York City soaking up the teachings of muckraker Wayne Barrett of the *Village Voice* by day, waitressing in Times Square by night, I was called back to Chicago where my sister was hospitalized in a psychiatric facility. Following my mother's illness, it was to be my second major caretaking role. My editor at the *Voice* had recommended I apply to work at the City News Bureau, an independent wire service, where Ernest Hemingway had gotten his start. So now twenty-six, I became a crime reporter working the night shift in Chicago at a time when homicides raged across gang territories in record numbers and the whole nightscape seemed to be on fire (Guthrie, 1999). By day, I spent most of my free time on the thirteenth floor of Rush Hospital, where my sister sat in the quiet room smoking cigarettes in a post-electroconvulsive therapy haze or circled the nurse's station dodging and weaving around her auditory hallucinations.

At 5:00 p.m., I began my shift at the morgue, where I received the nightly list of deceased persons, and ended it at 2:00 a.m., reciting the details of each person's demise to my editor. The deaths of junkies, gangbangers, and street people were usually deemed "cheap," meaning they were too banal to make headlines. I kept a thick notebook of quotes and anecdotes I'd gathered about their lives in my briefcase. Their untold stories began to haunt me.

Eventually the immersion into these darker worlds of psych unit and morgue, combined with a perpetual lack of sleep, took its toll. This is how I learned how secondary, or vicarious, trauma works: subtly over time. The emotional residue from chronic exposure to witnessing the suffering of others or assuming caregiving responsibilities is sometimes referred to as the "cost of caring," a kind of compassion fatigue (Figley, 1997). Its symptoms include changes in perception and memory; feeling either numb or in a state of hyperarousal;

and a sense of diminished safety, trust, and independence (American Counseling Association, 2011). Vicarious trauma is particularly rampant among those who inhabit the role of witness yet are denied a space to process the emotional, affective, embodied experience that accompanies such witnessing. In my own life, family and friends called me "resilient," but in my high-functioning haze, I was becoming increasingly detached from reality, disconnected from the full spectrum of my emotions, and sidestepping important reflexive and even grieving processes.

Perhaps unsurprisingly, many of my fellow earnest, hardworking reporters and, later, fellow activists or academics, all of whom were covering complex content about human behavior and immersed in deadline-driven, high-performance, high-stress work contexts with few spaces for relief, were heavy drinkers and workaholics who struggled with intimate relationships. In the humanitarian groups I work with today, I have seen how trauma and chronic stress shapes even the cultures of these crisis-driven care-work organizations in the same way they shape the worldview of individuals. Patterns of "relentless stress," such as repetitive emergency situations, may lead organizational cultures to act from a place of "chronic hyperarousal" similar to individuals who experience trauma (Bloom, 2011). In these environments where no spaces are consciously created for relief and admission of vulnerability, compassion may be shunned in favor of an atomized stoicism. A chronic gallows humor can insidiously infect an entire culture with cynicism. I still recall the cheeky banner at the City News Bureau that read, "If your Mother says she loves you, check it out!"

That Christmas, I worked until 3:00 a.m. and then trudged home and paused, as was my habit, in front of a little temple—a yoga seminary that featured stained glass mandalas and leafy plants in its huge plate-glass windows. It reminded me of California and my mother. Once home, I cracked open the photo albums I had stashed deep in the closet and revisited her life—our lives as a family—before the diagnosis, all the love and joyful moments. The year before cancer, she had gone through some kind of awakening. She had managed to eliminate her commute by working from home, and she found time in her everyday life to paint, take brisk morning walks along the bay, join a "stitch and bitch" club, and practice yoga and meditation.

We all noticed the change—how she seemed to be perpetually humming a tune and radiating some inner light. She had always left a trail of loveliness in her wake, repurposing everything from furniture to clothing, like her mother had done since the Depression. But now it all seemed so *intentional*: the stitched pillows or arrangements of poppies. I turned a page and saw that scrap of stationary in which she'd written from her hospice bed a list of qualities she thought we shared: "courage, loyalty, determination, strong opinions, empathy, healthy skepticism, artistic dramatic flair, sense of humor, a love of poodles and the outdoors and LOVE, LOVE, LOVE."

In spiritual traditions, we often affirm that the essence of courage is vulnerability and love. The Japanese art of repairing pottery with gold or silver lacquer, known as *kintsukuroi*, recognizes that the piece is more beautiful for having been broken. Tibetan Buddhist Chögyam Trungpa Rinpoche (1984) wrote, "To be a spiritual warrior, one must have a broken heart; without a broken heart and the sense of tenderness and vulnerability that is in one's self and all others, your warriorship is untrustworthy."

I closed the albums and felt something stirring deep within. After years of "paying my dues," I realized I had consistently served as a confidante for my (mostly male) colleagues and supervisors who were progressively showing signs of "leaking" from the rigid compartmentalization they had created to structure their front- and backstage selves. The ability to be present amid vulnerability was actually my gift, not this front of stoic resilience. The next day, I woke up and walked into that temple and signed myself up for the seminary. I began to offer yoga in church basements and YMCAs. Through these classes, and later in running my own studio for more than a decade, I left my detached silo and met people from all walks of life who shared their stories of rupture, usually prompted by death or loss, and their own struggles that resulted from denying this deep, seemingly irreconcilable rift between their public and private selves.

Having created a disciplined practice and "sangha," or community, I began to strengthen my own bridge between these stages and selves, gauging more skillfully when and with whom it was prudent and safe to share different aspects of myself and not grasping for more with others. With my sister, who had been cultivating her own meditation practice, this owning of my own vulnerability was a critical step toward an authentic, rather than an enabling, engagement in our relationship. Over time, I was able to cultivate the discernment I needed to gain the narrative competence to (re)tell my story (Frank, 2010).

Stage Three: Integration and Returning Home

During my pregnancy, I accepted an applied medical anthropology position with a large, midwestern urban hospital on a project addressing health disparities in the African American community across five Baptist churches. I spent the summer attending Bible studies and sermons to gain an understanding of the church environment, its resources, and its needs; the language and meanings that surrounded wellness and faith; and church members' resistance to biomedical approaches. In many ways, participating in this project reminded me of my experience on the reservation in Montana, with its ritual spaces and shared commitment to addressing structural violence. I was also back in my role of cultural translator and *accompagnateur*, which I felt I had the skills and capacities to perform. What I did not anticipate was what I *received* that summer.

At some point, participation overtook observation in a physiological sense as I stood in those pews. Awash in pregnancy hormones as my baby grew, I spontaneously opened up to the visceral, sensory experience of which I was a part. The main vehicle was call-and-response sermons, in which prayer, preaching, singing, saxophone or organ playing, and testimony were layered into multidimensional worship of sweating, swaying bodies with stamping feet, gesticulating and clasped hands, and powerful voices shouting, "Amen! Hallelujah! Praise the lord!" Other times, the gospel singers' voices swelled with such volume that the room vibrated. I often felt an increase in fetal activity for hours after such sessions, my baby bouncing and kicking gleefully in her amniotic sac.

After church on those summer nights, I walked outside our neighborhood, the passionate words of the evening's sermon swirling in my brain. I encountered circles of karma as I edged past Lance, the harmonica-playing homeless man the same age as my sister, snoring in his sleeping bag on the floor of our studio. My sister was now living on her own, taking "one day at a time" in recovery and counseling family caregivers struggling to understand their family members' mental illness. I could finally see how these circles of interconnection and compassion were woven through all the layers of my life. I was regaining faith. I came back from church, from these spaces of praise and worship, cupping my growing belly, letting the feelings wash over me like weather.

Mothering and Porosity

According to French psychoanalyst Luce Irigaray (1993), "'Porosity' references the anatomy of the woman to emphasize permeability and interrelationship over autonomy. The placenta is both permeable tissue and a nourishing envelope that mediates birth."

Chodorow (1999) asserts that, through the lens of gender identity, girls, or the feminine psychic structures in all of us, are more relational than boys, the masculine psychic structures in all of us. In general, women come to experience themselves as less separate than men, as having more permeable ego boundaries because the father figure remains the catalyst in which offspring begin to individuate from the mother. Regardless of how we self-identify in terms of gender identity, our ways of relating to others form somewhere along this spectrum of a rigidly bounded psychic position coded as the autonomous masculine or a porous or sensitized ego coded as the empathetic feminine in a broader misogynistic society that still suppresses the symbolization of femininity in its public discourse and pathologizes the female body.

As masculinity is constructed through symbols of an autonomous self, a body sealed and self-contained that penetrates but is not penetrated, the symbolic feminine, whose body is regarded as shape-shifting and porous, is viewed as monstrous. Many cultures reference a figure—*Selkie*, mermaid, Siren, Medusa, *Ciguapa*, witch—who represents the shape-shifting or seductive feminine principle and evokes fear of the insatiable feminine appetite, a sight imagined as irrational, emotional, and devouring of the autonomous self. In the Dominican Haitian village where I lived between 2006 and 2009 interviewing sex and romance workers negotiating the circuits of their intimate economies, my neighbor, a witch, once showed me the raised line of scar tissue on her scalp where her husband had cut her with his machete. He needed to "bleed out" her magic so she would stop flying at night.

As Irigaray (1985, p. 106) notes, "The supposed intrinsic leakiness of the female is a threat to well-being, a breach in boundaries of selfhood that blurs distinction between self and other." Leakiness can trigger a sense that one's identity has become unmoored. This fear of an unstable, incoherent identity prompts more anxious and often misogynistic individuation to reaffirm an unstable autonomy against this destabilizing desire. And yet, in many areas of life, we revel in this desire, the intersubjective enmeshment and blurring of the "I": sacred spiritual accompaniment, as revealed in the ecstatic poems of Rumi, or nursing children as the infant's suckling stimulates the release of oxytocin, which stimulates milk production and eventually a sense of being lost in the child's big, luminous eyes. And enmeshment is certainly highly desirable to fall in love or achieve "la petite mort" (the little death) of the orgasm.

Through a series of paintings that depict caregiving scenes between doctors and patients, Harvard University psychiatrist Arthur Kleinman (2015) shows medical students encounters that reveal the intercorporeal enmeshment that is a part of such devotion and attention: the blurred face of Goya with his doctor; the fusing of heads of a patient and visitor in a Picasso; the Madonna holding her crucified son, a painting that offers rich meaning around the depth of care as much as of suffering. In fact, Kleinman refers to compassion fatigue not as a kind of wearying from overcare but as resulting from conditions or environments that *diminish or prevent* one from being able to enact compassion. Those who enact presence are energized, not depleted, and they themselves have a network of nourishing relationships to draw from. "Presence is what makes care nonmechanical, gives care a vividness, a fullness," he says.

Of course, in many social and institutional contexts, exposing one's susceptibility on the front (public) stages of one's life is dangerous. The conditions that create the psychological safety needed to be vulnerable involve deep levels of trust and a secure social contract. As strategic social actors interested in self-preservation before self-actualization, we must skillfully maneuver between enmeshment with others and regulation of our emotions while protecting our bodily borders, contingent on the circumstances of the encounter. In this way, identity work, or the construction of ourselves, is always the suture point or temporary meeting point of our interactions that (re)forms us and enables us to act (Stuart Hall, cited in Watts, 1992).

In our interactions, we may also encounter ruptures to our cosmologies that create too much incoherence for our sense of self to sustain. As Lingis writes, "Trauma unmasks regularly functioning phantasms ('me,' 'my life') *as* phantasms. This is precisely why trauma is traumatic. It strips the world bare of the illusion that it isn't an illusion" (quoted in George & Sparrow, 2014, p. 54). But for others, (re)writing our life narratives resembles those old "choose your own adventure" books where, as we encounter those forks in the road, we are able to choose one path in the spirit of adventure without foreclosing the existence of another. Our sense of self does not collapse because we know other possibilities are available. At the same time, when one identity is threatened, on a practical level, we can import confidence from other domains of our lives when one domain is threatened and persevere (Cohen & Sherman, 2014).

Drawing from the metaphor of mothering from the field, might we envision new relations of intercorporeality? "In place of . . . the masculinist economy that reduces difference to a property relationship, our selves could form in the dynamic contact with others, not according to a fixed ideal but in a transformative encounter in which neither self nor other is a predictable, calculable identity with inviolable boundaries" (Shildrick, 2002, p. 118). And as social scientists studying patterns of meaning in culture, we can avoid the detached observer perspective from which "objective" scientific theory is formulated by emphasizing that we are capable of capturing only little bits of knowledge and are always interacting in dynamic ways with others that are ever emerging, changing, and ever vulnerable.

In many ways, the disembodied, detached, objective observer is still the preferred standpoint of the credible researcher. And the ideal fieldworker is still framed in terms of either empowering or demystifying the other. An ethic of reciprocal, if uneven, exchange is not at the heart of the encounter. We owe it to ourselves and each other to subvert this heroic narrative and to consciously and strategically create the bridge between the back- and frontstages of our lives. As researchers, we can mother by acknowledging that we are sensate beings intimately involved in encounters with others and be open to giving and receiving care and presence in this fragile world where we all share yearning and heartache. This can be done while acknowledging the various privileges and hierarchies in which we are ensconced.

Conclusion: The Antiheroic Narrative

The experience of caregiving is not romantic, and it may leave us at times feeling exhausted and bereft. Yet the commitment to accompany others in the spirit of service, to center their well-being as one's vocation, to journey with them regardless of outcome, is at the heart of what affirms the humanitarian mission, and what it means to mother in the field. My job these days is to also raise a little person named Ella Saige with as much love and care as I can muster to be her own kind of ethical cosmopolitan. At the same time, I support others who have dedicated their time and skills to social justice projects to mind their own inner development and limitations as they seek to be a force toward social change.

In this role, I have met many exceptional people who care for others on the front lines of challenging field contexts all over the developing world. They are technically skilled and proficient but also, at times, fragmented, incoherent, and lost. This situation seems inevitable given the nature of their task: witnessing the enormity of suffering on behalf of those of the global North and saddled with the label *change agent*. Sometimes the trauma is vicarious, absorbed through the knowledge wrought by treating women who are beaten or raped or by diagnosing patients who lack access to the cure. Sometimes it is direct, like surviving a bombing and being evacuated from a war zone, having to leave one's comrades behind. Occasionally, sweet moments occur; the treatment is available and provides the cure, or at least the alleviation of symptoms, or the program provides a refuge to empower others. More often, the results are mixed, temporary, and insufficient to meet the enormity of need.

The "art of life," according to Kleinman (2017), is less about an ego-driven "sticking it out no matter what" and more about coming to terms with the "insufficiency of our own resources and yet still acquiring enough wisdom to endure, to live into acts of service, knowing that life is dangerous and uncertain" (personal communication, October 25, 2017). It's about developing ourselves as human beings within a relational and ethical system of care. Through these relationships and the codesign of resources that support both the inner and outer journey of social justice work, careworkers tell me their own field stories of leaving home, rupture, incoherence, reintegration, and coming home. Together, we try to cultivate inner capacities needed to navigate the minefield of existential threats that surface and repair the harm we often inflict upon each other (using circle process, see "Practical Tips").

The ability to imagine new kinds of "heroes" (e.g., female, queer, disabled, from the global South) is important. Yet the elements that constitute these stories need to be critically reimagined, set in the larger ecological web of life, to be *sustainable and communal*. Perhaps inspired by the feminine, maternal principle in all of us, a new journey story for the humanitarian antihero could reflect iconic choices faced by mothering/caring and the different values that often animate women's lives.

Consider, for example, the choice to have or not have children; the ever-elusive search for a sustainable rhythm between home and work; or valuing family, friends, and lovers. Such a story might consider the transformative power of creating a culture that prioritizes the flourishing of children and the creation of human relationships to counter the boundless pursuit of self-interest. In contrast to the iconic lone hero on a solo adventure, our heroine understands that she is part of the collective. Her goals may be as protective or nurturing as they are operational, placing the care of more vulnerable others first. Like Persephone or Inanna, she also has the capacity to extend down into the depths of her own shadowy underworld and examine the forgotten and ignored parts of herself. While she takes accountability for her own journey-experience, she is not afraid to ask for help or seek out companions and wise guides along the way. Her eventual reentry into the greater community as an elder is honored for the living wisdom and experience she represents to be passed on to new generations. Her transformation may be external or internal. But she is empowered to fly, this monstrous mother–social scientist.

Practical Tips: Guidance for Facilitating Circle Spaces

- Request a space conducive to group conversation and plan within time constraints.
- Identify stakeholders.
- Rotate facilitation responsibility.
- Use a talking piece to encourage attentive listening and appreciative inquiry.
- Invite agreement to circle ground rules centered on respectful speech, confidentiality, and prosocial values, such as repairing harm through strengthening community and locating resources.
- Model prosocial behaviors: intentional speaking, active listening without judgment, taking accountability, compassion, presence.
- Allow for silence and spaciousness.
- Honor your own body's messages while tending to group's well-being (stretch/movement, food, rest, bathroom breaks).
- Cultivate high tolerance for ambiguity and polarities.
- Encourage dialogue; use the "both/and" approach.
- Use metaphors, poems, and personal objects to mediate topics and approach them "on the slant" (Palmer, 2004).
- "Story is the heartbeat of circle. Lived experience is our common denominator" (Jane Nicholson, Restorative Justice and Peace Circle facilitator).

- Create rituals to support a purposeful meeting with intentional openings, check-ins, breaks, transitions, and closing check-outs.

References

American Counseling Association (2011). Vicarious trauma. Retrieved from https://www.counseling.org/docs/trauma-disaster/fact-sheet-9---vicarious-trauma.pdf?sfvrsn=2

Bloom, S. L. (2011). Trauma-organized systems and parallel process. In N. Tehrani (Ed.), *Managing trauma in the workplace: Supporting workers and organizations* (pp. 139–152.). London, UK: Routledge.

Campbell, J., Cousineau, P., & Brown, S. L. (1990). *The hero's journey: The world of Joseph Campbell: Joseph Campbell on his life and work*. San Francisco, CA: Harper & Row.

Chodorow, N. (1999). *The reproduction of mothering*. New Haven, CT: Yale University Press.

Cohen, G., & Sherman, D. (2014). The psychology of change: Self-affirmation and social psychological intervention. *Annual Review of Psychology*, *65*, 333–371.

Cunningham, L. (2012, October 3). On leadership: Exhaustion is not a status symbol. *Washington Post*. Retrieved from https://www.washingtonpost.com/national/exhaustion-is-not-a-status-symbol/2012/10/02/19d27aa8-0cba-11e2-bb5e-492c0d30bff6_story.html?utm_term=.7597a8c484b6

Diamond, J. (2005). *Collapse: How societies choose to fail or succeed*. New York, NY: Viking.

Figley, C. R. (1997). *Burnout in families: The systematic costs of caring*. Boca Raton, FL: CRC Press.

Frank, A. (2010). *Letting stories breathe: A socio-narratology*. Chicago, IL: University of Chicago Press.

George, B., & Sparrow, T. (Eds.). (2014). *Itinerant philosophy: On Alphonso Lingis*. Goleta, CA: Punctum.

Gorman, J. (2012, December 17). Ancient bones that tell a story of compassion. *New York Times*. Retrieved from http://www.nytimes.com/2012/12/18/science/ancient-bones-that-tell-a-story-of-compassion.html

Gupta, A., & Ferguson, J. (Eds.). (1997). *Anthropological locations: Boundaries and grounds of a field science*. Berkeley, CA: University of California Press.

Guthrie, D. (1997, March 1). Environmental racism on Montana reservation. *Z Magazine*. Retrieved from https://zcomm.org/zmagazine/environmental-racism-on-montana-reservation-by-deirdre-guthrie/

Guthrie, D. (1999, January 7). Body count. *Chicago Reader*. Retrieved from https://www.chicagoreader.com/chicago/body-count/Content?oid=898124

Halifax, J. (2009). *Being with dying: Cultivating compassion and fearlessness in the presence of death*. Boulder, CO: Shambhala.

Irigaray, L. (1985). *Speculum of the other woman*. Ithaca, NY: Cornell University Press.

Irigaray, L. (1993). *An ethics of sexual difference*. (C. Burke & G. Gill, Trans.). Ithaca, NY: Cornell University Press.

Jackson, M. D. (2011). *Life within limits: Well-being in a world of want*. Durham, NC: Duke University Press.

Kleinman, A. (2009). Caregiving: The odyssey of becoming more human. *The Lancet*, *373*(9660), 292–293.

Kleinman, A. (2015, June 9). Enduring caregiving: The moral transformation of ordinary people. YouTube. Retrieved from https://www.youtube.com/watch?v=IogC9lwyiYQ

National Academies (2016). Recommendations. *Families Caring for an Aging America*. Retrieved from https://www.nap.edu/resource/23606/Caregiving-Recommendations.pdf

Palmer, P. J. (2004). *A hidden wholeness: The journey toward an undivided life*. San Francisco, CA: Jossey-Bass.

Paterson, J. G., & Zderad, L. T. (1976). *Humanistic Nursing*. New York: Wiley.

Remen, R. N. (2017, August 6). Helping, fixing, or serving? *Lion's Roar*. Retrieved from https://www.lionsroar.com/helping-fixing-or-serving/

Rinpoche, C. T. (1984). *Shambhala: The sacred path of the warrior*. Boulder, CO: Shambhala Publications.

Shildrick, M. (2002). *Embodying the monster: Encounters with the vulnerable self*. London, UK: Sage.

Solnit, R. (2016). *Hope in the dark: Untold histories, wild possibilities*. Chicago, IL: Haymarket.

Watts, M. J. (1992). Space for everything (a commentary). *Cultural Anthropology, 7*(1), 115–129.

15

Two Notes on Bringing Children Other Than Your Own in the Field

●●●●●●●●●●●●●●●●●●●●●

APRILLE ERICSSON,

DAWN ERICSSON PROVINE,

ARIELLE ERICSSON WHITE,

MIKAE PROVINE,

PIERRE ERICSSON,

BAHIYYAH MIALLAH MUHAMMAD,

AND MÉLANIE-ANGELA NEUILLY

This chapter provides a family perspective on mothering in the field. The first part was written by Mélanie-Angela Neuilly based on a compilation of notes and interviews conducted by Bahiyyah Miallah Muhammad with Aprille Ericsson, PhD, her nine-year-old daughter Arielle, her sixteen-year-old niece Mikae, and her adult nephew Pierre, about their experiences as Aprille mothered them in her field of aerospace engineering at NASA. In the second part, Aprille's sister, Dawn Ericsson Provine, provides her own first-person perspective on how she mothered in the field while attending medical school and later as an ob-gyn. Their combined practical tips are presented at the end.

Introduction

Dr. Aprille Ericsson's early childhood memories bring visions of standing in the main control room of the New York Metropolitan Transit Authority staring at the large, lit-up display board. She proudly remembers that this is where her maternal grandfather worked, and this is where her initial understanding of engineering stems from. She also remembers visiting her mother while she worked at Brooklyn College and attended the school of dentistry. These experiences shaped her life so deeply that she has strived to pass it forward to the next generation, even when having children of her own seemed out of reach.

When she left MIT and went on to graduate school at Howard University in Washington, DC, she found that the Howard University motto of "Veritas et Utilitas [Truth and Service]" complimented the MIT motto of "Mens et Manus [Mind and Hand]." These have served as personal mantras for Aprille as she has always aimed to create value for the world through both science and service. She does that by balancing her mentorship of young people in the sciences as well as through her dedication to her various communities and educational boards (from being graduate student council president at Howard University, HU Board of Trustees, board chair of HU Middle School of Mathematics Science, to serving as president of her daughter's school PTA).

Of her experience at Howard, she says, "Studying with my sepia-hued, yellow-tinted, red-boned and white-skinned brothers and sisters I came to realize early in my academic endeavors, 'We may have all come on different ships, but we're in the same boat now,' which Dr. King anecdotally stated."

Mothering from the Field as an Aunt and a Mentor

> I did not have my daughter until late in my Aerospace career. My daughter is nine years old, while my career spans some thirty-five years, between graduate work and working at NASA. Even though most of my career has taken place prior to the birth of my daughter, I have always made it a point to include young family members in my job.

Aprille's involvement of young children into her job and her discipline has been expressed in a wide variety of ways. Following the example set for her by her grandfather and her mother, both Aprille and her sister, Dr. Dawn Ericsson, brought a number of family members to work or work-related events:

> My oldest nephew, Pierre, started off with first coming to school with me at Howard University when I was doing my research. Then, when I started working at NASA Goddard Space Flight Center he would often come down and visit me for a period in the summer and I would take him with me to work

and I would drop him off at some of my colleagues' electronic labs. He would also come along with me on speaking engagements, and in one instance he had the opportunity to be with me when we did rocket launches demonstrations for Rosa Parks and I was one of the few speakers that presented to her at the time. I talked a lot about the historical STEM contributions of our ancestors and the work we do at NASA.

Later on, she had two nieces apply and successfully go through the S.I.S.T.E.R. Program, a program at the GSFC aimed at exposing young women and girls to engineering and science disciplines.
In Mikae's words,

I think one of the things I remember on the first day is that they gave us ID badges and we all felt so important driving around and looking at the different sites. So for example—I think they'd been bringing in a new satellite [James Webb Space Telescope components] on one of the days that we were there so we got to see that come in. It was super super cool … and everything that was super super awesome. We did a lot of demos. A lot of people came in and spoke to us and I think one of the things that shocked me the most about being there was being able to meet so many like-minded individuals about the same age. I felt like everyone there was super super accomplished. I mean as you can be for a middle school and it was really nice having those people around me.

FIGURE 15.1 Dr. Aprille Ericsson and nephew Pierre Ericsson pictured with Rosa Parks during her visit to NASA Goddard Space Flight Center (GSFC) in 1996

Fun is another way in which Aprille brings science to children, whether they were her own, her family's, or children in the community: "One summer, I had thirteen children from the family stay with me and we did math and science with sports related activities. We built rockets, we went to Howard University's Dental school to see their automated lab. We went to a baseball game and did the statistics for all the players. We went swimming and talked about buoyancy. We called it the Family Science Camp."

As president of her daughter's school PTO, she has organized Family Hallo-STEAM night, which includes hands-on STEAM (Science, Technology, Engineering, Arts, and Mathematics) activities, a STEAM costume parade competition, and a trick-or-trunk in the school parking lot involving a family car decorating competition. In Aprille's words, "We have a really good time and I'm the mad scientist at the event. I usually do an electricity theme and I have my little plasma ball. I've got mechanical hand, snap circuits—yes, we got it all. I have this stick that if you connect people together, the electricity will flow through and light up the stick because of the electricity in your body and so I talk to kids about electricity."

As a Black woman engineer, Aprille takes her outreach role very seriously and makes it a point to go above and beyond in both "Mind and Hand" and "Truth and Service." She also works with students involved in robotics, organizes competitions, facilitates a wide range of STEM and hands-on activities for Girl Scouts, and mentors high school and college students. She has traveled throughout the United States and abroad to speak to students about her aerospace career.

Mothering from the Field When Your Field Is NASA

When most people think of a lab, they think more of biology or chemistry labs. But we do a lot of lab work [as NASA engineers]. Much of it is in small spaces, for things like circuitry, but we also do lots of testing in a laboratory-type environment, and that's the kind of engineering lab space that is most conducive to bringing children around. Now of course, larger testing facilities with flight hardware are not the best place for children, but we may allow undergraduate students to do internships and be mentored and shadow people there.

In terms of creating a family-friendly environment, NASA has seen a true culture shift over time, with more and more women participating, and thus having family leave, and changing the nurturing environment. This includes having a lot of family-oriented activities throughout the year but also on-site childcare facilities.

Like many of us, Aprille had to get back to work after about three months postpartum. Unlike many of us, it was to begin to work on a proposal for a spacecraft mission. Like many of us, she brought her baby along: "She was probably only about three or four months old. I would be doing two days, and two or three days off, and I would rotate those days. There were always secretaries who were willing to keep an eye or friends on the team who would agree to keep her for an hour or so while I had a meeting. Overall, we were always trying to get the work done and tag team if necessary."

Much as she had done with her nieces and nephew before, Aprille did not stop bringing Arielle to work with her past infancy:

> As late as this week, as I am writing this, my daughter roams around the suite and gets into doing stuff or sitting in a corner and not necessarily in my office. She plays with her toys, writes on my board, draws, and a lot of the time, I give her little science kits that we have at our facility to read through. It can be tough to keep her entertained and make sure she does not spend her day on her cell phone. But at this phase of my career, now that I am a senior leader in the division office, we have a dozen offices, a huge conference room, two secretaries, a kitchen, and a bathroom inside our suite, so she more or less wanders. I have had to teach her office etiquette. Nevertheless, she has been exposed to many very smart people, and she is never ever bashful about asking questions.

Bringing the children in their family to work is something that Aprille and both of her sisters, Dawn and Trina, have done. This early field exposure has impacted them all in positive ways.

The Impact of Mothering from the Field on Children

Aprille's story illustrates how deep the impact of being exposed to complex reasoning and a wide range of experiences and activities and ways of thinking from a young age can be. But it also shows us the importance of having role models who look like us.

The impact is very direct. Arielle, now nine years old, wants to be an ob-gyn. As she says herself, "I feel like I'm a part of a world history. How people make stuff, how they do amazing stuff to help our world be alive. . . . Every time I go to my mom's job, I get to see all of these wonderful things that I'm never going to see at school or places that I barely go to. I get to see all of this science and all of these wonderful things."

Pierre is now a mechanical engineer at Budweiser, and Aprille is mentoring his own fourteen-year-old daughter: "I am super thankful for everything that my aunt did for me . . . but it feels different as a father. I mean the person that mentored you somehow can mentor your daughter, you know, you never think that that reach can extend through generations, you just think it's more direct."

In this case, familial mentorship is intergenerational. Pierre never imagined that he and his daughter would share similar mentoring experiences through his aunt Aprille. As a father, Pierre now sees his daughter's interest sparked in ways that only a woman could facilitate. It is no longer just about him being mentored but all the children in the family being exposed to the wonders of science, technology, engineering, and math. Pierre's experience has helped maintain the bonds that tied him to Aprille and, now, to his daughter.

And beyond providing mentoring, mothering from the field is about strengthening family ties. In Aprille's niece Mikae's words,

> I guess when I was staying with Aprille and her daughter it was almost like being in college for a little bit. Like I was away from home but I was living with someone who I trusted and was fairly close to and I think that whole experience made me more excited going into the future about being more independent and maybe living around. . . . When I go to college I plan on not being too far from family wherever they may be. And I think that's kind of given me a new look on family in general and independence.

As we ponder what mothering from the field looks like at different times in women's lives, Dr. Ericsson's experience reminds us that mothering from the field can be more than an organizational strategy. Instead, she tells us, it is an act of resistance, a radical act of education and emancipation; it is a civic duty and a service to family and community. This simple act, bringing your children to your place of work, whether out of necessity or choice, is always a transgression challenging the status quo. In Aprille's case, she makes visible what did not exist before her, embodying the model her family needed but also embodying a legacy of family exposure to site-based fieldwork.

Mothering from the Obstetrics Ward

Dawn Ericsson Provine, MD

"Mothering from the field" is an interesting phrase. In my mind, it conjures up an image of African American ancestry working in the fields with little ones wrapped snuggly to their backs. Mothers did the work of the day and kept their little ones close. It was a way to protect them and teach at the same time. Additionally, there was little room to question, "How will I raise this child and work at the same time?" It sparked creative ways to do so out of necessity.

Fast forward: African American women are seizing the opportunities increasingly presented to them over the last century. The more we, as African American women, seize these opportunities and succeed, the more positive a momentum we create for the future. So we press on because we also strive to create better opportunities for our offspring.

"Mothering from the field" came somewhat naturally to me. I was "mothered from the field," going to college classes with my mom when I was just two or three years old. I can recall the biology labs, seeing lab mice, and interacting with my mother's colleagues. The beauty of this was that I never questioned it. It was the only norm I knew. I remind myself often of that important point. As mothers, we often beat ourselves up for not creating a "normal" schedule. Our children's norms, however, are what we make them. Exposing them to educational and productive work environments is not the worst thing we could do. It is quite the contrary. We set their expectations and standards a little higher by exposing them to high achievers, do-ers and go-getters. This applies to our own children and the children of our village—cousins, nephews, nieces, and the children of friends. I have always enjoyed mothering the children in my village. There is great pleasure in seeing them learn, question, and develop their own ideas. When I was in medical school, I brought my first cousin, Antoine Hill, at the age of ten, into my theater-styled classroom of one hundred future doctors. From one of the top row, Antoine raised his hand and asked the biochemistry professor a question. It didn't cross his mind that he was there as an observer and not to learn and inquire, nor did he think that he was too young to speak up. I was so proud of him. Now an adult, he continues to be a critical thinker and still questions me on medical issues. There were many times where I also brought my nephew Pierre Ericsson to campus with me and introduced him to colleagues and administrators. These subtle experiences and interactions gave my cousin and nephew exposure to the hierarchy of certain environments and the kind of interactions people had in those environments.

Oftentimes, there is the *need*, not just the desire, to "mother from the field" because our busy schedules dictate it. For me, this was definitely so. I hosted my cousin and nephew at my apartment during my school years; otherwise, I would've missed out on their company. The rigors of my school schedule did not permit the usual family visits and outings. Such were the visits with my niece, Ciarra Jackson, years later. When she was a teenager, I told her that if she came to visit with me, I would take her to my office every day. She eagerly packed her business attire and came. For a week, she shadowed me and assisted at the office front desk. We spent so much more time together that way, and she learned about the responsibilities of a job, particularly one in the medical field.

The need to "mother from the field" presented itself many times during my medical career and with it, creative ways to do so were born. I married my Yale college sweetheart, Colin, during the beginning of medical school. My school, SUNY Stony Brook Medical Sciences Center, was one hundred miles from Colin's company, Honeywell, Inc., in Morristown, New Jersey. To make it work, we lived exactly in between both locations. Both of us commuted one hundred miles round-trip, over urban terrain, to school and work each day. A year later, our son Kaori was born, and I took a year off and returned to school. Having an infant, a long commute, and the challenge of medical school dictated that I get creative to manage everything.

Kaori rode with me early every morning, and I dropped him off at day care near campus. At school, equipped with my tape recorder, I sat in the front row for every lecture. I recorded every class throughout my day, listened attentively, and asked many questions. When I drove to and fro with Kaori, fastened in his car seat, I listened over and over to every lecture, rewinding and reciting where necessary. I did not have time to pore over textbooks in the medical school library, nor study in groups, as did most of my classmates. The recorded lectures were critical to me, and Kaori didn't seem to mind not listening to nursery rhymes or music in the car. He didn't complain that the drive took one, and sometimes two, hours. When his dad went on a week-long business trip during a critical exam period, creativity was needed again. I booked a hotel near campus and packed up a playpen, toys, diapers, and food for the week. Empathetic to my juggling, a school colleague came over every night to babysit at the hotel while I went to the lobby to study. If you keep key elements present in a child's life—core people and family, lots of love and stimulation, favorite toys and foods—children will thrive in many different situations. A child's compass for the norm is set by what is presented to them and, more importantly, their observation of people's demeanor in their surroundings. So if children see that mom is busy and on-the-go and seems happy doing so, they will likely follow suit.

While in medical school, I gave birth to two children. My second child, Mikae, was born ten days before graduation. For the first ten days of her life, she and my mother rode with me to school so I could do my final clinical rotation. During my class breaks, I popped in and out of class to nurse Mikae. Graduation came and two and a half months later, I started my ob-gyn residency training at St. Barnabas Medical Center in Livingston, New Jersey. This next step was fraught with an ominous overnight-call schedule. At its worst, I worked two months of thirty-six-hour continuous work calls every other night. I was very fortunate to walk away from a car crash where I totaled my car, tired and drowsy after work. I was one block shy of picking up my children from day care. Months later, I visited the day care as the special guest of the day in my son's classroom. The preschoolers were thrilled to try on oversized hospital scrubs, masks, shoe covers, and gloves. They listened intently as I talked about the dangers of opening medicine bottles. They eagerly placed pictures of organs where they should be on an outline of the body. Indeed, Kaori felt special and popular that day.

Generally, getting family time was challenging, so my husband frequently brought Mikae and Kaori to the hospital. They spent countless hours sitting

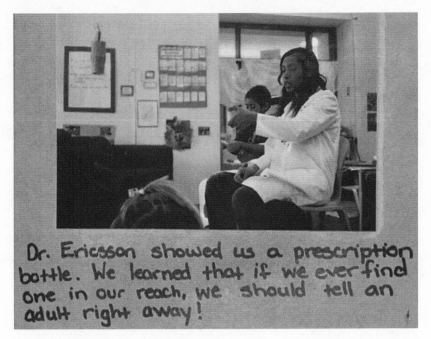

Dr. Ericsson showed us a prescription bottle. We learned that if we ever find one in our reach, we should tell an adult right away!

FIGURE 15.2 Dr. Dawn Ericsson Provine visits her son's day care early on in her career in 2004

with me among the buzz of fetal monitors, doctors, nurses, unit clerks, and patients passing by. I multitasked, entering patients' orders in the computer, combing my daughters' hair, and doing things with my children that they felt were special. We did things like peeking through the newborn nursery window; getting apple juice, Jell-O, and graham crackers from the patient pantry; or visiting my call room—a cramped room with bunk beds, desks, lockers, books everywhere, and resident traffic. We have a picture of us in my tiny call room with a little cake to celebrate Kaori's birthday. The children are smiling, oblivious to the unusual setting for a kid's birthday celebration. My kids, so accustomed to this setting as years went by, actually began asking to spend the night at the hospital with me on call. They were fine with packing up a cot and overnight stuff, getting snacks from the doctor's lounge, and watching television in a tiny call room. They didn't seem to care that I popped in and out all night between checking on various patients.

Just before my last year of residency, I had my third child, Kamora, and she too grew accustomed to the norm of my professional life. Early on, she and Kaori expressed an interest in entering the medical field. When she was nine, I began taking Kamora to do hospital rounds with me on weekends. We wheeled the computer up and down the hospital hallways. While I went in and out of patient rooms, Kamora had the task of putting together the billing sheets and keeping track of who I saw. She was eager to do it. At age sixteen, Kaori signed up to volunteer at two different hospitals where I worked. He gained critical experience venturing to do his volunteer tasks, aware of his invisible safety net—mom working on the third floor. It was great to eat lunch with him on those days, hear his enthusiasm about what he saw, and provide him with feedback. In that environment, he quickly developed his own relationships with doctors, nurses, technicians, clerks, and security personnel. Having an official electronic badge was an experience, and carrying out volunteer responsibilities, Kaori discovered the inner workings of the hospital. We could not wait until he turned eighteen years old, becoming eligible to officially shadow me in everything I did at work. Over time, I brought him, his friends, and many family friends to shadow. They came to my office and the hospital while I saw patients. They saw how I handled emergencies in the emergency room and obstetrics triage and watched full-blown surgeries and procedures and, best of all, babies being delivered. Today, Kaori is a sophomore at Vanderbilt University, completing premedical and predental requirements. He intends to enter the medical or dental profession.

My daughter Mikae, although not interested in entering the medical profession, was "mothered from the field" as a hospital volunteer as well. She appreciated her experiences working in the hospital gift shop. She currently wants to volunteer with hospice patients by bringing them comfort with her guitar and songs. Mikae had the additional benefit of being "mothered from the field" by her aunt, Dr. Aprille Ericsson. Mikae stayed at her aunt's house in Washington, DC, throughout the time she attended NASA's summer program, S.I.S.T.E.R. She recounts her experiences fondly among a multitude of engineers, scientists, and other like-minded young girls from various parts of the country. My youngest, Kamora, has spent her seventh-grade summer in a medical program at a medical school and hospital campus. She learned anatomy and physiology and made ongoing friendships with peers who are also interested in health careers. At the program's closing ceremonies, Kamora presented her own PowerPoint presentation on diabetes. This summer, she will rejoin the program and learn how to exercise her memory with techniques like mnemonics and problem-solve by studying the game of chess.

In sum, I feel fortunate that despite the many obstacles and constant juggling in my medical career, my children were able to learn about the medical field and not become victim to its rigors. Undoubtedly, obstacles lie within every career path, particularly for mothers.

Practical Tips

Here are some key points to take away from Aprille's experience:

- Mothering from the field is not just about your own children: mothering from the field can and should also refer to any and all nurturing activities we may engage in while in the field, whether it be while you are raising young children or whether you are mentoring your niece or nephew by exposing them to your activities.
- Mothering from the field is not just about mothers: bringing children to our places of work, when our places of work involve rockets, or foreign countries, or whatever else we study, can have an impact on them that we should never underestimate. For children, seeing their mothers or other role models in their lives shine at their peak professional competence is something that no books, movies, or more remote role models can replace.
- Mothering from the field is not just about children learning about your day-to-day: exposing children to site-based work can provide them with real-world examples of positive attributes such as teamwork and the importance of effective communication. Their experiences can be used to reinforce concepts that they learn in school and could benefit them in the future.
- Mothering from the field can help promote diversity and inclusion: in STEM fields specifically, bringing children to the workplace, can show them and reinforce the importance of diversity in the workplace—for example, by bringing girls into male-dominated fields and vice versa or bringing African American children into nonmajority fields.
- Mothering from the field is not just about the mentor/mentee relationship: being exposed to site-based work can set the stage for additional relationships to be made. It can be used as early professional development opportunities, especially when it exposes children to unknown summer camps or weekend-long programs. The full effects of a child's exposure to fieldwork are unknown. Therefore, it is important to conduct research in this area and continue to expose family and children to these opportunities.

Here are a few key points to take away from Dawn's experience:

- We often lament that we create irregularity in our children's schedules, do not see them enough, and nurture them less. When "mothering from the field," we mitigate those perceptions and provide benefits that are not available when "mothering from home." We can provide early, hands-on exposure to our careers, countering the typical influences that groom children to believe particular careers are unattainable. We can also regain the time we miss with our children by bringing them to our work spaces. At the same time, they can literally or metaphorically stand on our shoulders for support in their ventures.

- Through exposure to many areas early in life and viewing them as the norm, children find their voices more easily, leading them to do things like confidently ask title-bearing professionals unadulterated questions. Children brought into the field also become more aware of unique educational programs and supportive funding.
- Finally, these children can find like-minded peers earlier in life and create early networks that will support them for years to come.
- As for professional mothers, I believe *we* benefit by garnering the respect of colleagues who observe what we do. Undoubtedly, the feeling we enjoy from helping others, particularly our own children, is usually reward enough.

Here are a few key points to take away from Arielle's and Mikae's experiences. Adult fieldworkers should consider the following:

- Always ask your children if they want to attend. Never assume that they are interested in your work. Being forced to participate can have long-lasting and negative effects on children.
- Give children the opportunity to ask questions and have their opinions incorporated in decisions that are made about them.
- Don't assume that your work will be exciting to children. Rather, share your work experiences with them to allow them to choose what they are most interested in.
- When permissible, allow children to bring a friend along.
- Expose children to the field early in life—especially during junior high and high school. This experience may help them select classes and declare their major or minor field of study.

Children who may enter the field should consider the following:

- Be quiet, listen, and learn.
- Ask a lot of questions.
- Always keep an open mind. Try to shadow your parent for at least one day to see what happens because you might enjoy it.

Part VI

Practical Solutions to Complex Problems

• •

Because Mothers
Can Do Anything!

BAHIYYAH MIALLAH MUHAMMAD

While this whole book is proof that mothers do in fact conduct field research, it also illustrates that it is rarely, if ever, an easy feat. This final section of the book is a reminder to us all that complex problems can be solved with practical solutions. But as part of providing a counternarrative to the self-reliance trope, we also introduce concrete policy solutions that shift the responsibility of mothers' success in the field from the individual to the institution.

Here, Ryanne Pilgeram shares her practical solutions for successfully combining motherhood and fieldwork. She offers three main components and discusses them each in detail with her personal perspective weaved throughout: being a supportive partner, providing good childcare, and supporting a feminist epistemology. I, on the other hand, focus on practical solutions to saving money while conducting fieldwork without watering down the work. During a time when resources are limited and pooled, this cost-benefit analysis is needed. Here readers are introduced to the dollars and cents behind fieldwork.

We all know that mothers can do anything. But really, is mothering from the field worth it? It is worth all the fuss? Is it worth the support? Is it worth the methodological revolution? We are here to tell you that the answer to all those questions is a resounding yes!

Section-Specific Takeaways

- Find mentors in situations similar to yours. Utilize the advantages on online communities to build your network.
- Spend the extra time needed to locate childcare you are comfortable with. This will work out best for you and child.
- Prepare in advance before going into the field. Pack a to-go bag with all of your research supplies and small toys for emergencies.
- Finally, it is reasonable and acceptable to adjust your research agenda to better align with your life. You should not have to fit your life around your research.

16

"I Don't Know
How You Do It!"

● ●

Countering a Narrative
That Presumes That
Researching and Mothering
Are Incompatible

RYANNE PILGERAM

Learning the Hard Way

In summer 2007, I held the most beautiful baby in the world. He was perfect, and my pregnancy, labor, and delivery—though unpleasant from beginning to end—were what might be described by a doctor as "uneventful." At nearly the same moment he was born, I received page proofs for my very first peer-reviewed article. The culmination of my master's thesis, the paper was the result of in-depth interviews, ethnographic fieldwork, and countless hours spent perfecting the language, the theory, its every detail. The paper, in fact, was a "conditional accept" at the first journal I sent it to. My thesis adviser was thrilled with it but told me she was not surprised. For the first time, I felt like maybe, just maybe, I would become a *real* sociologist.

I also felt the way I assume most of us mere mortals feel after having a baby—especially a first baby: emotionally raw, exhausted, and in a lot of pain.

So as I sat with my new baby and saw the e-mail giving me a short few days to review the proofs and return them, it became immediately apparent that my academic career was over before it even started. I just couldn't read the proofs, let alone have them returned in a few days. It seemed the only option I had was to cry. My partner (also an academic), sensing that this moment called for more than just a supportive shoulder or pep talk, looked the proofs over for me and returned them by the deadline. Having survived that moment, I continued to swallow the bitter pill that my academic career was doomed. What was I thinking? It certainly didn't help that I was the very first of my friends to have a baby.

More than a decade and two more children later, I look back at that moment and realize how few models I had for negotiating my roles as mother and academic. I had taken my comprehensive exam at thirty-five weeks pregnant and then taught a four-week intensive summer course—administering the final exam on my due date. I had struggled through twenty weeks of severe nausea and vomiting, barely able to make it to class and sometimes not making it to class at all. I negotiated the pregnancy with very little grace, but I somehow managed. I had assumed that the pregnancy would be the hard part. But the inability to read the proofs left me feeling hopeless. I realize only now that I made the mistake of assuming that becoming a mother meant feeling the way I did at three days postpartum for the rest of my life, but how would I know that three days postpartum is not motherhood?

It turns out that at some point I started feeling human, my son started sleeping well, and I got my groove back, but it took almost a year. It was a different groove, but a groove nonetheless. After he was born, I wrote my dissertation proposal, conducted my fieldwork, moved cross-country for my husband's job, started writing my dissertation, got pregnant, got a tenure-track job, defended my dissertation, moved cross-country again, started my tenure-track job, had my second son, published some stuff, wrote some grants, conducted some more fieldwork, wrote some more stuff, published some more stuff, got pregnant and had a daughter, submitted my tenure packet, and got tenure. So I am writing this as a newly tenured academic mother. In other words, I am speaking publically and candidly about how I combined motherhood and fieldwork.

So here's my secret (knowing full well that it might not be the secret sauce for your journey): I managed to combine motherhood and a career that requires fieldwork by doing what I needed to make it work. Perhaps that sounds more obvious than it seems, but I've spent a considerable amount of my academic career feeling like I was cutting corners to combine motherhood with academic work. To some extent, this reflects the imposter syndrome that many academics experience; it also reflects an academic culture that values busyness. It was only recently, after I put my tenure packet together, that I realized that I had a strong CV. Perhaps it's because it was a natural point of career reflection that it finally occurred to me that everyone's research and careers can go in a variety of ways and that I chose the one that seemed to fit best with my dual roles as mother and professor. I wasn't cutting corners—I was making a life.

The Secret Recipe

I feel torn then in this chapter. If you just look at my results, it looks completely doable to combine motherhood and fieldwork (because it is). If you look behind the scenes, it's more complicated. On the best days, everyone gets dropped off at school or day care, and everything on my to-do list gets a check next to it. But there are entire seasons where that "best day" is fleeting. Mostly, I am stymied by ear infections and teacher in-service days, which never seem to overlap. There are also all the other parts of my job that are always calling to me: the student who needs extra advising to graduate, the lecture that fell flat and needs more examples, the committee that needs that chair.

For me to successfully combine all this has required three things: (1) a supportive partner who also has a somewhat flexible career, (2) a preschool/school system where I feel good about leaving my kids, (3) a feminist epistemology (for me this is reinforced by an amazing group of feminist academic friends) to counter the predominant cultural narrative that in a million ways seeks to undercut women and especially mothers in the academy.

So in an ideal world, I recommend finding a great partner for sharing the load. It helps if they are good looking and funny, have a flexible career, and are an excellent cook. Some people win the life lottery. If you have, congratulations! If you haven't, it's not impossible; you'll just need more of numbers 2 and 3.

Onward to childcare: find one you love. For me, this is hard because I feel guilty leaving[1] my children with anyone. I have gone to extraordinary lengths to not use childcare or use it as little as possible because of a combination of cost and guilt. I wrote my dissertation in a YMCA rec room because I could leave my son at the YMCA preschool program for two hours a day. The only catch was that I couldn't leave the building. It was just me and the Silver-Sneakers senior workout group in there every day. They would share their baked goods with me, and then I would put on headphones and write (I may be the only person who has ever gained weight after getting a YMCA membership). I have no regrets because through this I learned that I can be significantly more productive in two hours than I ever realized. My son was just potty-trained, and if he had an accident I would be summoned, so knowing that my writing for the day might end at any minute also kept me very productive. From the time our oldest son was born until I started my tenure track when he was three, he was only in ten hours of childcare a week. When our second son was born, we upped the childcare to fifteen hours per week. My feminist friends, however, have helped me recognize that I'm a little crazy. Looking back on those years, I can see that they were right. With their help, I found childcare that I love. I think I really believed that this wasn't possible, and so for many years, I just avoided looking. I sent my kids to the campus-affiliated center, which was good but not a good fit for our family. Finally, I took the time to start looking more widely and found a place where my kids love going and where I feel like we're part of a big, extended parenting family. The hours are also more flexible, and it's less expensive: the proverbial "win-win." The fact that I enrolled my eight-month-old there for thirty hours a week is testament to the fact that over time, my feelings about childcare have evolved in a dramatic way.

Having some combination of supportive people and trustworthy childcare is essential for the practical aspects of combining fieldwork and motherhood, but for me, a feminist epistemology and network are actually the most important.

It's essential because the neoliberal economy and by extension academy seek to remind us all that we are but cogs in the wheel, monkeys in the machine. That message is especially loud for mothers because at the heart of neoliberalism is the idea that anything that makes us human, that suggests that we are somehow embodied and attached to the world outside of our ability to produce and consume in and for the market, is superfluous. Most the time, the hardest part of combining my roles is getting over the idea that they are somehow conflicting. When I experience this conflict, it comes from the fact that I often don't have enough hours in a day, which is different from believing that motherhood can't fit with being a researcher. In other words, combining motherhood with academic life can be fraught, but my children give me a perspective I would not have had without them. They help me see that my career is only part of my life, and it will never be the most important part of my life. My work, however, doesn't have to be the most important thing in my life in order for me to be great at it. For me, the hardest part of combining motherhood and academia has been the unrealistic expectations of what I thought I should accomplish when my children were tiny babies and the narrative that comes from a handful of people and the culture more broadly, which suggests in a variety of subtle and not so subtle ways that motherhood is not compatible with academia. The more I am able to quiet this narrative, the easier it gets.

I certainly do not mean to imply that any of this is easy—if you are reading this with an infant under the age of twelve weeks, go take a nap. If your baby is less than six months, go take a walk. I have essentially given up on using my brain for the last two months of pregnancy until my babies are six months old. I have found other things to do. Editing a book during my pre- and post-natal periods was the smartest thing I've ever done. I stayed busy and got to be productive but wasn't trying to collect or analyze data. Instead of looking for balance in my life, I have decided to embrace the idea of seasons. And for me, the season of impending and new motherhood is better spent on the most nontaxing projects. Realistically, I'm going to need to check on the internet to see what size fruit my baby is every few hours for the last few months of pregnancy, and then after the baby is born, I'm going to want to check to see how many wet diapers they are supposed to have in the first few weeks. I now know and embrace this season of my life because I know it's temporary and because having a baby is really hard work. After my first son was born, I spent the first six months of his life absolutely overwhelmed with the idea of writing my dissertation proposal. I would sit at my computer and try to write until I could almost see smoke coming out of my ears and maybe produce a few convoluted sentences. But for me, at six months, a fog lifted, and I wrote the proposal in a month.

Applying the Recipe in the Field

That dissertation proposal was my first hurdle of mothering and academic life. The timing meant, however, that I wrote hyper-aware of how I was actually going to do a dissertation project with a baby. When I began graduate school, I was drawn to studying women in agriculture. My master's thesis was the culmination of interviews with women farmers on their farms and many hours of participant observation at a livestock auction. I had imagined reframing and expanding this project for my dissertation research. My advisors, however, suggested that studying alternative agriculture would better position me for the competitive job market. I wasn't thrilled by the change; I loved interviewing and interacting with conventional farmers, but I trusted my advisors and wanted a job, so I adjusted and though I can't know what would have happened had I written a different dissertation, their advice certainly didn't steer me wrong.

When I look at that pragmatic decision, I don't second-guess what I did nor why I did it. When I look at the decisions I have made in my research agenda to effectively combine my responsibilities as a mother with those as an academic, however, I have often felt guilt or embarrassment. But if people don't know the backstory on my research—how I'd planned on my research projects being bigger, or bolder, or more in-depth, or having more interviews, or longer interviews, or interviews on that day that my oldest was up all night with strep throat and I had to cancel the interview and haul him to Quick-care and then snuggle him and dose him for the next two days, and that my research schedule got blown to hell—if I don't mention that, if I just let show what I did get done, I look fine. More than fine—I look like a real academic who does real research.

My dissertation project included a summer of participant observation at a farmers' market and in-depth interviews and farm visits with a handful of farmers involved with the market. When my friends left that first summer to do their dissertation research in Appalachia or Alaska or sat down to organize extended road trips to interview transmen in the south or former professional football players around in the Midwest, I truly felt like a fraud. I chose this project because it was interesting and important but mostly because I could do it in my community. My son was not even a year old, and I didn't want to leave him. Taking him with me on a project seemed difficult because he didn't really sleep anywhere except in his crib, and he was finally sleeping and I didn't want to mess it up. So I picked a dissertation project based on a combination of my son's sleep schedule and my committees' advice. The former made me feel deep shame; the latter seemed like a good idea.

The participant observation at the farmers' market for my dissertation meant sometimes bringing my son with me in a carrier and taking my field notes with him on my back. Though I had brought him with me due to a scheduling necessity, I realized that his presence made me more approachable (or perhaps having him with me made me bolder). When I began to organize my field notes, I realized that on the days he was with me, I had more inter-actions with people at the market. These observations lead me to important observations about the role of the white, heteronormative family at farmers' markets—an observation that became a key idea in a dissertation chapter and later became one of the first articles I published on the tenure track and connected me with an editor who asked me to write a book chapter based on the idea.

Furthermore, a person just knowing that I was a mother was often an important source of entrée for establishing rapport with a respondent. As I pulled up to one farm to conduct an interview and farm tour, the farmer who met me immediately noticed the car seat in my backseat. She wanted to see pictures of my son, and the interview began with her telling me that too many women are putting off having children and how you can't really trust a woman without children. Though I didn't necessarily agree with her, I did immedi-ately realize that our shared experience of motherhood made for a more can-did interview and tour.

With the practical experience of running an ethnographic research proj-ect under my belt, I revaluated my next research project with two equally important goals in mind: I wanted a project that I found more interesting, and I wanted a project that fit with my now expanded family responsibilities. I was able to get funding for a project exploring how women farmers access farmland. For this project, I once again decided to interview people close to where I lived. Furthermore, I decided that while I enjoyed getting out to farms, it was reasonable to do interviews via phone when necessary. Once again, it wasn't necessarily motherhood that compelled this decision—it was a variety of circumstances beyond my control. Specifically, it makes sense to interview farmers in the winter when they aren't as busy on the farms, and that winter was particularly hard in the Pacific Northwest. My plans to drive out to farms often ended when the farmers told me that their road was snowed in. Despite this, I was able to squeeze in interviews all fall during the hours my children were in school.

I am more opportunistic about finding research projects than I might otherwise be, and I see research projects in a more fragmented way than I might otherwise see them. A workshop on alternative farming becomes a day of data collection and an article. New films on sustainable agriculture become data to compare against my fieldwork and become an article. Rather than just talking about writing an article with my colleague about our overlapping research interests, we signed up for a summer writing retreat and spent a week writing a book chapter. For me, mothering forces me to work while the preschool is open and no one is sick. I have decided that I am OK with getting an interview a week completed during a term. Of course, getting lots of interviews completed in a few weeks might be preferable, but it's not always doable. It's the practical solution for me.

My post-tenure research transition also aligned with the end of pregnancy, newborns, and toddlers in my life. These multiple transitions marked a shift in my academic and research agenda as well. First, I took it as an opportunity to shift my research focus. Thus I applied for and received a small grant to fund a new project. Though the funder does not allow childcare to be included in the grant, I asked someone who I knew was an ally to have lunch with me and then asked her how I might include money to fund childcare in the grant in a way that would be acceptable. The two things I need for my research are money for transcriptions and childcare. My ally encouraged me to include a summer salary for myself, which is typically not funded, in order to cover childcare. To cover myself, I did not actually discuss my childcare needs in the grant, but I was careful to explain why I would have to conduct research in the summer that focused on the community I was researching.

This new project examines issues of rural gentrification in a small town in Northern Idaho. The fact that it's my hometown and that I had family and friends there who I can farm my children out to (and actually afford to pay them for their work or, more precisely, pay them to be able to take off of work to watch my kids) is one of the reasons I decided to study this particular community. Over the course of a year, I conducted thirty in-depth interviews and assessed a tremendous amount of archival data.

Planning when to conduct my interview and archival days meant planning my interviews around the days that my kids had school and I had off from teaching: the beginning of Thanksgiving break, early January, late spring. This meant I could spend several days at my research site without the children, but their dad could solo parent without being overwhelmed (this is no judgment on his ability to parent—I only mean that three kids is a lot, alone, for many days). During the days that we all came to the field site, it meant hauling the family with me and taking my kids swimming in the morning and starting interviews or archival research when the littlest one napped at grandma's house. It meant drinking beers on my mom's porch while the kids climbed and ran around when I would have benefitted from being alone and writing field notes and memos about the day.

In the past, I would have told myself at a million points during the process that I had no data, that this is not how a real researcher does research. But miraculously, that voice was nearly silent this time. In fact, there were moments where I felt almost euphoric in the field. It was clear that I was getting better at running a research project: more organized, more confident, better able to see what I needed and didn't need in an interview.

I have almost quit kicking myself for not asking enough follow-up questions because I was worried about the kids being hungry or missing me and rushing the last few minutes of some interviews, convincing myself that a single missed follow-up question is all that stands between me and my magnum opus. I know better than to tell myself that I'll write the book manuscript after the kids go to bed. Nothing happens after they go to bed because here's what actually happens: when kids get older, they magically want all your attention at precisely the moment you are exhausted. They are like babies that way. So the preteen that barely talks needs to discuss all his worries, thoughts, and dreams but only after 8:45 p.m. But I gave up trying to get stuff done at night years ago.

I still have less grace for myself than I'd like but more than I used to have. I think I am coming to understand that this is a long road, and the seasons of my life don't get exactly easier, and yet it is easier somehow. My colleagues take a sabbatical to collect data. I take a sabbatical to write up data. It means my data collection is sometimes piecemeal, but nevertheless, I have a huge folder of material and a full term for uninterrupted writing. And so using the lessons learned from my dissertation writing, I will hole up for two or three hours a day without internet but with baked goods and write (and I will get a little chubbier). And in a few years, in spite of all these things that looked like barriers, I will hold a book in my hands and it won't say all the things I didn't do that I thought I should have done. They will be our secret.

FIGURE 16.1 Dr. Ryanne Pilgeram conducting the archival research for her project on Dover, Idaho, as represented in a LEGO diorama by her ten-year-old son in 2017. As this unsolicited diorama suggests, our children are watching the work we do, listening to us talk about it, and feeling a sense of pride in it. For parents of young children, you may be most interested in the fact that your children will go into the basement and play with LEGOs, color, or do God knows what for hours at a time without interrupting you and then bring up a very flattering LEGO likeness. You may be moved to tears by the generosity of it all.

You CAN Do It

I often hear that academic work and motherhood are incompatible. But I actually cannot imagine not being a mother and an academic. Perhaps this stems from the fact that I had my children when I was fairly young and new to academic life. My son was born a few weeks after I finished up my coursework, so for me, academic work has always meant either being in class or trying to teach and research with a child. Academic work has few boundaries. My children taught me the art of creating boundaries through necessity. As someone who studies gender and work, however, I'm also careful about how I talk about my children at work. While acknowledging the problematics of this approach, I don't use my children as an excuse—ever. I blame all the other things my colleagues blame for not being able to schedule a meeting. My Tuesday/Thursday afternoon meetings have for the last five years been my after-school pickup time. Recently, I was asked to chair a committee for my college, and we had a very difficult time finding a meeting time. The administrator for the group suggested we meet on Tuesday afternoons, and I felt a great deal of pressure to say yes. But I thought about how much joy I get picking my children up from school, how easy it is to catch up with the teachers if there are any issues, and I said a polite but firm "no, that just won't work for me." Later, I found out that a major issue in the scheduling was that someone on the committee sets aside two full days a week for writing and research. The three hours I am not available during the work week were not really the issue, but because I knew that those were three hours a week that I was not available because I was "mommying," I felt guilty. I have colleagues who make no qualms about not meeting because they don't like to get up early, they work out over the lunch hour, or they don't come to campus on days they don't teach.

It bears repeating—none of this is easy. But realistically, I don't think being an academic is easy for many people. I don't think being a parent is necessarily easy. Furthermore, people who don't have children feel similarly pulled in many directions. Perhaps my motivation for writing this is to counter the "I don't know how you do it!" narrative that is constantly directed at me. Though I believe that this narrative comes from a place of good intentions, it nonetheless reinforces the notion that being a mother and being an academic researcher are incompatible. It's the idea that if I'm succeeding at academic work, I must by definition be a bad mom or vice versa. And it's a narrative that is so pervasive in the culture that I have convinced myself that making strategic decisions about combining academic work and motherhood kept me from being a real researcher or a great mom. It's only been the critical, feminist work that I've engaged in that has forced me to actually examine the data—these data being my own research record and the relationship I have with my children. The truth is, when I look at the data, it's pretty clear that I've got this. And the less time I spend wringing my hands, the more time I have to do the things that matter to me.

Practical Tips

- If you are turning to this book while pregnant or with an infant, remember that mothering a baby is hard, and it gets easier, so have grace for yourself.
- Find other people who are in a similar situation—if you can't find them in your own community, there are online communities.
- Find childcare that you feel good about. You will be more productive if you're not worried about how they are doing.
- If you attempt to conduct research during the course of your everyday demands, you will need to be incredibly organized. Before you start your project, get yourself organized—print every form you'll need, prepare your research folders, buy and test your equipment, take a

refresher class. You will want to be able to grab your bag with your research equipment and run between class, day care pickup, and that meeting you forgot about.

- It's reasonable and acceptable to adjust your research agenda to better align with your life.

Note

1 I'm looking at this word *leaving* and want to change it to *having my children in childcare*. The term *leaving* gives you a glimpse of my psychology around this topic.

17

Ethnographic Research in Africa

• • • • • • • • • • • • • • • • • • • •

The Hidden Costs of
Conducting Fieldwork for
Mothers with Children

BAHIYYAH MIALLAH MUHAMMAD

When mothers make the decision to go into the field to conduct site-based research, there are various tolls they must pay. Throughout this anthology, we have learned about these situations through personal perspectives. We highlighted how mothers deal with the trials and tribulations that come along with fieldwork. One such trial pertains to the financial burden fieldwork can impose on researchers.

We do not often discuss the economic strains that fieldworkers face, especially those fieldworkers who are women and more specifically those who are mothers. Mothering in the field brings with it the additional concerns regarding the well-being of family, whether they are brought into the field or left at home. While gender in field research has been considered (Warren, 1988), the focus has been mostly on how it shapes field access, data collection, and the interpretation of one's findings (Schenk-Sandbergen, 1995). Although important to consider, what is left out are whether female researchers incur hidden costs compared to their male counterparts. We know too well the story of the male site-based researcher who conducts his fieldwork while his wife is at home taking care of the day-to-day. But what about the mother who travels into the field with babies, without babies, with others, alone? Is her story less worthy of being told? Are her needs the same as those of the lone male fieldworker?

In this chapter, I challenge this comfortable archetype by putting to rest the gender-imbalanced field researcher story. That story is no longer a reality for this twenty-first century. Before research funding can be allotted to provide financial assistance for mothers who conduct fieldwork, we must have a better understanding of the costs specific to mothers conducting fieldwork. What follows is my story of the hidden costs associated with the ethnographic research I conducted in Africa with my children in tow, which I discussed in chapter six of this volume.

Field Expenditures

When considering actual field expenditures for the typical site-based researcher, especially those of us who conduct long-term fieldwork, financial support becomes very important in helping facilitate the entire research process from predeparture to study completion. Thus at the start of my tenure-track position in 2013, during my job interview, I was prepared to discuss my research, which would include my family accompanying me in the field. To begin negotiations about my start-up grant, I had a working budget and international research proposal in hand that included my proposed global work with children in tow. The overall argument was my ability to merge my research on children of incarcerated parents with first-person perspectives of how I included family in the research experience as a means to not "sell my soul" on the tenure track (Rockquemore & Laszloffy, 2008). From the very beginning, I shared my research and publication plan.

My publication goals went hand in hand with the support received. In fact, I triangulated mothering from the field with my global comparative research of populations affected by incarceration and my optimal success on the tenure track. This was the strength of my proposal: I was able to speak to the elephant in the room by answering the question that repeatedly came up. Each department and college that provided support wanted to know how mothering from the field would help me be promoted and secure tenure. This was a question that I could speak directly to. I connected my global research project with a manuscript on my experience. This was considered a satisfactory response, and my research proposals were fully funded from combined resources coming from the Office of the Provost, the College of Arts and Sciences, the Department of Sociology and Criminology, and the Graduate School. The combined total amount of funding from these colleges and departments was $17,500.

Specifically, these internal grants included the Reginald Lewis Travel Fund ($1,000) through the Office of the Provost, a start-up grant ($4,500) through the College of Arts and Sciences, research funding ($5,000) through the Department of Sociology and Criminology, and a summer research grant ($3,500) through the Graduate School at Howard University. Although most of my financial support came through numerous departments and colleges at my university, I also supplemented these funds with my personal savings ($2,500). In addition, an HU ADVANCE-IT summer grant ($1,000) was used to purchase some equipment for my field research.

All of this budgeting was made easier for me, as the organization that sponsored me to connect me to their local prisons and to families and children of incarcerated parents had provided me with a budget that was created specifically for my field research project. This included the accommodations previously mentioned, as well as access to all meeting venues, meals throughout the day, round-trip transportation to and from the airport, transportation to the field around Kampala for each day, and transportation from the residence to the field sites outside of the city limits. Lastly, compensation was included in costs for incarcerated subjects, families, and child subjects. There was also an administrative fee for my entire stay. This allowed me access to their administrative building with access to office space with Wi-Fi and a computer. This budget was very helpful in averting hidden costs.

That the majority of funding came from internal grants that were discretionary in nature allowed for greater flexibility in how funds could be used. My husband was included on the grant as a media team leader supervising the work of a graduate and undergraduate students. As a lead member of the research team, his round-trip airfare and that of the two students working on the project was covered by internal grant funds. All of the media crew volunteered their services in the field. As staff on the project, their round-trip airfare and accommodations were covered by grant funds.

International Travel Costs

International travel can be expensive for a single person. When considering the costs for a family, expenses reach new heights. We booked through the university travel agency; this meant that we did not have to pay any out-of-pocket costs for our travel except for any additional luggage costs at the ticket window. By using the university travel agency, we received double savings. This included reduced rates on flights, hotels, and round-trip travel from the airport to the hotel. In addition, the agency allows for your travel to be attached to your travel and/or hotel rewards programs. So although my start-up funds were used to cover these costs, I also received reward points on my travel and accommodations. The flights to Uganda cost $1,200 round-trip for me and my husband. My eldest child paid a child-sitting fee, which was $600, and my youngest child was a lap child, so I was only required to pay the taxes associated with her seat. These charges totaled $150, which made for a family international travel total of $3,150.

The majority of costs for my site-based research went toward accommodations, travel, site-based study costs, and miscellaneous charges. The costs associated with moving my family of four from the United States to Africa for three months were by far the highest. Our accommodations included housing for the full research team, which composed of a three-person media crew, a senior research assistant who kept an eye on the girls a few times, and myself as primary investigator on the project. My family arrived first to ensure that everything was in order for the arrival of the rest of the team. The media students and research assistant arrived one month after my family, and their stays were staggered in time.

Accommodations for our research team included a family-style suite with four bedrooms and four bathrooms. This also included a fully stocked kitchen, an en suite washer and dryer, a living room, and a balcony. This family setting worked great for us. My husband and I took turns cooking for the household. I was able to use my per diem to purchase groceries, and with the exchange rate in Uganda, we were able to stock up on food and snacks for the household. When anyone wanted something "special," they purchased it. We all shopped together, and this saved on trips into the field and saved on gas by carpooling into town.

My daughters really enjoyed all the company in the house, although everyone resorted to closed-door rooms when we weren't sharing a meal together. Most of our time was spent in the field, taking pictures and conducting observations and interviews throughout the week. On weekends, we were able to fully enjoy the "research home" space. This site-based field project had an extended family feel, and we all worked as a team to ensure that project expectations were met. We reminded ourselves to have fun and enjoy all the beauty that Uganda has to offer.

Hidden Costs: Dealing with the Unexpected

Even with the best of planning, things happen. During my field research in Uganda, there was an emergency travel advisory put on through the embassy of the United States because of a specific threat to attack Entebbe International Airport by an unknown terrorist group. As a direct result of this advisory, the two students who were part of the media team had to reschedule their flights, which resulted in additional fees that were not a part of the approved travel authorization. Because the original tickets were arranged through the university travel agency, this process was a lot easier than if I or the students had purchased their tickets. Because the fees resulted from an emergency outside of my control, the university absorbed the costs and did not require me to pay out of pocket. Having university support is an advantage and really makes field research less stressful.

With university support, there are still field research expenditures that will not be covered. I expected that my immunizations and that of my children would be covered through our university family health center, but this was a privilege that was offered to students and not faculty. The health center has an international travel office, however, where I was able to get travel immunizations at a cheaper rate than those offered outside of the university. They also provided up-to-date information on the immunization specifics needed for entry into any country. In addition, they provided immunizations to my family and had the capacity to provide prescriptions for travel medications. It worked in our favor that our university has the Howard University Hospital, where predeparture and follow-up visits could be scheduled.

With insurance, our costs were substantially reduced. For example, the yellow-fever shots we were all required to get prior to departure cost us (two adults and two children) around $200 rather than the estimated $150 to $350 per person without insurance coverage. And we of course had many other shots and pills to pay for. Specifically, our recommended malaria pills for the entire family totaled $550.

Even with all these resources available on campus, the costs of such services were not covered by any of my grant funding. The costs associated with predeparture travel were all out-of-pocket expenses. The total of these expenses was approximately $1,150. This is typically the amount I save to cover my predeparture expenses for any international site-based research, based on prior experience with such types of expenses. Because these predeparture costs are medical in nature, I always increase my flexible spending (or health savings) account deductions in years I know I will be traveling for international fieldwork.

Included in predeparture fees are also visas and passports costs. We usually are all current with our passports, but passport costs for our family of four can run us around $575. These are initial costs that must be considered if you or your family don't have current passports. For our travels to Uganda and Kenya, the cost of a multiple-entry visa was $100, which may vary depending on the country you are entering. We thus had to pay $400 for the four of us to enter Uganda. Even before leaving home to conduct my site-based research, I was required to spend more than $1,000 just on travel documents.

Even with the support of your university, there will be additional costs that must be considered. For me, these costs included predeparture costs, paying mortgage and other bills for an empty house back home, and dealing with field emergencies that result in added expenditures. Many of these costs are not covered through any grants and are often not considered eligible expenses.

Table 17.1
Funding for field research

Funding source	Funding/grant type	Application requirements	Costs (USD)
Office of the Provost	Reginald Lewis travel grant	Letter request Meeting	1,000
Howard University Graduate School	Summer faculty research grant	Application Research proposal Budget Competitive	3,500
College of Arts and Sciences	Start-up funding	Letter request Research proposal Publication plan Budget	4,500
Department of Sociology and Criminology	Seed funding research grant	Letter request Research proposal Publication plan Budget	5,000
HU ADVANCE-IT	Mini research grant	Application Research proposal Publication plan Budget Peer reviewed Competitive	1,000
Personal savings	Out-of-pocket funding	N/A	2,500
Total			17,500

Practical Tips

- Before you begin any field research position, be it in the academy or in an organization, become familiar with the support they offer parents.
- It is never too early to create your budget. Whether you desire to conduct your work with or without your children in tow, begin calculating all the costs associated with your proposed study. Start this process by establishing two separate budgets: one for yourself and one for your family (however this may be defined). Look at both budgets to identify ways in which they merge. The more costs that can be merged with your needs, the more likely they will be funded or reimbursed.
- When negotiating the use of your start-up funds, make sure to include what will be needed to conduct your work with or without children being brought into the field. Make sure to negotiate this with your university.

- Start-up funding can be used in more flexible ways than some federal funding. Also consider foundation funds, which can also be used in ways that incorporate travel needs specific to mothers with children, babysitting needs during fieldwork and/or professional conferences, and supplies, including things needed for younger children who accompany you into the field.

- Open up a travel account through your credit union or bank and have automatic deductions taken from each paycheck in anticipation of your international field research. With my credit union savings account, I use the funds as on-hand cash while in the field. All costs will later be submitted for reimbursement. Upon reimbursement, I put the funds back into the savings account to be used during future fieldwork. Save for your fieldwork in the same way you might save for a vacation.

- Join professional organizations that support the needs of women, mothers, and their children. My professional organization, the American Society of Criminology, offers babysitting services at conferences for additional fees. In instances such as these, your university may be more likely to cover costs, as they fall under the larger umbrella of "conference costs."

- In terms of predeparture costs, such as immunizations, visas, and other expenses, check with your college/university to identify what resources are available to you as faculty. This may include free services and/or discounted services. Compare the associated costs of college/university services to outside services. The key is to do the research in advance to ensure that you are getting the most bang for your buck.

- Make sure to be reimbursed for all your travel expenses—especially for the extra costs that have been preapproved through your college or university. Always check with an accountant to see how to maximize your professional travel expenditures.

- Use your flexible spending account or health savings account for predeparture medical costs. This may mean that you will need to increase your monthly deductions to account for the extra costs associated with international travel requirements.

- Strongly consider field research when your children are young. As it pertain to travel purposes, children under the age of two can fly without out a purchased ticket simply by sitting on your lap, which is either free of charge or only amounts to the cost of travel taxes. If planned properly, you may be able to benefit from not having to pay the hefty costs of international travel with a child older than two years of age.

References

Guest, G., Namey, E., & Michell, M. (2013). *Collecting qualitative data: A field manual for applied research*. Los Angeles, CA: Sage.

Muhammad, B. M. (2009). Counting children of incarcerated parents: A methodological critique of past and present literature. In R. Muraskin & A. R. Roberts (Eds.), *Visions for change: Crime and justice in the twenty-first century* (5th ed.) (pp. 568–585). New York, NY: Pearson Prentice Hall.

Muhammad, B. M. (2011). *Exploring the silence among children of prisoners: A descriptive study*. Retrieved from Rutgers University Electronic Theses and Dissertations. (Accession Order No. EID.00061087)

Muhammad, B. M. (2018). Against all odds: Resilient children of incarcerated parents. In L. Gordon (Ed.), *Contemporary research and analysis on the children of prisoners* (pp. 141–154). Newcastle, UK: Cambridge Scholars.

Muhammad, B., & Muhammad, M. (2014a). I don't understand: Questions among children of incarcerated parents. *Corrections Today*. Boston, MA: Pearson Learning Solutions.

Muhammad, B., & Muhammad, M. (2014b). *The prison alphabet: An educational coloring book for children of incarcerated parents*. Atlanta, GA: Goldest Karat.

Muhammad, B., & Muhammad, M. (2018). *Does my parent have Facebook in prison? Over 200 questions and answers to help you engage children of incarcerated parents in critical dialogue*. Atlanta, GA: Goldest Karat.

Rockquemore, K. A., & Laszloffy, T. (2008). *The black academic's guide to winning tenure without losing your soul*. Boulder, CO: Lynne Rienner.

Schenk-Sandbergen, L. C. (1995). Gender in field research: Experiences in India. *Economic and Political Weekly, 30*(17), ws38–ws45.

Simmons, T., Muhammad, B. M., & Dodd, K. (2018). Kick in the door, wavin' the four-four: Failure to safeguard children of detained and arrested parents. In L. Gordon (Ed.), *Contemporary research and analysis on the children of prisoners* (pp. 85–99). Newcastle, UK: Cambridge Scholars.

Warren, C. A. B. (1988). *Gender issues in field research: Qualitative research method series 9*. Newbury Park, CA: Sage.

Conclusion

●●●●●●●●●●●●●●●●●●●●●●

BAHIYYAH MIALLAH MUHAMMAD

AND MÉLANIE-ANGELA NEUILLY

Mothering from the field can take on many shapes. In this volume, we have presented fieldwork conducted in the humanities and social sciences as well as in the physical and life sciences, fieldwork conducted locally or internationally, for intermittent or long periods of time, alone, with children, or with entire families. We have even presented how mothering from the field evolves over one's life course, reminding ourselves and our readers that, as Anne Hardgrove concludes in chapter 10, "for a parent, and a mother, there is no 'end' to the adventure of parenting and fieldwork" (p. 168).

Mothers in the field are far from a homogenous group. Presented in previous chapters are the voices of women who became mothers earlier on in their lives and careers, those of women for whom it happened later, voices of single mothers, of married mothers, of mothers of single children, multiple children, young children, grown children. We have included mothers from differing socioeconomic backgrounds and racial and ethnic identities. We even included fathers' and other family members' voices, and yet many more voices remain unheard. What is considered the field in site-based research also covers a wide range of realities. We have included a broad range of disciplines from both the social and physical sciences, sites close and far from home, exotic or more mundane, traditional as well as more innovative. This is important because as we question the constraints imposed on what field research should be by our patriarchal framework, showcasing the reality of what site-based science looks like is revolutionary.

At the onset of this book, we sought to share our experiences of mothering from the field, hopeful that these personal narratives would serve to empower other mothers to charge forth with their field research plans by providing them with a template and a community. Now, almost four years later, in what can be seen as an entirely different political landscape, our narratives resonate more as manifestos. We talk of resistance, we talk of persistence, we talk of resilience. Through an empowering dialogue that breaks down the patriarchal model of field research, a new hope emerges when we look to each other for guidance and fortitude. Those children of ours, those we brought to the field with us, they are whom we are truly writing for. As we make sweeping recommendations for change in academia and science, we are truly advocating for a better world for them, more diverse future for up-and-coming female field researchers whose work must be respected in all academic circles and seen as the science it has always been. Here we provide evidence for a shift in what is considered science and who is supported to achieve such scientific pursuits, a shattering of the glass ceiling that has oppressed women and mothers for far too long. A much-needed fixing of the leaky pipeline.

As made clear in section one, the very foundation of the academia in which we stand is based on the exclusion of women, mothers, and the private sphere they are supposed to represent and inhabit. None of it is clearer than in the field of anthropology, where the ideal field scientist is the lone white male fieldworker going to faraway places for lengthy periods of time. Therefore, it is no surprise that women have struggled to find a place in the field and have not had many opportunities to tell the stories they feel are important. The issue, though, is that in trying to fix this problem, the onus has continuously been placed on the individual women, forcing them to reconfigure themselves to better fit within the existing mold, rather than addressing how problematic the mold is in the first place. The underrepresentation of minorities, women, and mothers in STEM and site-based disciplines speaks volume of this issue.

In the rest of this volume, we break that mold by establishing the validity of mothers' narratives and standpoints on their research. The richness of contributors' perspectives is the perfect illustration of how baseless mothers' insecurities about the righteousness of their standing in their fields truly are. Whether they have completed their research alone or with a support team, whether they have experienced hardships beyond the pale or simply within the bounds of a mother's balance struggles, our contributors exemplify how the important lesson in field research is not as much to ensure that its circumstances are perfect but rather to contextualize any and all findings within the research conditions, whatever they might have been. Thus breaking the patriarchal mold involves making visible what had traditionally been left invisible.

This could be discussing how you had to cancel interviews because your child's day care was closed or they had the flu, or it could mean uncovering the reality of a spouse taking the lead on parenting while you have to devote most of your time to doing field observations. It could also look like explaining how being a mother was a rapport-building asset in one set of research situations but a hindrance in another. But first and foremost, what it does is break the patriarchal mold of field research and demand that we recognize field researchers as humans with an existence that lives beyond their fieldwork. As mothers, we know this reality all too intimately, as we have second shifts to tend to when we get done with our day in the field, as we have to juggle phone calls from our children amid a conference presentation or endure the relentless physiological demands of pregnancy and breastfeeding all the while attempting to find intellectual stimulation in our careers.

In this volume, field methods are redefined by centering the experiences of women and mothers. Through the projection of personal narratives from a diverse group of dynamic mothers, this population is humanized. This is not done for any sort of sympathy for their unique circumstances; rather, these stories are highlighted to provide contextual underpinnings to the research of women with children. Although history is evidence that these stories have led to important scientific findings, the mother-researchers of the past have not been outwardly recognized as such, and policy has failed to address their personal and professional needs in order to pave the way for more mothers to conduct site-based research. It is now time to begin supporting mothers of the academe in ways that other researchers have been provided a helping hand. Following this section is a working list of recommendations that can be used to begin this important work.

Our recommendations are broken down by audience: first, policy recommendations intended for universities, funding agencies, and other administrators along with legislative representatives and government officials; second, recommendations pertaining to changing perceptions and acceptance of research topics and methodologies that do not conform to the age-old academic cannon and yet absolutely conform to the scientific endeavor of knowledge creation and discovery; finally, practical tips for individual researchers and their families and networks of support. While these individuals, their children and families, and their research are the most important to us, we want to make it clear that ultimately, it is not incumbent upon them to figure out how to solve their "children problem" in the field. It shouldn't be considered a problem in the first place. This is why this book prioritizes policy and methodological recommendations, placing them at the onset. Knowing that such change will be slow, readers are also provided with some "life hacks" of sorts. It may continue to be hard because mothering and parenting in general are not easy and because field research in general is challenging, but we show here that it is not impossible.

Policy Recommendations

While each contributor in this volume has her own voice, her own perspective, and her own set of recommendations for others, a definite chorus emerged from within this diversity. These themes repeated themselves throughout the volume—most of them centered on tangible policy recommendations and are detailed here.

- Whatever family-friendly policy solutions we may come up with here will never gain any traction if we do not first find a way to solve the root problem that women in site-based research disciplines face: underrepresentation. Helping women and mothers once they have managed to win against all odds and have reached the level at which they are expected to juggle family responsibilities with their research expectations is important. However, they are destined to fail unless conditions are created in which women and mothers are no longer the minority. The way to do this for site-based research disciplines is to start a lot sooner than graduate school. We need to attract and retain girls in STEM disciplines from early elementary education on. It is only when gender disparities in academia are solved at the source that any downstream solution will actually gain traction.
- Policies promoting inclusivity in academia or any other work environments need to be tailored to acknowledge that women and underrepresented minorities should not be treated as one group. Their needs vary, and policies that do not recognize the diversity within this "diversity" category will only benefit the few (middle-class, heterosexual, cis-gendered, white women) instead of the many (everybody else who is neither the above nor a middle-class, heterosexual, cisgender, white man).
- Funding agencies should provide support for more than the researcher and include support personnel in grant budgets beyond spouses. This financial support should also extend to payment for childcare if needed as well as multiple entries into the field if shorter / more frequent field trips are necessary to better accommodate work-life balance.
- No matter what it is called—work-life balance or work-life integration— it must not be driven by the "work" side of the equation. In a culture in which we are constantly reminded that more is more, something needs to change. We must put balance back in the equation and apply

the French principle of *un petit peu de tout* (a little bit of everything). While most of the literature on work-life balance seems to hinge on individuals' ability to restore the equilibrium, we do not believe it to be a reasonable expectation. Instead, if a culture change is to happen, if we are to restore meaningful balance to our work and personal life worlds, unions are what will lead the way to broker such discussions. As researchers, we need to embrace the reality of our labor status as workers and realize that collective bargaining may be our only salvation.

- Of course, while none of this was touched upon by any of our contributors, it goes without saying that equal pay should be at the center of any policy reform that seeks to benefit women and mothers. Nationwide, women researchers are paid substantially less than their male colleagues. Balancing the pay scale can benefit those women who desire to complete site-based work by affording them more financial flexibility. Fieldwork can be expensive, especially when considering being accompanied by children and/or other supports. Regardless of one's decision to go alone or with others, one should be able to have access to enough personal funds as to not feel strapped while in the field or, worse, refrain from conducting field research in the first place because of financial strain.

Methodological Recommendations

A methodological revolution is needed—one that recognizes the radical importance of acknowledging researchers as human beings.

- This means that we need to make sure various forms of research, including fieldwork, are accessible to all and not just a few. Practically speaking, this would be made possible by implementing the policy recommendations listed earlier. Those policies will not be enough to solve the problem, though. We must also acknowledge that if the doors of fieldwork and other methodologies are to be opened to all, our very definitions of fieldwork need to widen and broaden. This means that we cannot expect fieldwork to take precedence over family life or that both be kept hermetically separate from one another. It means understanding ourselves and our standpoints as crucial design elements that cannot be ignored and having these standpoints accepted within the research community at large. In practical terms, it means a broader inclusion of a wider variety of methods and questions in textbooks and a bigger push by peer-review gatekeepers as well as publishers to include those varied types of research in their outlets. This would allow for the topic to be streamlined into the curriculum for research methodology courses everywhere.

- This also means that all research, whether conducted in the field or in laboratories, whether qualitative or quantitative, needs to be acknowledged as being conducted by human beings and thus emerging from specific standpoints. Not only would such a methodological revolution be beneficial to individuals who conduct research that falls out of the bounds of the ideal worker positivist framework; it would also benefit science at large. Not only is it good for science to open its doors to a wider diversity of researchers asking a wider range of questions; it is also good for all of science to become more reflexive.

Practical Tips

While we do not want to put it on individual women to have to solve their "mothering from the field" problems by themselves, we also know from experience that no amount of policy recommendations will help when it comes to dealing with a colicky baby or a partner lost in translation. For whatever they are worth, what follows are the little things that worked for us. It is important to remember that each situation is different, and even within one family, fieldwork will always bring new challenges. Again, mothering from the field is something that cannot be mastered.

- Things may be tough, but make memories. Take advantage of your location and of the fact that you cannot be working 24-7 because of your children. Take pictures of the good times. The hard times may never truly fade away in your memory, but at least you will have pictures to remember the good times. These photos may also be used to support a future publication.
- Additionally, remember that if your child is big enough to remember these field trips, they will most likely not remember them as hard. Instead, these trips will be the foundation for lifelong learning and incomparable experiences. And whether or not they come along, our children absorb everything we do. When we are at our best, which many of us are when we are in the field, our children benefit the most. They see in us real-life powerful role models. They also get exposed to various work and life environments and to the complexities of research.
- We may live in a world that expects us to always be doing more, conquering bigger, working harder, but let's remember that it is also perfectly acceptable, important, and interesting to conduct your field research in your own backyard. Adapting your research interest to fit

your personal circumstances is a great way to achieve work-life balance while recognizing that the best research is completed research.

• Think through the total costs of conducting your proposed fieldwork project. Include extra funds for hidden costs that may emerge unexpectedly while you are in the field. Consider these costs when negotiating your start-up packages or applying for internal or external funding for research.

• Finally, take the initiative to mentor or be mentored by another mother researcher. Or better yet, organize a "mothering from the field" chapter in your university, join an online community, and find the mentors you may not find at your doorstep. Do not wait for someone to assign you to someone who is in the same situation. Having a mentor and a community throughout the process will be very important. And when you are done, pass it forward! Be a mentor, share your experience, and make sure your voice is heard and others can be inspired by it. This book makes clear the importance of sharing field narratives. We can all be a part of this.

Of course, quite a few of us have also conducted fieldwork as we were working on this book and experienced how different it was to do while knowing this community existed. It was also different because our children had of course changed, and so did our standpoints. We do not anticipate for this volume to be the be-all and end-all of the conversation, and we understand that this is a conversation that has been going on, albeit in less public forums, for as long as women started joining the ranks of fieldworkers worldwide. What we do hope for with this volume is to participate in pushing the conversation of women who mother and conduct fieldwork closer to the public. We hope to provide a community to which mothers can turn and find solace and comfort along with some helpful tips. We hope that it spins out more conversations and helps foster more communities inclusive of LGBTQI families and their narratives, stories of fathers and their evolving experiences in the field, information from those conducting fieldwork while caring for aging parents, and so much more.

The #pregnantinthefield hashtag is a current example of how such stories are already gaining traction thanks to social media (Carter, 2017). The increased scrutiny of field safety for women is another (Flaherty, 2014; Flaherty, 2017; Nelson, Rutherford, Hinde, & Clancy, 2017). And the website *Faces in the Field* (http://facesoffieldwork.com/gallery/) provides an illustration of the humanity of scientists. This serves as an important reminder that we must continue to humanize scientists. Sharing their stories and showing their faces and that of their families keeps them at the forefront of policy implementation and practical solutions for making methodological advances and revolutionary change in the academy. This shift includes rather than excludes when

FIGURE C.1 Coeditors Bahiyyah Miallah Muhammad (right) and Mélanie-Angela Neuilly (left) include their growing daughters in one of their final remote work sessions. This photo was taken by Muntaquim Muhammad.

things go wrong. Finally, the #fieldworkfail hashtag is definitely the best and most hilarious example of how the full story must always be told—we can't emphasize the good and swipe the bad under the rug. Rather, we have to stay true to ourselves and our contrasted experiences and keep it authentic. This is how we can level the playing field because the fieldwork of mothers is serious, it is scientific, it is scholarly. The fieldwork of mothers is needed.

References

Carter, I. (2017). Pregnant in the field: Have trowel, will travel. *The Guardian*. Retrieved from https://www.theguardian.com/lifeandstyle/2017/jul/01/pregnant-in-the-field-blog-photography-have-trowel-will-travel

Flaherty, C. (2014). What happens in the field. *Inside Higher Ed*. Retrieved from https://www.insidehighered.com/news/2014/08/13/researchers-react-study-about-sexual-harassment-scientists-field

Flaherty, C. (2017). Harassment in the field. *Inside Higher Ed*. Retrieved from https://www.insidehighered.com/news/2017/10/17/follow-study-misconduct-academic-field-sites-says-clear-rules-conduct-and#.We4ntSX_4So.email

Nelson, R. G., Rutherford, J. N., Hinde, K., & Clancy, K. B. H. (2017). Signaling safety: Characterizing fieldwork experiences and their implications for career trajectories. *American Anthropologist*, *119*(4), 710–722, http://onlinelibrary.wiley.com/doi/10.1111/aman.12929/epdf

Acknowledgments

On July 8, 2018, as we were finalizing this book for production, Kelly Anne Ward passed away suddenly following an accident. From the beginning of our conversations about this book, Kelly had played an intricate role. As an expert on higher education, women, and motherhood, we had of course read her work. But beyond academic knowledge, Kelly had been a true mentor and friend to Mélanie from early on in her career at Washington State University. News of Kelly's passing resonated throughout the Washington State community and beyond as all the women Kelly had personally mentored throughout the years started sharing their favorite Kelly stories. We all remember her humor, her love of horses and on-point nail polish, her preference for mentoring while walking, her commitment to improving the status of women in academia, and her dedication to work-life integration and making time for her own family. This book is what it is in large part because of Kelly. Thank you.

Contributor and renowned higher-education expert
Kelly Ward, who unexpectedly passed away as we
were putting the finishing touches on this volume

Notes on Contributors

STACEY L. CAMP is an associate professor of anthropology and director of the campus archaeology program at Michigan State University. She has worked as an archaeologist in Ireland and the western United States. Her research has examined the politics of commemoration and memory as well as the archaeology of migrants living in the late nineteenth- and early twentieth-century western United States.

KIMBERLY GARLAND CAMPBELL is a research geneticist with the USDA-ARS in Pullman, Washington. She is an adjunct faculty member in the Department of Crop and Soil Sciences and a member of the Molecular Plant Sciences graduate program at Washington State University. She received an MS in 1988 and a PhD in 1991 in crop science from North Carolina State University. She also received a master's in theological studies from the Lutheran Theological Seminary at Philadelphia in 1985. Kim conducts research in wheat breeding and genetics, specifically for club wheat, a specialty class of soft white wheat. She works with collaborators throughout the United States to improve wheat for resistance to stripe rust and soil-borne diseases. She and her husband have three daughters and a son, and she has mentored twenty-eight graduate students and postdoctoral researchers over her twenty-five-year research career. Her commitment to education extends from kindergarten to doctorate, given that she also serves on the Moscow Idaho School Board. She takes special care to motivate and provide support to her children, students, and young faculty, especially women, as they negotiate life transitions, join the scientific community as women of color, and seek to excel.

LYDIA ZACHER DIXON completed her PhD in anthropology at the University of California, Irvine, in 2015 and is currently a junior scholar of the social science network there. Dr. Zacher Dixon has published on midwifery and obstetric violence in Mexico and is currently working on a book manuscript. Since completing her fieldwork, she has gotten married and had another child. She lives with her family in a rural California town, where she continues to struggle to balance her academic and family lives.

APRILLE J. ERICSSON is an aerospace engineer who has held numerous positions in education, technically and athletically. While attending the Massachusetts Institute of Technology (MIT), she worked in the Space Systems Laboratory and worked on a fiber optic gyroscope in the Physics Laboratory. Dr. Ericsson's early research at Howard University (HU) was developing control methods for orbiting large space platforms like the International Space Station. She has served as an adjunct faculty member at several universities. Currently, she sits on engineering academic boards at the National Academies and MIT and previously at HU as a trustee and as the chair of the HU Middle School of Mathematics and Science.

DAWN ERICSSON, MD is a native New Yorker. She attended Yale University as an undergraduate, where she satisfied her premedical requirements and received her BA in history of science and medicine. She graduated from medical school at the State University of New York at the Stony Brook Health Sciences Center. She then completed her residency in ob-gyn with New Jersey's busiest program, St. Barnabas Medical Center, where she was the first female African American graduate.

Dr. Ericsson has been married for more than twenty years to her husband, Colin, and they have three children. She enjoys spending time with her family and also participates in a myriad of organizations in her community. She is on the Board of Trustees at Academy Preparatory School Tampa and is an active parent at Berkeley Preparatory School, where her husband serves as a board trustee. She chairs the teen group of the Greater Tampa chapter of Jack and Jill and is an active member of the Tampa graduate chapter of Alpha Kappa Alpha Sorority, Inc. Dr. Ericsson is board certified in ob-gyn and holds membership as a fellow of the American Congress of Obstetricians and Gynecologists. She has been an active member of the Hillsborough County Medical Association, Florida Medical Association, American Medical Association, Medical Society of the State of New York, Bay Area Medical Association, and Student National Medical Association.

In 2016, Dr. Ericsson was voted Tampa's Best Obstetrician/Gynecologist by her peers.

In practice, Dr. Ericsson provides thorough and compassionate care to her patients. She is currently incorporating integrative medicine and aesthetics into her practice. She also enjoys mentoring, networking, baking, traveling, learning foreign languages, comedy, and sports.

PIERRE ERICSSON is currently a manufacturing mechanical technician for Anheuser-Busch in Jacksonville, Florida. He has been in the mechanical engineering field since 1995. His introduction into this realm of study was supported by his entire family, especially his aunt, Dr. Aprille Ericsson. While attending high school at Northbrook Senior High in Houston, Texas, he received a prestigious academic two-year $35,000 scholarship from Chuck Norris personally through the Linda Lorrelle Scholarship Fund.

In 2002, after completing only one year of college at Texas Southern University for computer science, he further pursued this passion with his entrance into the U.S. Navy as a gas turbine mechanical engineering technician. While serving his country for fourteen years, he continually engaged in multiple engineering platforms including pneumatics, hydraulics, thermal dynamics, physics, heating and cooling mediums, marine propulsion, and electro-mechanical energy principles. In 2015, he opened his own business in Jacksonville, Florida, called Revitalized Electronics. This business was created around his desire to pursue electronics repair.

Upon his honorable discharge from the military in 2016, he decided to obtain his mechanical engineering BA from a private and highly esteemed college, Jacksonville University. During his admittance into college in late 2016, he landed a great employment opportunity to work for Anheuser-Busch AB InBev full time, leaving his studies at Jacksonville University.

DEIRDRE GUTHRIE is a research professor on the Wellbeing at Work program at the University of Notre Dame. She received her doctorate in medical anthropology from the University of Illinois, Chicago. Prior to graduate school, she worked as an investigative reporter for the *City News Bureau* and *Village Voice*. Deirdre has written on a wide range of topics from indigenous environmental justice to contemporary circus life. Following her leadership role for Rush Hospital's Department of Preventive Medicine on the ALIVE Project, she will be developing a study on the well-being of humanitarian health-care workers for the Wellbeing at Work team as well as supporting current studies. Deirdre flourishes as a yoga and mindfulness meditation student and teacher. Her favorite place to practice is in her partner Ray's art studio, surrounded by his paintings, with her daughter, Ella, by her side.

ANNE HARDGROVE holds a PhD in anthropology and history from the University of Michigan, Ann Arbor. Her primary fieldwork for her dissertation and first book took place in Calcutta (now Kolkata), India. She is a tenured professor in history at the University of Texas in San Antonio, where she teaches courses on Asia and global studies. Her subsequent research and fieldwork experiences have been shaped by the growth of her family, including a spouse and a rapidly growing son, who was diagnosed in early childhood as having special developmental needs.

JOANNE KARRAM is a retired kindergarten teacher, mother to three, and grandmother to five. She has actively supported her children in their many adventures, including helping John and Grace move from Fiji in 2008 and editing four versions of Grace's thesis. Although Joanne is formally retired from education, she enjoys her part-time work as the organ and choir master at St. Paul's-on-the-hill Anglican Church.

SARAH KELMAN is a PhD candidate in the anthropology department at the University of California, Santa Cruz. She conducted field research in Kuala Lumpur, Malaysia, for eighteen months with her partner, her then six-month-old, and her cat. She is currently writing her dissertation on Islam, ethics, and entrepreneurship in the tech start-up and creative art, design, and media sectors.

LINDSEY ALYSSA MARCO is a doctoral candidate in the counseling psychology program at Washington State University. She is currently out of state on internship, serving in the U.S. Air Force as a clinical psychology resident. Her main interests include understanding and fostering resilience, military populations, trauma, and recovery.

BAHIYYAH MIALLAH MUHAMMAD is an assistant professor of criminology in the Department of Sociology and Criminology at Howard University. She received her doctorate from Rutgers University's School of Criminal Justice. Dr. Muhammad's major research interest is familial imprisonment, focusing specifically on those issues pertaining to children of incarcerated parents. She has conducted hundreds of interviews with affected children, parents, and caregivers in the United States, Europe, Uganda, Cambodia, Vietnam, Malaysia, Thailand, United Arab Emirates, and various Caribbean islands. Her most recent work revolves around success and resiliency among children of prisoners.

Dr. Muhammad is cofounder of Project Iron Kids, an initiative to educate and empower children of incarcerated parents. She copublished the first coloring book for children of the incarcerated titled *The Prison Alphabet: An Educational Coloring Book for Children of the Incarcerated*. In addition, Dr. Muhammad spearheaded a Howard University Alternative Spring Break experience connected to her *Prison Inside Out* course: Making Our Memories

Camp at a federal prison in Alderson, West Virginia. During this once-in-a-lifetime experience, incarcerated mothers spent an intimate week engaging with their children behind bars.

MUNTAQUIM MUHAMMAD is an international videographer with expertise in documentary film and action photography reflecting the lived experiences of children. Muntaquim has worked as personal assistant and road manager to actor Michael K. Williams, known as Omar on HBO's *The Wire* and Chalky White on *Boardwalk Empire*. His ongoing photo series, *Merging Cultures*, highlights children of incarcerated parents residing in Africa, Asia, Europe, UAE, New Zealand, and America. In addition, Mr. Muhammad works alongside his wife, Dr. Bahiyyah Muhammad, with *Freedom Productions* to create an animation film on children of prisoners. Currently, he serves as assistant director of *Served*, a short film highlighting the collateral consequences of parental incarceration and a full-length documentary, *Love among Young Sisters*, starring his two daughters, Jaelah-Millah and Jian-Alaa. He is cofounder of Project Iron Kids and coauthor of *The Prison Alphabet: An Educational Coloring Book for Children of Incarcerated Parents*.

MÉLANIE-ANGELA NEUILLY is an associate professor with the Department of Criminal Justice and Criminology at Washington State University. She received a PhD in criminal justice from Rutgers University in 2007 and a PhD in psychology from the Université de Rennes in France in 2008. Mélanie-Angela conducts qualitative comparative research on violence and violent death—more specifically, she explores issues surrounding measurement and data collection processes as they pertain to medico-legal practices of classifying death and homicide. Her research has so far compared medico-legal practices in France and the United States, in various sites as well as at various times in history. As the mother of a four-year-old daughter, she became interested in issues pertaining to women and mothers in society in general, in academia in particular, and specifically with regard to field research.

During her twenty-five-plus year tenure with NASA, Dr. Ericsson has worked as aerospace engineer, technologist, project and program manager, and executive. In 2017, she assumed the position of new business lead for the NASA GSFC Instrument Systems and Technology Division. Just prior, she served as the capture manager for a proposed astrophysics midsized class explorer called STAR-X. She served as a NASA Headquarters program executive for earth science and a business executive for space science.

Dr. Ericsson has won numerous awards. She was the first person of color to receive the prestigious "2016 Washington Award" from the Western Society of Engineers. Dr. Ericsson is the first female to receive a PhD in mechanical engineering from Howard University and the first African American civil servant female to receive a PhD in engineering at NASA GSFC. She received her BS in aeronautical/astronautical engineering from MIT.

RYANNE PILGERAM is an associate professor in the Department of Sociology and Anthropology at the University of Idaho whose research focuses on food and social justice. Her work on issues of social inclusion and social justice within sustainable agriculture has recently appeared in *Race, Class & Gender*, *Environmental Communication: A Journal of Nature and Culture*, and *Rural Sociology*. She is also the director of the Certificate in Diversity & Stratification program at the University of Idaho and the recipient of the 2014 Hoffman Award for Teaching Excellence and the 2016 Virginia Wolf Distinguished Service Award.

MIKAE PROVINE (daughter of Dawn Ericsson Provine) is a high school junior at Berkeley Preparatory School in Tampa, Florida. She competes with her school's selective a cappella group, the Mello Divas. She also plays guitar, piano, and ukulele. Mikae has performed in establishments in Ybor City and on the local radio station, WMNF. She has earned acceptance into the National Junior and Tri-M music honor societies. At school, she has also been a member of the science, model UN, crew, archery, and JV volleyball teams. She currently serves as a student library proctor and is excited to be the next executive director of the school's Diversity Program. In the Greater Tampa chapter of Jack and Jill of America, she is serving her second year as a recording secretary. She attended NASA's S.I.S.T.E.R. Program as a rising freshman and was classified as the program's top applicant. Mikae is interested in attending a liberal arts college after high school.

KELLEY SAMS is a postdoctoral researcher in social anthropology at the Norbert Elias Center in Marseille, France. She holds a PhD in medical anthropology from the University of South Florida and a master's in international public health from Tulane University. She was awarded a Fulbright-Hays Grant from the U.S. Department of Education and a Michael V. Angrosino Research Achievement Award for her research on trachoma elimination in Niger. Kelley engages ethnographic photography and other qualitative methods to study the circulation of medication and public health initiatives in sub-Saharan Africa. Her recent project focuses on the circulation of Chinese artemisinin-based malaria medication and Chinese health and development work as a part of the collective research project "The Political Life of Commodities."

MARYLYNN STECKLEY is an instructor I in the Department of Global and International Studies at Carleton University in Canada. She received her PhD in geography as a graduate of the Migration and Ethnic Relations Collaborative Program at Western in May 2015. In her doctoral research, she explored local responses to the encroachment of the global food system in rural Haiti. Her dissertation, titled "Agrarian Change and Peasant Prospects in Haiti," explored the trajectory for rural Haiti in the post-earthquake period. This included an examination of how race-based social hierarchies (legacies of colonial slavery) influence peasant diets and agro-productive practices in ways that undermine peasant agriculture and rural self-provisioning and also how peasants are struggling against disadvantageous trade regimes, land grabbing, and culinary colonization. As a result of this research, Marylynn is now fluent in Haitian Creole. In 2014, Marylynn was one of five winners in the Storytellers Competition for the Social Sciences and Humanities Research Council's Impact Awards. Her doctoral research also inspired a recent episode of CBC Radio's Ideas program titled "Just Trying to Help." Marylynn has also conducted field research in Cambodia, Indonesia, and Thailand and has spent more than five years in Haiti, where she worked in Advocacy and Food Justice Movements and where she conducted critical ethnographic field research to understand the linkages between identity, consumption, and peasant struggles for land. Her work in food systems, prejudice, and inequality has also contributed to her recent interest in the indigenous food systems and land struggles in Ontario.

GRACE KARRAM STEPHENSON is a full-time mother of two and a part-time post-doctoral fellow at the Ontario Institute for Studies in Education (OISE), University of Toronto. She graduated from OISE in 2016 with a PhD in higher education, and she regularly assists Dr. Ruth Hayhoe in teaching comparative higher education and international academic relations. Her research interests include the internationalization of higher education, study abroad design and marketing, college student development and spirituality, and university governance. When Grace is not writing about higher education, she is at Toronto's High Park Zoo visiting the llamas with her children.

JOHN M. STEPHENSON is a program officer at Prosper Canada, where he develops nationwide programs to financially empower low-income communities. His previous work at All Saints Church Community Centre allowed him to take paternity leave with both his children as well as a five-month leave to join his wife Grace on her fieldwork in Dubai and Malaysia. John loved being the full-time dad during these travels and exercising his superpower of eating everything in his path.

CECILIA VINDROLA-PADROS is a research associate in the Department of Applied Health Research at University College London and an embedded qualitative researcher at University College London Hospitals NHS Foundation Trust. She holds a PhD in applied medical anthropology from the University of South Florida. She has been involved in studies aimed at evaluating complex health interventions, the health care needs and preferences of children, and the availability and sustainability of existing health-care infrastructures. She is coauthor (with Linda Whiteford) of *Community Participatory Involvement: A Sustainable Model for Global Public Health.*

KELLY WARD was vice provost for faculty development and recognition and a professor of higher education in the College of Education at Washington State University. Her research examines different aspects of faculty career development, including work, family, and academic careers. She is coauthor with Lisa Wolf-Wendel of the book *Academic Motherhood: How Faculty Manage Complex Roles.* Kelly Ward unexpectedly passed away on July 8, 2018.

ARIELLE ERICSSON WHITE (daughter of Aprille Ericsson) is a very active nine-year-old scholar athlete. Currently, she is a "Principal's Honor Roll" fourth grader in the DC Public School Montessori Inspired education track. She has played on competitive T-ball and baseball youth teams. She also participated on her school's tennis and academic team and girl scouts. Since the age of three years old, Arielle has been taking lessons to play the piano and dance ballet, tap, jazz, and hip-hop. Arielle loves all STEAM-related activities. Arielle aspires to be an ob-gyn; she says she would like to deliver babies in space. At the age of six, in first grade, Arielle was her school's guest speaker for the kindergarten graduation. That same year she joined her mother, Dr. Aprille Ericsson, as a guest speaker for a national conference cohosted by the White House, the U.S. Department of Education, and the Georgetown Center on Poverty and Inequality on "Front and Center: Bringing Marginalized Girls into Focus in STEM and Career and Technical Education."

BRIAN C. WOLF is an associate professor of criminology and chair of the Department of Sociology and Anthropology at the University of Idaho. He holds a PhD in sociology from the University of Oregon. Dr. Wolf's research centers on the intersection between organizations, crime, and social control. He has published research related to corporate environmental crime, controversies in policing, and international criminology. An ongoing research project, "Good Trouble," considers how deviance and deviant behavior may be a source of positive social change. Much of his research contains a broad international and comparative perspective. For example, he has conducted teaching and research projects in Europe and Southeast Asia. Dr. Wolf was awarded the 2015 University of Idaho teaching award. Dr. Wolf is married to Mélanie-Angela Neuilly, and together they raise a vivacious daughter.

LISA WOLF-WENDEL is a professor of higher education in the Department of Educational Leadership and Policy Studies at the University of Kansas. She is also the associate dean for research and graduate studies in the School of Education. Dr. Wolf-Wendel is the author of numerous books and refereed journal articles on topics related to equity issues in higher education. Her research focuses on faculty issues, including studies of the academic labor market, the needs of international faculty and faculty from historically underrepresented groups, and several recent research projects pertaining to the policy response of academic institutions in the wake of demands for dual career couple accommodations and work/family balance. She is an editor of the *ASHE Higher Education Monograph* series and serves on the Editorial Board of many publications in higher education, including *Research in Higher Education*, the *Journal of College Student Development*, and the *Journal of Student Affairs Research and Practice*.

Index

access, 70, 77, 144. *See also* entrée/entry
aerospace engineering, 240–241, 242–243
affective labor, 191–192, 197; and men, 132–133
agriculture, 171–172, 174–176, 257–259
androcentrism, 30, 31, 32, 35, 37
anthropology, 30, 77–78, 273; concepts of, 76; cultural, 34–36, 189; feminist, 35, 155; history of fieldwork in, 157, 188; as immersive, 189, 190, 192–193; interlocutor relationships, 186, 194, 195; medical, 78–80; reflexive, 70, 72, 86
Antink-Meyer, A., 72
Appadurai, A., 77
archaeology, 28–33, 34–39; and children, 37–38; collections research, 32, 39; and cultural anthropology, 35; feminist, 31–32, 35, 37–39; history of, 28, 31; as masculine endeavor, 28–29; processualist, 35; reflexive, 36; romanticization of, 28–29
aunts, 240–241, 248

Badruddoja, R., 87
Bailey, L., 82
Battle-Baptiste, W., 29, 36
breastfeeding, 82, 141, 142, 143; and rapport, 101; and water safety, 104
budgets, 144, 265–266, 269, 275
Buenos Aires, Argentina, 78

career mystique, 19–20
caregiving, 223, 229–230, 233, 235. *See also* childcare; spouses: as caregivers

care vs. service, 225
Cassell, J., 77, 86
childbirth, 62–63; in the field, 81, 206–207
childcare, 176, 255–256; access to, 39, 69, 73; by family and friends, 115–116, 259; in the field, 190, 211; opinions on, 193–194
children: as academic inspiration, 51–52; as assisting research, 56–57, 175, 248; education, in the field, 65, 73, 211–212; illnesses of, 52, 83–84, 176, 212–213; as incompatible with career, 16–18, 20; life circumstances, 169; packing for, 73–74, 104, 252; perspectives of, 51–52, 55–57, 59, 182; preparing for the field, 96–98; and rapport, 98, 112, 164, 169, 210, 258
circle spaces, 236–237
Claassen, C., 32
Clancy, K., 30
Clark, S. M., 20
class: and gender, 130; and parenthood, 131; and privilege, 156, 157, 206–207
collaboration, 13, 22, 72, 185–186
community, 83, 115–118, 203, 262, 273, 278. *See also* support: networks
Conkey, M. W., 30, 31–32
coping mechanisms, 142–143, 225; of children, 158
Corcoran, M., 20
criminology, 92–93, 98, 140